MW01067787

THE
ANDREW
GAZE
STORY

A Kid, a Ball, a Dream

ANDREW GAZE
WITH GRANTLEY BERNARD

Hardie Grant Books

Published in Australia in 2005
by Hardie Grant Books
85 High Street
Prahran, Victoria 3181, Australia
www.hardiegrant.com.au

All rights reserved. No part of this publication may be
reproduced, stored in a retrieval system or transmitted in
any form by any means, electronic, mechanical, photo-
copying, recording or otherwise, without the prior written
permission of the publishers and copyright holders.

The moral rights of the authors have been asserted.

Copyright © Andrew Gaze and Grantley Bernard 2005

Cataloguing-in-Publication Data is available from
the National Library of Australia.

ISBN 1 74066 329 2

Jacket and text design: Nada Backovic
Photograph section design: Lou Kubicki
Front jacket photograph: Greg Elms
Back jacket photograph: Newspix
Typesetting: Pauline Haas, bluerinse setting
Printed and bound in Australia by Griffin Press

10 9 8 7 6 5 4 3 2 1

This book is dedicated to the sport of basketball
and everyone who has ever played the game

Foreword

Didn't everyone grow up living next to sporting stadiums? Doesn't everyone's dad go to Channel Seven on a Sunday morning and joke with Lou Richards on television about sport? Don't all kids go to Essendon Airport just to play?

My childhood with my brother Andrew didn't seem extra-ordinary, and it was only after we left our cottage next to the basketball courts at Albert Park that we started to appreciate how different our upbringing really was. It afforded us a youth shared with people from all walks of life, from every economic background and from all corners of the world. Albert Park Basketball Stadium was a melting pot for basketball followers from around the state and at times the country, and it produced a generation of basketballers and people the like of whom may not come again.

That old tin shed brought us together to sweat it out in the summer and freeze during the winter. It may have been state of the art at the time, but you still had to sweep the possum droppings up before you could play, and be careful not to run into the poles at the end of Court One. In this setting, Andrew honed not only his skill as the country's best basketballer but his ability to negotiate with not-always-understanding officials, speak languages that enabled him to get the whole team playing together and find a humility that allowed him to be benched just one more time.

He was lucky that he sometimes had a physical advantage in his chosen sport. But a trait that some may say cannot be learned was, I believe, his greatest asset. Perseverance. Andrew has never given in. From the time he could hold a basketball, he has been practising. Before he could get the ball anywhere near the ring, he has been throwing it at one. People who were regulars at Albert Park would know to steer clear of him unless they wanted to be drawn into just one more game of one-on-one, or around-the-key or first to twenty-one. This attribute has brought him great success in his sporting life and has set him up for life beyond it.

As siblings, we are both echoes of our parents' modesty, acceptance and humour, traits that were sharpened on every one of those nine Albert Park courts. These qualities now resonate through our children, on other courts, in another time. But in sport, as in life, our youngsters still have to accept the referee's decision as final, they still have to learn to speak the language that their point guard or forward will understand and they still have to sit on the bench.

They are lucky that their sport allows them to share the court with names as diverse as Brancatisano, Kwok, Lee and Phillips. They are lucky that their sport teaches them modesty, acceptance and humour. And they are lucky that a humble sportsman by the name of Andrew Gaze paved the way for them.

Janet Gaze-Daniels

Contents

Foreword v

1 The World's Best Playground 1

2 Father, Mentor, Coach 15

3 An Olympian, Once and Always 31

4 Whatever You Do, Don't Mention Angola 48

5 The Communist Block 57

6 A Basketball Education 69

7 The Biggest Dance of All 87

8 Not So Super Sonic 102

9 A Matter of Perspective 113

10 The Italian Job 126

11 No Reign in Spain 144

12 My Country's Captain 154

13 Title Time 168

14 A Shot with The Bullets 191

15 All Greek to Me 203

16 Almost Bronzed Aussies 217

17 Glory without a Guarantee 237

18 Gaining the NBA Spurs 249

19 Have You Got a Minute? 269

20 All in the Family 291

21 Can You Keep a Secret? 300

22 Let the Games Begin ... Please 318

23 Medal or Bust 329

24 For Love, Not Money 339

25 The Last Lap 354

Acknowledgements 372

Statistics 375

chapter one

THE WORLD'S BEST PLAYGROUND

THE old Albert Park Stadium was massive. Massive to a little kid, anyway. With its nine courts, it was gigantic and you could always muster up an echo if you yelled loud enough when the place was empty. Sometimes you only needed one bouncing ball to hear the reply in the near distance. It seemed so big it would be easy to get lost there. But maybe the best part was that I knew my way home. That's because it *was* my home. We lived at the stadium.

My dad Lindsay was the Victorian Basketball Association's general manager and one of his responsibilities was to be caretaker of the stadium. With the GM's job, which he started before the place was even built, came the caretaker's residence, a small brick cottage that was nestled between the basketball stadium and the badminton stadium. So our home's close proximity to the basketball courts was very handy the first time my mum Margaret took me to basketball training. I was about six when mum took me on the short walk down to Court Nine, which was at the front of the nine-court Albert Park complex, to train with the Melbourne Tigers under-twelve teams and officially get involved in the sport. She took me in, introduced me to the coach, then wandered off home. There were a lot of strange faces and bigger kids and it was one of the most intimidating, confusing and worrying experiences I'd ever had – in my six long years, anyway. I cried my eyes out – turned on the tears like you wouldn't believe – and pulled the pin on training. I made a fastbreak for home. Mum was a bit surprised to see me back so soon and so distressed, but she didn't growl or make me go back to finish the session. She just took me back the next week to start all over again. It was an inauspicious beginning, to say the least, and some would say I made a career out of sooking and whingeing on the court. But once I had started, it took me more than thirty years to break the basketball habit.

There are two things in my life I marvel at: the environment I grew up in and my genes. I consider myself to have been extraordinarily lucky on both counts. I was born into a basketball family, a basketball environment and a basketball influence. Whether that's fate or whatever, I have wondered how the hell I came out two metres tall. My dad's not that tall – maybe 185 centimetres in his prime – and my mum's not that tall. They may be slightly above average, but for some reason, I grew taller than average. So there's obviously a biological advantage I gained. And you'll probably need a sociological expert to qualify this, but I don't reckon you can underestimate the environment I grew up in at Albert Park.

The suburb of Albert Park and its neighbouring suburbs are among Melbourne's trendiest these days. But before World War II, Albert Park itself was largely swampland. During the war, the military built massive storage depots on the park site. When the war finished the facilities were used as Commonwealth storage depots and in the late 1950s were converted into stadia for badminton, table tennis and basketball, with a squash centre added later. As part of the upgrading and beautification of the Albert Park area, a golf course, lake and footy fields were thrown in.

Basketball has been played in Victoria since 1905, and in the early days it was often played in cramped venues like town halls and church halls, where the sidelines were sometimes a metre or more up the wall. After the war, games were played at bigger venues like the Exhibition Buildings in Carlton and at the Royal Melbourne Showgrounds in Flemington, but the Victorian Amateur Basketball Association had nowhere to call its own. Just when the VABA was about to build a two-court complex at Northcote, the chairman of the Albert Park Management Committee, Senator Pat Kennelly, proposed the conversion of the Commonwealth storage warehouses into a basketball HQ with six courts. My dad was appointed stadium manager in 1958 and the official opening was held on 6 April 1959 when a Victorian all-star team played a team of Mormons. Two courts were added to the back end of the complex a few years later and Court Nine, which became the centre of the women's basketball universe in Melbourne, was added after that, making it the largest basketball stadium in the southern hemisphere. Which was a nice tag to have, but the bottom line for the Gaze family was that it was our home.

It wasn't just a matter of being born into basketball. It was my destiny. My mum and dad met in Adelaide when dad was training with the Australian team in preparation for the 1960 Olympics. In fact, the Australian team played in the local Adelaide competition to make sure the players got enough games together before leaving for Italy. My mum was friends with a woman from the North Adelaide club, which took on the job of organising social occasions for the Olympic team. The occasions were nothing fancy – maybe a dance or something as simple as a television night, given TV was still a bit of a novelty in those days and not everyone owned a set.

Those social occasions brought Lindsay Gaze and Margaret Nation together, only to be separated when my dad went to Italy for the Olympics. But my mum moved to Melbourne to visit relatives, their courtship was renewed and they were married on 6 January 1962. They became parents when my sister Janet was born on 8 July 1964.

It should not surprise anyone that my dad was actually away on a basketball trip – playing in Adelaide – when I was born on 24 July 1965. When mum went into labour, her mother babysat Janet while she called a taxi. The only problem was the taxi dispatcher thought it was a hoax. He didn't think a pregnant woman would order a cab to collect her from the Albert Park Stadium, not realising we lived there. So after a second call to reassure the taxi company that it was a legitimate fare, mum headed to St Andrew's Maternity Hospital in East Melbourne, where she gave birth to the most beautiful bouncing baby boy anybody had ever laid eyes on. In those days, it was not the father's place to be in the delivery room assisting the mother, so even if my dad had been around he would have only been pacing the waiting room floor, or maybe just reclining casually. Since he was doing neither, mum rang the team's hotel in Adelaide and left a message to tell him Andrew Barry Casson Gaze was now of this world. Fittingly, my dad did not get the message until after the game.

Some early photos show me crawling around the floor at Albert Park, pushing a basketball. So when I say I've never known a day without basketball, that is the absolute truth. Before I could walk, I was living and breathing basketball. It was a unique situation and I can't honestly remember a day of not being involved in basketball or at least thinking about it. We had sliding doors at the back of the house and, when I wasn't much older than a toddler, dad put up a ring for me. I can still remember getting the ball in for the first time. Maybe that's why I remember: all along the ten-feet-high rings around me had been so high, but now I had something my size to aim for.

We had no neighbours, but we were in a highly sociable situation as people playing basketball came and went from 5.30 p.m. until about midnight almost every day. It became second nature to doze off at night to the sound of referees' whistles, score-bench hooters, argumentative losers, and car engines revving in the car park. It was an unusual lifestyle, but I didn't know any different and wouldn't have wanted anything different.

Even when games weren't on, there was something happening, sometimes when it shouldn't have been. Like fire alarms ringing or burglars breaking into the stadium to fleece the canteen or the little sports store. The security was minimal and I remember one time when my dad was up at 3 a.m. chasing burglars. Another time we noticed a basketball shoe sitting in the middle of the main court. It was dropped by a thief as he ran from the sports store to make his getaway through the emergency exit in the south-west corner. All that added some edge when my dad would lock up on Friday nights and occasionally forget to turn a light off in the change rooms. He'd ask me to run back and flick the switch while he waited. When the light went off, it was pitch black – you couldn't see your hand in front of your face – but I used to sprint out of there like Carl Lewis, worried the bogeyman would get me. Nor was it unheard-of to wake up some mornings and almost trip over a drunk or a vagrant who had curled up on our front doorstep or in the shed that housed the scoreboard numbers at Harry Trott Oval, which doubled as a very big backyard for us. One night we even had a few cows on our front doorstep, which was a novelty for us city dwellers. Apparently, a cattle truck had overturned on nearby Kings Way and some of the passengers had escaped and hightailed it towards the stadium. Stirred from her sleep, Janet woke my dad to inform him that 'the police are racing cows outside'. Although he assumed Janet was dreaming, my dad did take a look out the window just in case, only to see that the police were in fact herding cattle towards our house, given that there was no escape route beyond that.

I considered this all to be pretty normal when I was a kid but now I sometimes wonder about the safety aspect of a young family living in a house that was so isolated. It helped that my mum had the bravado to handle tricky situations. One summer holiday, when my dad was away, mum was taking Janet and me to the shop for an ice-cream. When the basketball comps closed down for Christmas–New Year, it was actually rare for people to be hanging around, so if there were two or three vehicles in the car park, you kind of sensed somebody might be up to no good. Anyway, on this day, my mum's car was parked in front of the cottage and there was a bloke lying underneath it. Mum bowled over and asked what he was up to. He came up with the highly believable response that he was look-ing for the toilets! So mum pointed him in the direction of the public toilets and sent him on his way. These days, you would think twice about confronting a situation like that, wondering whether it might be somebody on drugs or a vagrant ready to ambush and rob you.

In the main, though, the Albert Park Stadium and its surrounds provided a safe environment for my sister and me. You would run into other kids who might have been wagging school and people who were smoking or drinking, but I never felt endangered or exposed to bad things. I had good parental guidance in those areas and I didn't really have time to think about ending up on the wrong side of the tracks – maybe because sport was such a distraction. I've never smoked and I've only ever had the occasional celebratory drink of alcohol. Sport, especially basketball, took up too much of my time and focus.

I would often play cricket and footy in the basketball stadium, sometimes accidentally smashing a light or cracking a scoreboard. My mates and I just did what kids did. The thing for me was that, even though I played different sports, it was still in a basketball environment. When I just hung around the place, it was usually with a ball in my hands, dribbling, shooting, passing off a wall, all the while building up skills and feel without even knowing it. The thing that still surprises me is that I never got jack of it and tried to escape. I guess one reason I didn't get sick of basketball was, even though we lived and breathed it, I was never forced to play it. It was there, but it was my choice.

Fridays were always special because of two things: school was finished for the week and it was game night. Primary school, and secondary school for that matter, did not hold the same excitement and interest for me that basketball did. I certainly had the capabilities to be a good student but was probably classed only as average. Inevitably, the comments in my school reports had a familiar ring. They would usually say I was capable, but was easily distracted and did not have a total commitment to my school work. I'd say my teachers had a pretty good handle on that. Most of the time, when I should have been concentrating on my times tables, I was thinking about basketball.

As soon as school finished at 3.30 p.m. I'd race home – which only took a couple of minutes, given that Eastern Road Primary School was across the street, get changed into my playing gear and be ready to go, shooting around, willing tip-off time to arrive. Even when I was playing under-twelves, I would often play up in the under-fourteen C-grade team if it was short of players. I didn't need to be asked twice. Some nights I even sneaked in a third game with one of the Tigers under-sixteen teams to help make up the numbers. That was the beauty of living on site. If coaches were short of players, they knew I would be there. As an under-twelve kid, playing against under-sixteens was like playing against men, but I gained experience and learned to understand the game.

Having quickly overcome the shock of my initial training session, I was still only six when I played my first organised game with one of my cousins, Peter Gaze, in the Tigers under-twelve C team against kids who were ten or eleven. They were a lot bigger than us and for the first two years we got pulverised and didn't win a game. By the time we were nine or ten, we won a few but by the time we had turned eleven and were in the A team we were flying.

I also played with my Eastern Road Primary team on Saturday mornings at Albert Park and it wasn't unusual for one of my eager team-mates to tap at my window to wake me up. But we were the odd ones out. Throughout my school life, when most people asked what sport I played and I said basketball, they would look at me strangely. Most kids considered basketball to be either a girls' game or something from another planet. The way most of them played it, they had it covered on both counts. They didn't know what it was, and they struggled to know how to play it.

So even though I was in Grade Two, I actually played on the Grade Six team because I was the only one who knew what to do and the only one with a vague knowledge of the rules. Consequently, I saw a lot of the ball for our team and one day I scored a hundred points, stealing the ball and making lay-ups like I was a basketball conveyor belt. I thought it was a great achievement, but my dad thought I should have shared the ball more. He was always on about passing and getting my team-mates involved, but I couldn't comprehend it because I was trying to win. I wanted to know why I should pass when they couldn't catch and if they couldn't catch, they couldn't shoot, so they couldn't score, so we couldn't win. It wasn't that complicated to me. But to my dad, that wasn't what basketball and team sport were about. It was a long, long time before I finally understood what he meant. That didn't mean I agreed with it, but I understood it.

I also learned a lot about team play from one of my first coaches, Ron Anderson, who was a terrific bloke and a terrific coach with kids. Ron was very good at teaching fundamentals, we would run a structured offence and we were very disciplined. The only thing I didn't like about Ron, who coached me for six years until I was thirteen, was that if you weren't paying attention he would give your hair a tug to snap you back into tune. It didn't hurt and was just a little reminder, but I was always thinking, 'I hope Ron doesn't pull my hair.' I suppose if I had paid attention I wouldn't have had to worry. I was lucky to have Ron involved in my formative years. After initially training at Albert Park, the team later practised at Waverley, an outer suburb of Melbourne, and he would pick me up without fail. Ron was very committed to basketball and the kids, had a good understanding of the game and loved what he did.

Ron bought me the first basketball I ever owned. That might sound strange, given that I lived at a nine-court basketball stadium with any number of balls at my disposal. But while there were plenty available, I didn't own any of them. Ron coached me in a Saturday afternoon competition, we wore blue uniforms and played at Nunawading. That much detail I recall. I did well, we won the championship and as a thank-you gesture or a prize, Ron bought me my very first leather basketball. I might have slept with that ball the first week I had it. There is no doubt Ron was a significant influence in my early years and I owe him plenty.

One thing mum and dad taught me was to be responsible for my actions and to fulfil my commitments. They never forced me out the door to training, but if I didn't want to go, or I wanted to watch one of the frequent exhibition games on a Sunday afternoon at Albert Park, I had to telephone the coach and tell him.

My responsibilities increased as I got older and I soon embarked on one of my first money-making ventures. When I was about twelve or thirteen, I started refereeing for some pocket money. We learned how to referee on Saturdays from a woman named Margaret Gorman, who then let us loose on the girls' competition on Court Two. I refereed with David Maher, whose older brother Tom Maher coached the Opals to Olympic bronze and silver medals and is perhaps the finest coach of women's basketball this country has known. Once we finished our refs training, we got our C-grade badges and called games on Thursday nights, usually doing four games back to back, but skipping the last game of the night so that I could be in bed at a reasonable time. I loved doing the women's games on Court Six. The women were less hassle than the men over on Court Four. The men could get stroppy and scream at you, never realising they were terrible players and we were only kids. When you had to referee some of those games by yourself, you found out how much spine you had. Maybe that was why I only lasted about a year blowing the whistle.

There was always something for a young basketball enthusiast to do around the Albert Park Stadium, whether it be selling copies of *Time-Out*, a basketball publication that lasted a short time in the 1970s, or sweeping the floors or just shooting hoops. It was the place to be in Melbourne on Wednesday nights when the VBA State League was being played. The stadium was a mid-week gathering place for the who's who of Victorian basketball, especially among the players, and if I wasn't watching, I was down the back shooting hoops on the warm-up rings on the side wall near Court Five. It was the best.

Even when we moved from the stadium cottage to our house in St Leonard's Avenue in St Kilda, the Albert Park complex still remained the centre of my universe. Not that I didn't start to broaden my view of the world from St Leonard's Avenue, which was a dead-end street and a haven for the street-walkers of nearby Acland St when they had to turn a quick trick. It was quite an eye-opener for a naïve fourteen year old to peer out the front window of our house and receive a rather shocking and rudimentary lesson in human relations. Not that my astonishing viewing lasted long. While the ladies continued to conduct business in the street, my mum had a two-metre brick fence erected to at least separate them from our front window.

By the time I was about thirteen, my job responsibility had grown. A couple of mates, Peter Skadins and Peter 'Pee Wee' O'Mara, and I formed the crew that operated the scoreboard for the VBA games. We got maybe fifty cents a game and we'd go home with one dollar and fifty cents, thinking we were as rich as Bill Gates. It was big time, but the best thing was that we got to watch the top players in Australia up close every single week. We got to see most of the guys on the Australian team playing for their clubs in a competition that was easily the strongest in the nation before the NBL matured in the mid-1980s. Such was our eagerness to replicate our heroes' deeds that we would rush onto the court during half-time to take as many shots as we could before being shooed away by the referees.

One of the greatest treats was to see Eddie Palubinskas play. In his day, Eddie was Australia's top player and was flat-out one of the best shooters in the world, finishing second in scoring at the 1972 Munich Olympics before topping the list four years later at Montreal. Eddie was a bit of a nomad, but he would usually come back to Melbourne to prepare for the Olympics and World Championships. He certainly never lacked confidence. One Wednesday night, when Eddie arrived at Albert Park to play for the Caulfield Spartans, he asked what the VBA scoring record was. He then went out and hit 66 points to claim the record.

The place just buzzed when a guy like Eddie was around. Even though he was a shooting freak, Eddie worked hard on his game. One time, Eddie was working out on the back courts at Albert Park as I shot around on a nearby court, so I stopped to watch and admire his beautiful technique. As I watched, Eddie shot fifty free-throws with his right hand and fifty with his left. If he missed one, I don't remember it. From then on, I took a hundred free-throws, all with the right hand, to finish my solo sessions. If I was going to be as good as Eddie, as I dreamed as a kid, I had to do what Eddie did.

During this time I learned a lot about the game, the coaches, the players, how the players behaved and acted and what they did to score and win. I was young and impressionable and soaked it up like a sponge in a puddle. Watching these games was why I wore number 10 throughout my career, from juniors until I retired. The number 10 singlet for the Tigers was worn by Bruce Case, who was my hero as a kid and caught my eye with the way he played. Being so close to the players and the game unquestionably had a signifi-cant impact on my development. Being able to hone my skills and have the experience of refereeing, scoring and doing odd jobs was educational and gave me a better appreciation and understanding of the game. I was never blessed with great athleticism and that process of being immersed in the game was just as important as going out onto the back courts and shooting and shooting and shooting. It was a personal development and understanding of the game from the absolute grass roots to championship basketball.

A lot of parents have asked me what they can do for their kids to help them progress in basketball. They've got them on a weights program or a stretching program and they're doing this and that. Times have changed, but I tell people about my own experience: that I never lifted a weight until I was nineteen or twenty and I never did a stretching course. All I did was play and play and play and play. People try to find some secret program or some guarantee for success. There isn't one, except hard work. It's important to get the basis for fundamentals and my dad and coaches helped me with technique. But I learned the rest from playing. So that's my advice: let the kids play as much as they can, anywhere they can. They should never feel they're too good or not good enough because they will always learn something or be able to hone something in whatever game they play. I played in any game going, no matter the level. Usually it was because teams needed players and I felt obliged to help. But it forced me to adapt to different players of different standards and I had to learn how to get involved in the game and get my team-mates involved. It makes me laugh when kids or their parents say they don't want to play too much. As a kid, I never felt tired. I rested when I slept and I never thought I could get too much basketball.

When I was in the under-twelves and under-fourteens, I wasn't a dominant player. I was extremely uncoordinated, very clumsy and not particularly athletic. A few people would say some things never change. I made Victorian teams when I was top age in under-twelves, under-fourteens and under-sixteens, but I never made those rep teams in my first year in the age groups. As an example of where

I was with my game, I played in a very good Tigers under-sixteen team with Olympian Bill Wyatt as coach. The starting five was Chris Dimattina, Peter Gaze, Russell Wyatt, Simon Wigg and Greg Bartlett. I was on the bench with Ray Gordon and Michael Dimattina and, although we didn't lose a game in under-sixteens for two years, I still had plenty of work to do on my game.

In the second year of under-sixteens I started to make some progress, playing in VBA Division Two and training with the Tigers' senior team a bit. In fact, I made significant improvement to the point that in my first year of under-eighteens, as a fifteen year old, I played senior basketball and started to establish an advantage over my junior peers. I was taller than most of the other kids, but because I always played in higher age groups and levels, I had to handle the ball and play the guard positions, which meant I developed good ball skills under pressure.

The next and, perhaps most important, step in my basketball education was far less formal but far more demanding than anything I had done. When I was about fourteen or fifteen and waiting for my Friday night junior championship games, I would often join the 'jungle ball' session on Court One. It was mainly a gathering of the Americans who played locally and they would scrimmage against each other in a high-quality, highly competitive and sometimes highly charged atmosphere that actually once provoked a stabbing. When they only had nine players, I was often roped in as the tenth player to make two teams of five. But within twelve months I was pretty much a regular alongside guys I looked up to and admired – Brian Goorjian, Al Westover, Bruce Palmer, Casey Jones, Ray Shirley and Bennie Lewis. There was a lot of talent on the court every Friday and there were two things that were imperative: you had to be good and you had to be able to handle yourself.

It was a full-on situation and, since I was the junior member of the group, I was pretty submissive. There was a lot of ego involved and, as we called our own fouls on defence, I learned quickly that even the slightest hint of touching someone was enough for me to admit to a foul. I also saw how the others operated – what they got away with, what they tolerated – and I applied that to my own game. We would go hammer and tongs for every minute, but when it came 5.45 p.m., it was knocking off time. We'd go and have a shower and there were no grudges. While I would prepare to play a couple more games in the junior ranks, the older guys would head to the nearby Rising Sun Hotel for a few beers and plenty of exaggerating. Talk about the school of hard knocks ... the jungle ball scrimmages were the masters degree.

The demolition crews tore down the old Albert Park stadium in 1997. We had moved to our house in St Kilda years earlier and the cottage that was home for the first fourteen years of my life had been through various lives of its own. After we left, the house was converted into a small dormitory for visiting teams and later into Pete's Bar, which was a hive of post-game activity on Wednesday nights. I'm pretty certain my mum never had so many beer drinkers in her kitchen at any one time as they did on those Wednesday nights.

In 1997, the Victorian government built the Melbourne Sports and Aquatic Centre just down the road as part of the revamping of Albert Park to accommodate the Formula One Grand Prix. Before the bulldozers and wreckers' balls got too busy, some of us went down to the stadium with a circular saw to get some souvenirs. I have a small side table at home that is made of the timber from the bleacher seating in Court One, which the Tigers graced for the last time in an exhibition game against the University of Arizona on 24 May 1997. Those bleachers were actually made from the timber floor for the 1956 Olympic Games basketball tournament at the Exhibition Buildings. It is nice to have some basketball history, but it's even nicer to have a piece of the place that was and always will be my first home – as a person and as a basketball player.

chapter two

FATHER, MENTOR, COACH

AS a kid, winning a trophy is the ultimate. Your name is read out, your chest puffs with pride and you're not sure whether to run or walk to get that prize. The Melbourne Tigers under-fourteens had beaten Bulleen in the grand final of the Moomba Tournament at Coburg, so when my name was called during the presentation ceremony, I stood up among the hundred or so kids on the main court, puffed up my sunken chest as best I could and headed for the man with the microphone and the trophy. It was a proud moment to say the least.

But instead of warm applause, or any applause at all, the crowd booed. It didn't hit me at the time. I just shrugged it off as I went to get my prize as tournament Most Valuable Player for my under-fourteen age group. It was only later it dawned on me. The crowd hadn't booed me, Andrew Gaze. They had booed Lindsay Gaze's son.

After the awards ceremony, a couple of people mentioned that the reaction was not nice, but I didn't worry. I didn't think much of it until I came home to our cottage at Albert Park Stadium. A friend of mum's dropped in and I overheard them talking. Mum's friend said it was disgusting how people booed me. Mum agreed it was disappointing and that night I got upset because I thought my mum was upset. With all these other people talking about it, I realised it wasn't a good thing.

It wasn't the first time people had reacted badly towards me, which was maybe why I handled it with indifference myself. At the time, my dad was the Australian men's coach, was coach of the Melbourne Tigers and was general manager of the Victorian Basketball Association (now Basketball Victoria), so he had a fair influence on what happened in the sport. Not everybody agreed with that and sometimes they channelled that displeasure through me.

The basketball community was pretty small and whatever went on was well known – there weren't many secrets. So when I played in the under-twelves and under-fourteens, everyone knew who I was, or rather whose son I was, and some made me a target for comment. Whether it was because I didn't have to pay to get into Albert Park Stadium and everyone else did, or the fact that my dad was national coach and declined to pick certain players, or people were jealous or they weren't brave enough to confront my dad, I don't know. But other kids sledged me on the court with schoolyard trash talk. It wasn't sophisticated, but I knew what they meant.

It even happened outside Victoria. We went to a tournament at West Adelaide when I was fourteen and I copped sledges and abuse for being Lindsay Gaze's son. Maybe they hadn't forgiven the old man for not picking Werner Linde, South Australian basketball's favourite son before Phil Smyth inherited the title, in the 1976 Olympic team. It wasn't dramatic, but there were always elements of it and I was able to get accustomed to it.

I just never knew any different. My dad was national coach from when I was five, which was before I had played my first game. It was always something I had to deal with and mum would say 'don't let it bother you' or 'just ignore it, they're silly and don't understand'. I faced this issue – an issue other people had – from the start, so it was almost second nature. A lot of times I didn't understand about the particular details, but it still had to be endured.

My parents taught me to turn a blind eye. They took a passive approach of not giving back to the aggressor, of not letting on we could even hear them. It was a case of 'That's their problem'. We knew the truth: that none of us had ever had anything easy. In fact, knowing the way my dad operated, I probably had to work harder for things because he wasn't going to just give them to me, and other people certainly weren't. I was never going to gain an advantage because of who my father was.

My dad never talked to me specifically about the sledging, but I remember something that will stay with me forever. During an under-fourteen game, a kid from the other team kept belting me and trying to intimidate me. I had perfected the art of playing on and not getting involved. But the night this happened, my dad gave me an insight I'd never thought of. Sometimes, he told me in his wise and informative way, when you're getting belted, you need to be patient and selective because sooner or later you have to stand up for yourself. You don't have to get even straightaway, but there are times when you have to give someone a sharp, sly one in return, just to settle the score.

Whacking someone was against the grain of everything I'd been taught. I didn't even realise you could do that and, naturally, I'd never contemplated it. If someone belted me, I was taught to cop it and move on. I was an innocent, always prepared to take the moral high ground. Now my dad was telling me if I hit someone and the referee sees it, that's stupid. But there may be an instance in which I could bang one back and only two people in the whole world would know about it. That was when I started to realise there was more to my old man than I knew. But I could never bring myself to take this type of action and have never had the conviction to put it into practice.

My dad is from a humble background and leads a humble existence. He has never been motivated by any kind of financial return and he's not laden with enormous resources. That was surely a product of his upbringing.

My grandmother, Pat, basically raised her three sons – Barry, Tony and Lindsay – on her own. If times were tough around the world, coming out of the Depression and into World War II, they were even tougher in the Gaze household. My paternal grandfather, whom I never met, left the family when the boys were young. Albert Gaze was a magician and entertainer, with an itinerant and transient lifestyle. The number of houses the family lived in as they moved around would have kept one or two real estate agents busy if they were managing such a property portfolio.

Unfortunately, there was more than constant house-moving. My grandfather, for the time he was around, made life hard for his family with physical and mental abuse. It wasn't a happy situation and much of my dad's childhood was spent wishing he could grow up fast so that he could protect his mother from his father.

Much as my grandfather was an unknown stranger to me, I saw Nanna almost every day, especially when I was young. She was just as involved in Albert Park Stadium as the rest of the family. She ran the canteen and paid me a few bucks a week to make sure the pies were in the warmer and the hot dog cooker was turned on. Before that, Nanna had a shop in Prahran and Lindsay Fox delivered briquettes in the truck that grew into a multi-million-dollar empire.

My grandmother's relationship with my dad and our family could not have been warmer or closer. When she died in 2003, we discovered a bunch of letters my dad had written to her while overseas on tours as a player and coach. The letters were incredibly detailed, no doubt written with the idea that if Nanna couldn't have been there with him, she would at least feel like she had. There were many examples of how well my grandmother raised her sons. One might have been my dad winning the Victorian Father of the Year in 1992. That was an award for all the family to savour, especially Nanna, who did a pretty good job against the odds.

It goes without saying that my dad was a strong influence on me and my basketball. He could write a much more interesting book than me, I'll give you the drum. But his lifelong involvement with basketball happened by accident. My dad's eldest brother Barry was the first Gaze to fall in love with the game and it took him more than a year to convince my dad and their older brother Tony to have a go at basketball. Barry's younger brothers were initially reluctant because they were more interested in football and thought basketball was a 'girl's' game. It wasn't until Geoff Swan, the coach of the junior Tri-Boys Society Youth Club team, pleaded with them to play in a game at a nearby community hall in South Yarra that my dad's passion for the sport was sparked. A few years later when he was a teenager, my dad was hanging around the Melbourne Showgrounds one cold day while a basketball game was being played. He was approached by a man who gave him a jumper to keep the chill at bay. That simple act of kindness by Ken Watson gave rise to a partnership that provided the base for basketball, certainly in terms of participation, to be the success it is in this country today. Ken, who coached Australia at the 1956 Melbourne Olympics and is considered the father of basketball in Victoria (if not the nation), got my dad playing and involved. The rest, as they say, is history.

One day, someone will spend the time and energy to write a history of Australian basketball. They will sketch the evolution of basketball from humble beginnings and they will profile some wonderful contributors to the sport. Ultimately, just exactly how much of the contribution has come from my dad and Ken Watson is unknown. It is invaluable and incalculable.

Many people look at basketball from an NBL standpoint, so if you ask them how many basketball courts Lindsay Gaze has been responsible for building, they wouldn't have a clue. To most people, he's the bloke who coached the Melbourne Tigers in more than six hundred NBL games. In fact, he's coached since the 1960s and he coached the national team at four Olympics. But if you want to compare basketball in other states with basketball in Victoria, in terms of the facilities or how the sport has evolved and how some-one had the patience and vision and ability to work through a process of going from 1500 registered players to about 100,000, a lot of that was to do with my dad and Ken Watson. Those of us who have played in the modern era are fortunate that men like Ken and my dad, who love the sport so passionately, had the vision, knowl-edge and drive to make things happen.

Ken and my dad were not ego driven and have not self-promoted their achievements. Quite the contrary, actually. They don't want kudos and they don't seek it. They followed the path of being guardians of the sport so their legacy will be to leave it in better shape for future generations. As pioneers of the sport, they have qui-etly gone about their business and the story goes largely untold.

For some people, the history of Australian basketball starts at Michele Timms and ends at Lauren Jackson. If you went to kids in an under-eighteen comp these days and asked them who was Eddie Palubinskas, one of the greatest players Australia ever had, they wouldn't know. That's why someone needs to sit down with my dad and Ken Watson and document the history of the sport. Ask them about the Baltic immigrants who had an amazing passion and fire, and the Mormons who became the first American imports, and the church groups who played in halls so small the sidelines were actu-ally painted half a metre up the walls. I've heard those stories, but lots of people haven't. That's unfortunate because the sport needs its history known to give it more meaning.

I've been there, seen it and lived it. I've seen my dad up at in the dead of night chasing burglars out of Albert Park Stadium. I've seen him administer comps to get more people involved. I've seen him help build a system that enabled Australia to become more than competitive in world basketball. I've heard and dreamed about the mystique of the Olympic Games. My dad played a role in all those things.

My first recollection and impression that my dad was doing something important came when it seemed we were at Essendon Airport a lot. When my sister Janet and I were little, going to the airport meant one thing: we got to ride on a great see-saw there. After a while it dawned on me we were there because the old man was off on another basketball trip, whether interstate or overseas. It was second nature since he was away so often, including the day I was born.

Dad was an absent father in the sense that he didn't work regular hours. He worked in the VBA office or at meetings around town during the day, and most nights he would play, coach or attend more meetings. That's just the way it was. But it wasn't like he was never there and often we'd sneak a peek through the window to see if dad was coming from the stadium next door with a lolly, as he often would. Although dad had tremendous influence on my upbringing, it was mum who usually meted out punishments and did the running around for training and games.

My mum, Margaret, would get emotionally involved in the game of basketball. She has a reasonable understanding of the sport, but I wouldn't call her an expert. That said, a more passionate supporter you will not see and she is not backward in coming forwards when the situation calls for it. If she gets a set on someone for their on-court demeanour or actions, they're history – forget it. But when the game is over, she sees the players as people again and treats them accordingly. She's a typical fan in many ways: very parochial and one-eyed when it comes to the Melbourne Tigers.

My mum loves just about any sport. Put her in front of the TV for a game and she'll yell at the screen. She can't be neutral, she gets involved in the contest. She'll call blokes idiots and fools. But the thing is, she has never played basketball, never even shot a ball. I've never seen her in an athletic contest. Never ever. But she loves to watch and be involved. One of her involvements was Gaze Sportswear, which she operated for the first ten or eleven years of my life. She had a shop in St Kilda, making basketball uniforms. Basketball at that time was almost a total Gaze production.

Mum was often my confidante and I used her as a sounding board. If I needed advice I would usually involve both mum and dad, just to remove the emotional element, which mum and I couldn't get past. When I needed a rational, level-headed response to something that might appear dramatic, my dad had a great way of putting things into perspective and finding a solution that removed that dramatic element. Mum and I have always been more emotional about issues and some people might have noticed that, on the basketball court, I tend to show my mother's side.

Interestingly, my sister Janet, who is a year older than me, has a bit of both mum and dad in her. More than one person, though, has said she has more of my mother in her than she might want to acknowledge. Not that that's a bad thing. Janet is easygoing, rational and much more intellectual than me and much smarter. I think she got the old man's brains and mum's emotions. Janet is very quick to pick up on stuff and very sharp, whereas I take a little time to hone the blade. Janet played basketball but never really took to it like I did. She enjoyed it and was quite a capable player and that was good enough for her. Janet's involvement with basketball was probably a great example of how our parents treated us. We were surrounded by basketball, the food on the table came from basketball, but we were never pushed to play basketball. It was our choice.

Janet has been very supportive of me during my sporting career, usually going to home games with mum and, later, her own three kids. Growing up, we had a good, close relationship obviously helped by the closeness of our ages. I was always only one year behind her through school, and it helped me no end that I got her notes and assignments to lead me in the right direction. Like our family in general, we don't make a big deal of our relationship but it's safe to say that if I ever needed Janet in a crisis, she would be there in a heartbeat, just as I would be for her.

Because my dad was so busy, he rarely saw me play a game of basketball in my younger days. I cannot recall, except for once in the Nunawading under-fourteen tournament, any time when my dad watched me play. It probably wasn't until I was in the under-sixteens that he got more involved, and that was because he coached the team. So he never coached me in a team environment until I was fifteen. Because he worked in the office at Albert Park and I was shooting around on one of the courts, he might have taken fifteen minutes on his way to a meeting to offer some tips on technique or whatever. But it was intermittent input – there was no structured regime and I never really asked for help. It wasn't like the one-on-one scene from the movie *The Great Santini* in which the father, played by Robert Duval, refused to be beaten by the son and gave him a mental hammering. My dad's input was informal, almost like I was any other kid shooting hoops and my dad wandered by.

I actually played basketball with my dad before I was coached by him. Long before professionalism was even thought of in Australian basketball, the Tigers men would train Saturdays and Sundays and Monday nights. After training on Mondays, dad would play in the Melbourne Association comp with a team called Prahran. By the time I was about thirteen, I often played in that team with my dad and a lot of older, senior players. Some of them were former Tigers or younger blokes looking for another game and I would often help out when they were short on players.

That was the closest we got, in a pure basketball sense, because my dad had his commitments and I had mine. He also might have been wary about keeping a distance, knowing his presence might only have added to any pressure I was feeling. While I did learn a lot about basketball from my dad in a coaching and teaching sense, a lot of his greatest lessons were about life.

One of the lessons my dad hammered home in his subtle fashion was this: 'Andrew, there's three main areas of life: sport, social and academic. If you try to do all three, you have a chance to be pretty good at all of them, but you're not going to excel at any of them.' Most of the time, he conveyed that message to keep me focused on studies. He said, prophetically as it turned out, that it doesn't matter how long it takes to get educated, as long as you get there. He said different people do things differently and he was very big on not being concerned about failing. In his book, there's no shame in going back for a second crack and doing it again to get it right. If it took a couple of extra years to finish high school, so be it. Maybe I took him too literally, though, when it took me eleven years to finish university.

While I might have been tempted to let my tertiary education lapse, it was partly out of an obligation to my parents that I completed my degree to become a Bachelor of Applied Science. Having decided early that sport and education would be my choices from the three options presented by my dad, it seemed pointless not to finish uni, even if it was a decade after starting. Through my parental influences and guidance, I understood the value of education, which was a factor in my determination to get qualified.

That degree doesn't make me any more intelligent than the bloke next door, but it is nice to have the certificate on the wall. It doesn't say how my marks were or how long it took to earn it. Nor does it say I had to invoke my dad's help to get there when I struggled to fulfil the course's requirements. I had to front a committee and explain myself, but they weren't convinced of my worth as a student. Fortunately, I got a second hearing and, with my dad's help, I convinced them to let me continue the course. Had they known that, because of Olympic Games and world titles and overseas tours, it would take eleven years, they might have had second thoughts.

When I did finally graduate, it made the front page of the *Age* newspaper. It was big news all round. And a big relief, too.

That philosophy of excelling at two aspects of life rather than being mediocre at three was the basis of concentrating on sport and school, or making sure they were priorities. When my dad spoke, he usually made sense, even if it wasn't what I wanted to hear. There was usually a moral or a lesson to the tale, too.

Like when he gave me a lesson in the appreciation of money and spending it wisely. I was about eleven or twelve and had saved my pocket money to buy a toy pinball machine. Finally, the day came when I would get the tram to the city and make the purchase of a lifetime. Only, I never got that tram to the city. My dad talked me out of spending my money on the pinball machine. He never straight out said not to buy it, but basically he said it was a waste of my hard-earned money. I was shattered. What my dad suggested was that, rather than buy the pinball machine, we could go to the local hobby shop and buy a model plane that needed to be built. Then there would be a sense of learning and achievement in following the plan and constructing the plane. It makes sense now, but it didn't then and I bawled my eyes out about not getting the pinball machine. In fact, I must have cried and sooked long enough for my dad to pay for the plane. So it actually turned out to be a win for me.

My dad has a real philosophical bent. He has an extraordinary depth of knowledge on a range of subjects and it's not unknown for him to explain a loss on the basketball court by weaving in some Candide, a character created by eighteenth-century French author Voltaire, who believes the world we live in is 'the best of all possible worlds'. There's a whole package of philosophy and pragmatism in there. If you asked him about any issue, he'd give you an explanation, some history and an opinion. He can talk about politics, religion, world affairs, sport, whatever, and relate to other experiences without coming across as an opinionated know-all.

In fact, my dad is well-known for his philosophy pertaining to winning and losing basketball games. One line he has often trotted out is that a billion Chinese don't care about the NBL results and how they affect the Melbourne Tigers. As we now have Chinese investors and sponsors in the club, he may have to revise his figures. Another line of his, which is my favourite, is one that confused me for a long time.

One night, we had lost an under-fourteen or under-sixteen game and I hadn't played well. So I was sooking it up and carrying on a bit. My dad and I were talking casually and he tried to tell me about what it meant to just play the game. He told me that, when it came to winning and losing, 'there are only two times in life when winning is important: in surgery and in war'. As a fourteen year old, I didn't have a clue what he was talking about. It didn't make sense, but I took it in and it stuck in my brain. It wasn't until I was well into my senior career, and felt the pressure of success and failure and dealing with the uncomfortable internal feelings you have, that the penny finally dropped. That philosophy often doesn't alleviate the emotion of losing, but it does bring an understanding and a perspective that is impossible to argue with.

I suppose my dad's perspective and broad intellect come from being involved with so many people over his life. He has an enquiring mind and knows education comes only from learning new things, which means meeting different people and being open to suggestion and to interpretation that might not be popular but at least stimulates thinking and debate. As for the number of people my dad knows, I couldn't even start to count them. There is probably not a country in the world where he couldn't go and find a contact, either directly or indirectly, to help with what he needs to know or do. That's saying something, and that one fact makes it much easier to appreciate what basketball has done for my dad and me.

One thing about the old man is that he has time for everyone. He's extremely tolerant and gets to know people. And although he might eventually walk away and make an assessment or pass comment in the negative, he has at least given each person a fair hearing. Nor does he wait for people to come to him. Getting the Chinese involved in the Tigers was due to dad's enthusiasm, vision and persistence. While the players were off looking for cheap DVDs during our tours of China, dad would head off in the other direction, either looking for cultural and historical enlightenment or going to a meeting with Chinese officials and businessmen about basketball, the Tigers and the future. Sometimes, with his grand plans for international tournaments and tours, he might seem like the nutty professor, but he chips away and cultivates contacts, finding common denominators. And you know that, eventually, he will achieve his goal.

While many members of the modern world are all about instant gratification and results, my old man still has the patience to work on long-term goals like making international tournaments a reality. It might be four or five years down the track, but he has the foresight and the patience to see it through. I just sit there and shudder to think about how much hard work it will be, but he has the determination to do the ground work. That is a massive strength in his character.

One strength that might also be a weakness is that he firmly believes if you want something done properly, you do it yourself. I've seen it in the way he was an administrator and the way he coached: his ability to delegate is virtually zero. It's not that he doesn't trust people, but to get a job done the way he knows it should be done, he'd prefer to do it himself. Another thing he has always been big on is that there is more to basketball than just playing the game. It's also about philosophy, work ethic, desire, determination, passion, dealing with winning and losing, and the pressures success and failure bring. This is a lesson he has passed on to me. I learned the dimensions of a basketball court by helping him paint the lines when we resurfaced courts during the Christmas holidays. I know how to make nets for the baskets because dad used to buy cord and weave his own nets, which were better than anything he could buy. More than just playing and coaching, for my dad basketball was an all-encompassing involvement that went from running competitions to helping build countless stadia around Victoria.

My dad has always been there to serve the game, and while some people have assumed he had an ulterior motive for being on committees and so on, the fact is that if he's asked to contribute, he'll never say no. It's true that he has sat on countless committees, both in Australia and overseas. In fact, he is still on the FIBA Technical Committee, which deals with the rules of the game and meets in Europe annually. But he never makes a fanfare of these meetings. He'd tell you on Thursday he was going to Geneva, fly out Friday, attend the weekend meetings, then be back at Tigers training on Tuesday. No big deal. He sees it as an honour and a privilege and a duty to the game to be on committees and there's certainly never any lobbying on his part.

He made that clear back in the early 1970s when Ken Cole publicly campaigned to take over from my dad as coach of the men's national team. While Cole, one of the most colourful and flamboyant characters Australian basketball ever had, was happily quoted in the media, my dad's only comment was that being in charge of the national team was not a job you should lobby for. That's pretty typical of his outlook. It was a position of honour, not politics.

Unfortunately, politics and the accusations that come with it are unavoidable in sport. So it has been for me and my dad, going back to the day I was booed at Coburg and continuing until the day we retired from the NBL. There were accusations of nepotism when he was Boomers coach and I was selected for the 1984 Olympic team, but many people were ignorant of the real situation of how my dad viewed selection. If I wasn't worthy, I wouldn't have been in the team. I can say that with a totally clear conscience.

In fact, I might have had to do *more* to prove I was good enough for that team. I *never* had an easy passage because of who I was and

I know for sure that my old man wasn't going to start handing our favours when it came to the Olympic team. Even when he coached me in juniors, I was never treated any differently because I was the coach's son. My dad treated all his players as his boys and as equals. It was almost to the point that he was a teacher as much as coach. If we had young players of limited ability at Tigers training, he would teach those kids as much as he would the NBL players. Sometimes this was frustrating as he devoted time to players who were not going to play in an upcoming game, but such is his nature that he was compelled to teach. That's just the way he was as a coach.

As for him and me, if someone who didn't know us spent a year with the Tigers and was asked at end of that year who was the coach's son, I don't think they would have been able to say. Others might think differently, but that's how I saw it. My Tigers team-mate Mark Bradtke had a different take on it. He used to joke that I got looked after because my mum was sleeping with the coach.

For me, it's hard to separate my dad the coach from my dad the parent because he was my basketball coach for more than half of my life. It's not like the lines were blurred for me when it came to him being a coach as well as a parent. It's just that my dad is very consistent in all facets of his life, whether it be coaching or parenting. He doesn't go through emotional highs or lows. He is very stable, very approachable and very reliable – as a coach and as a parent.

I do acknowledge that most guys wouldn't be able to hack it with their dad being so involved in what they did. But it's not like we're joined at the hip. We have separate lives, we do different things. It's just that we worked together, like two guys in a father-and-son accounting practice, except I reckon we had more thrills on game nights.

Nor did success change how we see each other. We wouldn't have a different relationship if I had not been a basketball player. The relationship my dad has with Janet, who didn't play much at an elite level, is no different from the one he has with me. When we're in a non-basketball environment, it's no different. We are who we are and we feel pretty secure about that. We don't have a really demonstrative relationship in which we hug and show our affections. I guess we're a little bit old school in that regard. But I know if I ever needed my dad, he would be there in an instant. Like when I was in hospital with the blood clot that went from my shoulder to my lungs. I thought I was going to die, but I knew that if my dad was there to reassure me everything would be fine. He has the ability of keeping things in perspective, seeing the positive and taking an even-handed approach, even when things seem most dire.

Even though I achieved a lot in my career, I have never needed my dad to tell me how proud he is of me. I know he is, but to go over the top is just not his way. That he was willing to travel around the world to see me play is proof of pride in a way. That he and my mum flew to Seattle on a weekend visit for the Final Four of the National Collegiate Athletic Association (NCAA) tournament when I was at Seton Hall showed that. My dad's reticence in demonstrating his pride or congratulations is not reserved for just me – it's the same for everyone. Achieving is not special to my dad. Your life should be spent *trying* to achieve. But I'll tell you one thing: when somebody is down, my dad will be one of the first to offer a hand up, whether it be with an overt gesture or something as simple as a letter of encouragement. Anybody can get pats on the back when they're doing well. My dad will usually have a pat on the back for you if you're not. That's just one reason why I'm proud to say I'm Lindsay Gaze's son, whether people want to boo me for it or not.

chapter three

AN OLYMPIAN, ONCE AND ALWAYS

THE train ride home from the Footscray Institute of Technology to St Kilda, via Flinders Street Station, was always the same. It never differed, from the stations we stopped at to the jerky swaying of the carriages and the rattle and hum of the engine. Just for once, only once, I wanted this train to be an express. Better still, a bullet from door to door. Didn't this train driver know I needed to get to the letter box? Today. Right now. It was Wednesday 2 May 1984. It was the day I would find out whether I was to be an Olympian.

As we closed our gruelling Boomers training camp the week before in Canberra, Phil Smyth asked me to call when I knew who was in the Olympic team. I knew what Phil thought. He didn't know what I knew: even though my dad was the national team coach, I would be the last person to know the team. Or at least

I wouldn't know until I ripped open the envelope I hoped was waiting for me when I got off that slow train. Phil reckoned my dad would drop the team to me early. But there was not a chance in the world. For one thing, I knew not to ask; for another, I knew there was a better chance of James Naismith, the creator of basketball, still being alive than of my dad telling me the team before the official notification. The postie had that honour.

I don't expect anyone to believe it – I wouldn't if I were them – but the honest truth is that I had no idea who would be on that 1984 Olympic team until the letters arrived, and neither did my mum. So it was probably fitting that as I started nervously lifting the flap on the envelope, my mum was right alongside me. Finally, I got the letter out and unfolded it. I was in. We probably jigged a couple of laps around the kitchen table because that was as far as the news could travel. The letter said to keep the selection information confidential until the next day when it would be officially announced to the public. I was in the Olympic team and couldn't tell anyone.

That night, the Melbourne Tigers, who were also coached by my dad, had a VBA State League game at the old Albert Park Stadium. Just about everyone I knew was there, playing or just hanging out, and the best news of my life had to stay a secret. As we warmed up for the game, the old man never even gave a glimpse of acknowledgment about my Olympic selection. The instruction was to keep it quiet and my dad, in his inimitable fashion, took it to the letter. That was my dad's way. He knew and I knew but it was business as usual. I was in the team, I deserved it, so deal with it.

We played the game and I was up in the old wooden bleachers watching the game after ours when Brian Goorjian approached me. Brian was a team-mate who eventually became the Boomers coach for the 2004 Athens Olympics. He stuck his hand out and congratulated me on making the team for the LA Olympics. Somebody, maybe even the old man, hadn't been able to keep the secret after all.

My dad being Boomers coach and the talk of nepotism never took the gloss off my first Olympic selection. Some people might think it would, but it didn't. It was because of my dad that I aspired to be an Olympian. It was because of my dad that I *became* an Olympian. I grew up hearing stories of the Olympic Games. My dad was involved in the 1956 Olympics at Melbourne as an emergency for the exhibition Australian Rules football match and he went to every Olympics as a player or coach through to 1984 in LA. He was in the Olympic Village when PLO terrorists slaughtered members of the Israeli weightlifting team at Munich in 1972. He was poolside when Dawn Fraser won gold in Tokyo in 1964 and he was at the track when Herb Elliott won the 1500 metres at Rome in 1960. He told me stories that encompassed the history and, perhaps more importantly, the spirit and deeds of those who competed at the Olympic Games. When I was fourteen or fifteen, I started to think, 'Why wouldn't you want to go to the Olympic Games?'

Those ambitious thoughts coincided with the 1980 Moscow Olympics. The 1980 Games were shrouded in controversy, with sixty-five nations staying away, most of them in support of the United States-led boycott protesting the Soviet Union's invasion and occupation of Afghanistan, but they were a watershed for me. While I was aware of the 1972 and 1976 Olympics with my dad coaching the Boomers, the Moscow Games were probably the first I had taken a strong interest in. In fact, the 1980 Games were a big motivating force for me to become an Olympian because the basketball games were on television early in the mornings. I loved watching the basketball, but we also tried to see dad on the sidelines, just to make sure the KGB hadn't snatched him from his bed.

In Moscow, the Boomers lost to Cuba by seven and weren't given much chance in the next game against Italy, who went on to win the silver medal. It was a game I'll never forget. Likewise for those who actually played in the 84–77 upset win. The images of Ian Davies, still a relative unknown in Australia after spending much of his life in the United States, dropping bombs on the Italians on his way to being the tournament's leading scorer were indelible. I recall Phil Smyth at these his first Olympics, running down the clock at the end and Gordie McLeod, who hadn't played a minute, running around like a celebrating lunatic, hugging my dad, showing just how much the win meant.

It was so exciting. It showed the Australians weren't bad at basketball and we could compete on the biggest stage available. It meant I could go to school that morning with my chest out and my pride overflowing. Unfortunately, not too many others felt the same way. When people heard we beat Italy, they thought it was no big deal. They didn't understand. They didn't know the history or what it meant. For the basketball community and for me, it was huge. It was a very important game in fuelling my fire to experience that mystique of the Olympics first hand.

Some time after the Moscow Olympics, the Gazes were doing the Sunday night ritual of lounging around in front of the television, waiting for the new week to start. It was at our old house in St Leonard's Avenue. I was on the couch, dad was on the floor and mum was in her favourite chair as we watched a documentary about the Olympics. That was when mum mentioned that it would be great if one day I made it to the Olympics. Mum thought 1988 might be my best chance. As a worldly wise fifteen year old still trying to make the Victorian junior team two years in a row, I tended to agree. My dad didn't.

To support his opinion, my dad quickly launched into a story, as only he can, of Olympic experiences and examples of people who achieved great deeds only because they aimed high in the first place. In his mind, successful people set the highest standards to aim for. He held up 1988 as a possible Olympic goal, but asked, 'Why shoot for 1988, when the 1984 Olympics are available as a target?' In his view, to aim for 1988 was what was expected. To aim for 1984 was a chance to excel. Set your goal as high as possible and at least give yourself a chance. If you set your goal at making the 1988 Olympics, then you've got no chance for 1984. My dad probably wasn't that specific and he didn't apply it to me and my Olympic aspirations, but he was saying to aim as high as you can and achieve as high as you can.

That talk hit the mark. What he basically meant was that you shouldn't feel ashamed or embarrassed or reluctant to set yourself high goals. It also put in perspective that maybe it was not out of the question for me to think about the Olympics. I was fifteen, LA was three years away and I started to believe it was possible. I would be only eighteen or nineteen by the time LA arrived. What were the chances? Long to very long, I thought. But it intrigued me enough to think it might be possible, that maybe if I aimed higher than I should dare, I might just achieve it anyway.

It was a fortunate moment that possibly shaped my life. If we hadn't been sitting there that night, if we hadn't been watching that program, if mum hadn't said what she did, I might never have had that conversation with my dad. The seed might never have been planted. That was a significant conversation and moment in my life. If my dad hadn't planted that seed, who knows whether I would have achieved what I did in basketball. Without the seed, I might never have contemplated the possibilities. Not so soon anyway. The other aspect of that conversation was my dad spoke purely as my dad, not as a basketball coach. Nor was it supposed to be about the Olympics, even though he used the Olympics as the example. It was about life in general, but those Olympic images certainly painted a powerful and lasting mind portrait.

When I didn't analyse or replay my dad's message from the carpet, I listened to a motivational speech that my dad had taped on a trip to America. I've still got the tape, but I don't need to play it to know what it says. I have listened to that scratchy recording so much I have almost memorised it. It's the worst quality tape, but the words from Reverend Bob Richards, an American known as the

'Vaulting Vicar' after winning Olympic gold medals in 1952 and 1956, as he addressed the Louisiana State University basketball team formed one of the most impressive motivational speeches I've ever heard. On the tape, Richards talked about setting goals and relating them to Olympic experiences, which was a bit like my dad's talk. As a slowly maturing fifteen year old just starting to eye senior basketball, it had a great impact and influence on me. I had probably been told a lot more significant things along the way that went in one ear and out the other. But when my dad or Bob Richards were in my head about the Olympics, nothing else mattered.

Some people thought, and maybe still do, that I made the Boomers team for LA because my dad was the coach. Public criticism and accusations of nepotism were nothing new to me. Remember, I was the kid who got booed at Coburg when I collected my tournament MVP trophy. So a few people making the suggestion that my father picked me on the basis of blood rather than merit was only natural. The accusations, though, could not have been further off the mark. Actually, at the time I didn't think it was much of a big deal. If there was some objective justification for my selection, it was that I was the leading Australian scorer in the NBL that season, hitting 29.1 points per game (or ppg) and winning the NBL Rookie of the Year award. To me, and my dad, statistics and awards were irrelevant in the selection process. But it gave the general public, who didn't see a lot of basketball or understand the selection process and philosophy, some evidence for them to grasp. They could see, even though I was only a teenager, that I was the leading Australian scorer in the NBL.

There was never, certainly from my point of view, any hint of nepotism or favouritism from my father. Ever. When I was selected in the Olympic team, he didn't say anything because he didn't have to. That's how he was with everyone. You need to understand the relationship and the personalities involved for it to make sense. When you think of a stereotypical family situation, you would say there would be a feeling of nepotism even from within. There wasn't in our situation. For me, it was an opportunity.

My first Boomers selection in 1983, which never gets talked about, might have been a more debatable point. I had just been to the junior world championships in Spain and the Boomers were going to tour Canada and the United States as part of the preparation for the 1984 Olympics. My dad, as Boomers coach, had looked a little down the track and had spoken to the Australian junior team coach Ian Laurie and his assistant Pat Hunt about who would be worth taking on that senior tour. On their advice it ended up with me, Mark Dalton and Peter Wain being promoted, which I think was supposed to send a message to a few players to make sure they maintained their edge going into an Olympic year. That selection might have been subject to more scrutiny and question than in 1984 because the Tigers were not playing in the NBL in 1983. Although we won the second-tier South East Conference and I was a prominent player for the Tigers, that initial selection, I believe, was to see what I and a couple of others could do at that level as part of the national team's process of identifying, grooming and developing players for the future. If I couldn't cut the mustard, I would have been found out and the accusations of nepotism would have been allowed to gain substance. I wasn't found out and that should have been enough to quieten those with a beef.

I think I showed my potential to be a national team player over Easter 1982, when the Boomers endured their gruelling annual training camp at Albert Park. Twenty players were invited to the camp, but my dad called me in to make up the numbers when one of the invitees was a late withdrawal. It was a brutal camp but, at only sixteen, I had the time of my life as I played with Boomers regulars Phil Smyth, Larry Sengstock, Wayne Carroll and Ian Davies, who generated an intense level of competition that showed what was needed to succeed at international level. We had two sessions per day, with the twenty players split into four teams of five for the afternoon and evening scrimmages. It was just so physically demanding and, being a boy among men, I reckon it was the toughest Boomers training camp I ever endured. After the morning sessions, I would go home, get something to eat and sleep, ready for the next session. I didn't want to embarrass myself with these blokes, who were still my heroes from the 1980 Olympics, and I don't believe I did.

The junior world championships in 1983 were my first truly international basketball experience. In terms of a setting for a tournament involving virile young men, Palma de Mallorca, off the coast of Spain, was a disaster. On a holiday island later made infamous as the hideaway for Australian fugitive businessman Christopher Skase, there were plenty of female distractions, so it really was a test to see who was going to perform. At basketball.

There were some good players on that junior team and all of us went on to at least play in the NBL, while my roommate on that trip, Brett Flanigan, coached the Canberra Cannons for seven NBL seasons. I was the youngest player on the team and wet behind the ears in terms of the mysteries of life outside the basketball court. Flanigan, who was a lot more experienced in the social department, had it sussed. We stayed in a big tourist resort and Brett did not let something like the language barrier stop him from meeting plenty of the inmates. One time Brett tried to converse with a French girl, but he spoke no French and she spoke no English. That was where one of our big men, Sandy Caldwell, came in handy. Sandy spoke French and acted as interpreter for Brett, but I'm not sure that he was passing on Brett's lines as suavely as their original English intended.

That tournament turned out to be a good lesson in life and basketball. In the opening pool matches, we lost to West Germany and Brazil either side of a win over China, but that wasn't good enough to make the top-eight phase. In the consolation round, we beat Angola (a little different to the next time I was in Spain), Canada and Uruguay, and lost to the Dominican Republic for a tenth-placed finish. It was a mediocre effort, but I learned plenty about the international game and tournament lifestyle. World championships and Olympic Games are all about playing games over a two-week period. It's not like an extended league season, where you sometimes get a few second chances. In tournament play, one false move, one bad result, can ruin your chances of a medal. That's why you must understand and appreciate the urgency and importance of every single game at the big international events. You never give a sucker an even break and you always walk around with eyes open, looking for the next trip-wire to send you crashing.

I know my dad reflected on certain selection situations for the national team and wondered about what might have been for players had they been picked rather than left out at certain times. I've heard him talk about what sort of international career Michael Johnson might have had if he'd gone on that 1983 tour of Canada and the United States. Johnson was an outstanding perimeter shooter, one of the best the NBL ever saw during his long career with the Newcastle Falcons. But his international career with the Boomers was limited to basically a handful of games. For a player of his talent, you sometimes wonder what might have been. Another shooter in the frame for the 1984 Olympics was Darryl Pearce from Adelaide. There was talk that Darryl, who averaged 26.1 ppg that season, should have been in the team. But if anybody had a problem with my selection for the 1984 Olympics, they did not tell me. That said, there was one bloke from New South Wales who wrote to the now defunct *The Australian Basketballer* magazine claiming my selection 'can only be considered as pure nepotism'. Funnily enough he wanted Gordie McLeod and Ian Robilliard, both from New South Wales, in the team. Bill Palmer, a former player who went on to become the NBL's general manager, replied in the next issue supporting my selection, which was nice of him. But the bottom line for me was that I just wanted to go to LA, go to the Olympics, do the best I could with whatever opportunity I would get and try to enjoy it.

My dad's theory on the Olympic Games opening ceremonies was that you could see more and enjoy it more from the grandstand. But his strong advice was that if you had never marched in an Olympic Games opening ceremony, you should do it because it would be an experience you would never forget. He didn't need to tell me twice. The opening ceremony for the 1984 Olympics at the LA Memorial Coliseum was a flash affair and probably the first of the we-can-do-better-than-you openings that followed. There were grand pianos and a spaceman flying through the air, but the highlight might have come from team-mate Damian Keogh as we walked around the stadium track. Somehow, he spotted glamorous actors Linda Evans and Brooke Shields in the crowd. He yelled out to them, but that was about the extent of the communication: I don't ever recall Damo hooking up with the girls during our time in LA. For me, Linda Evans and Brooke Shields could have run naked through the Olympic Village and I might not have noticed – there was so much going on and I just tried to soak it all in. After all, how did I know if I would get to another Olympic Games?

Given that it was my first, if not my only, Olympic Games, the experience was obviously new and fresh, so there was plenty of head swivelling and jaw dropping, even if some things didn't quite match up to expectations. As the premier sports event in the world, the Olympics have a perception of grandeur, with five-star accommodation, everyone at your beck and call, the freedom to do as you please. The difference between perception and reality can sometimes be a rude shock. The first thing that struck me was the level of security. From the time we landed at LA International Airport and processed our accreditation, the security was enormously tight. Apart from the guards and police on the ground, there was a helicopter circling the village most of the time. I wasn't sure whether I should have felt safe or felt threatened. But after the massacre at Munich in 1972, you could not blame the organisers for looking after the athletes' safety, even if it meant going to extremes.

A unique aspect of the LA Olympics was the two athlete villages. One was on the University of California Los Angeles (UCLA) campus and the other, where we stayed, was on the University of Southern California (USC) campus. It was a negative splitting the village. Part of the thrill of the Olympics is the village, where the sporting world gathers and you are exposed to different cultures. That's a big part of the Olympics and some of it was missing in LA.

As for the standard of accommodation, just let it be said that three units between a twelve-man basketball team, its coaches and support staff did not make for palatial living. Each apartment had a small living room and kitchenette and two bedrooms with two bunks each. I shared a room with Damian Keogh and Mel Dalgleish, who grabbed the bottom bunk beds. Seniority ruled, so junior had to clamber up to the second-storey bed every night. Which was better than our team manager Bob Elphinstone, who slept in the living room. Once the tournament started, sleeping arrangements were the least of our worries.

At every Olympic Games I went to, the Boomers identified a game we had to win to advance to the crossover rounds against an opponent we thought we could beat. In LA, there were two: the opening game of the tournament against Brazil and another against West Germany. Win those two and, theoretically, we would go into a quarter final against a team other than the gold medal favourite, the United States, which had on its roster future NBA superstars Michael Jordan, Chris Mullin, Patrick Ewing and Sam Perkins under the coaching of fiery college legend Bob Knight. This was the team Charles Barkley didn't make, so they must have felt pretty good about themselves.

Brazil took us all the way to the buzzer in my Olympic debut and, I'm pleased to say, I made a valid and significant contribution. With a couple of minutes left, I had the ball with the shot clock (we had thirty seconds on each possession to take a shot) running down. I was way out. There was no three-point line under FIBA rules in those days, but I would have been well beyond the arc. I just heaved up this prayer and it was answered, helping us to win 76–72 after we trailed by four at the half. It was a massive win because we felt if we got by the Brazilians we would certainly make the top four in our group.

We lost the next game to European power Yugoslavia, then came the big game against West Germany. We won, 67–66, after being down five at half-time. We lost to Italy and then we beat Egypt, pulling away in the second half. What seemed like a regulation win over Egypt was also historic for the Boomers. It was the first time we had qualified for the Olympic quarter finals, with a chance to progress to the medal rounds. Unfortunately, we lost to Spain, 101–93, in the quarters and were eliminated from the medal race. In the consolation rounds, we lost to Uruguay and beat West Germany again to finish seventh.

The win over West Germany was more important than finishing seventh, which was our best finish at the Olympics. We should have been in the play-off for fifth and sixth, but the loss to Uruguay in the first game of the classification round relegated us to the play-off for seventh and eighth. It was a deflating scenario similar to the one the Boomers had faced in Moscow four years earlier. We still had some of that team in LA and it was interesting to see how they responded to our situation.

My dad often talked about 1980 at Moscow, when Australia got screwed in the infamous seven-point game between Cuba and Italy. There were three pools of four, so you had to finish in the top two to advance to the second round, which determined the four teams to play for medals. The Boomers lost to Cuba 83–76, upset Italy 84–77 and beat Sweden 64–55. Italy beat Sweden by 15 and Cuba beat Sweden by 12, so the Boomers were almost guaranteed a top-six finish. The only way they would miss was if Italy beat Cuba by seven points in the final group game. Then Italy and Cuba would advance. Any other result would be good for Australia.

There was no way the game between Italy and Cuba was fixed.

Far from it. Suffice to say that, once the game got near the finish and the margin was possibly seven, an element of cooperation was introduced between the teams. My dad was courtside and reckoned once the realisation dawned, late in the game, that Italy and Cuba could both advance, there was no reason to spoil what had suddenly become a beautiful basketball relationship. The most ominous sign for the Australians came with a few minutes left and one team shooting two free-throws, with Italy ahead by an even number. When the player made one and missed one, my dad turned to team manager Bob Staunton and said: 'We've got trouble here.' Sure enough, Italy won, 79–72. The seven-point margin meant Australia was heave-hoed back into the classification spots. The Boomers finished the tournament with a 6–2 record in eighth place while Italy, which played for gold after upsetting the Soviet Union in the crossover games, went 5–4 to show the vagaries and importance of every game in such a tournament.

The point of the story was not the Boomers' hard luck. Rather, it was the response from the team after such a shattering blow. It was something my dad always talked about: how the Boomers beat Czechoslovakia in their next game. He talked about that team demonstrating its character. After the shattering situation where playing for a medal was probable, the Australians now had to play for seventh at best. Rather than any great material reward, the Boomers were playing for pride and to show just what they were made of. It would have been a perfect time to spit the dummy over the seven-point game and get the sulks. But they showed their character against the Czechs and won.

We were in a similar situation in LA after losing what we thought was a winnable quarter final to Spain. Then we lost our next game in the classification rounds to Uruguay, which was a team we should have beaten. I thought about what my dad had said about the team in Moscow and whether this team in LA had that kind of character. Against Uruguay we didn't show much character at all.

After the loss to Spain in the quarters, some players relaxed totally, taking the attitude that because we couldn't win a medal, the tournament was over. Fortunately, the loss to Uruguay jolted everyone back to the real world. Faced with going all out or just turning up against West Germany, we had a fair dinkum crack and beat them in another close contest. We could have said, 'Stuff it, we're not interested.' But we came back to win it for the best ever Australian finish at the Olympics.

I held my own at my first Olympics without setting off a chorus of oohs and aahs every time I touched the ball. I played as the sixth or seventh man, averaging about fifteen to twenty minutes per game off the bench, and I was fairly satisfied with my effort. The one thing that probably put it all in perspective for me was that, even though I was an Olympian, I still had a commitment to play for the Melbourne Tigers under-twenty team every Friday night. Not that I thought that was unusual. It was all still just basketball to me. During the preparation for the LA Olympics, the Boomers played a series against the touring Cibona club team from Croatia. After the game in Melbourne, I flew out that night to Perth to play for Victoria in the under-twenty national championships.

That underlined my youth in the Olympic team. Playing-wise there was no problem; I was accepted by my peers. From a social point of view, though, I was not as advanced as the others. Mainly, we just hung out in the village between games, and training and village life was fine by me. I got an appreciation of the camaraderie that existed between the Australian Olympians from all sports, and experienced the special buzz when the first Aussie medal, and especially the gold medals won by swimmer Jon Sieben, heptathlete Glynis Nunn, weightlifter Dean Lukin and the men's team pursuit cyclists, arrived back in the village. There were other attractions in the village, such as the games arcade and the dining hall. It was all the food and Space Invaders you wanted. All free. How could you beat that? It turned out my dad could.

During the Olympic tournament, my dad was approached by a representative of Pony footwear. He had some cash available if six players wore Pony shoes for the rest of the tournament. Adidas was the official team sponsor, but footwear was a personal choice and some guys already had deals with Puma. Given that we were part-time athletes, maybe earning a few grand in the NBL, any extra cash was always welcomed.

After one game, a meeting was called at the back of the old school bus that drove us between the village and basketball venue, which was the Forum, famous as the home of the LA Lakers. It all seemed very clandestine as my dad explained the situation that Pony would tip in the money for us all to share if we got six blokes to wear Pony shoes. My dad left it up to the players to decide and there was never a problem getting the numbers. I would have been happy with a free pair of shoes, but when we had our six volunteers I continued wearing the shoes supplied by adidas, the official supplier to the Australian Olympic Committee. I think we got about a thousand US dollars a man in cash, which my dad distributed each time the Pony guy came good. It was all for the players – my dad never took a cent – but I don't think all of the players understood or appreciated that. It wasn't massive money, but it was better than the minimal per diem we got from the Australian Olympic Committee.

The one thing about my dad as coach of the Olympic team was that he would do anything to make sure we had a chance to give our best. If that meant getting us a few extra dollars or making a couple of controversial selections along the way, so be it. When you look at the teams he coached in 1980 and 1984, they both over-achieved with undersized rosters. Ian Davies was maligned for his defence, but he could score and he played his best basketball for my dad. Mel Dalgleish was a rough diamond, but he played at two Olympics and there was a good reason for that: dad picked teams for the Olympic tournament and international conditions. It's easy to pick an all-star team, but all-star teams don't do well at the Olympic Games. There was no better example of this then when the star-studded United States team, which had the best individual talent, finished third at the 2004 Athens Olympics. That was why blokes like Dalgleish and Damian Keogh got selected. They were tough, hard-nosed competitors and sometimes you needed to forget about niceties in international basketball and just work your butt off. We did that in 1984 and got a decent result.

I had always wanted to play basketball for Australia and be an Olympian. But it wasn't until that Sunday night conversation with my mum and dad that I started to realise maybe the dream could become reality. I always knew, though, I would have to earn that chance myself. That there would be no favours.

My dad once gave me a T-shirt that was given to Australian team members and I wore it to Tigers training one day. I wore it only once. My Tigers junior team-mates thought I was presumptuous wearing a shirt that purported to make me something I wasn't. I wore it because it was a basketball T-shirt that my dad had given me, but I never wore it again. Like the training singlet my mum gave me. She took one of my dad's old Australian playing singlets and tailored it to size, so I could use it as a training top. It was an ideal piece of clothing for that purpose. But I couldn't wear it: I had not earned the right to wear it. I understood the difference between the T-shirt and the singlet and there was no way I would wear an Australian singlet until I had been chosen to play for Australia.

Funnily enough, I did not keep a lot of my Olympic gear and I regret not retaining and collecting more memorabilia of my international career. In fact, after the LA Olympics, I tore the pocket with the Australian Coat of Arms off the team blazer and sent the blazer down to the nearest Brotherhood bin. Years later, a bloke contacted my dad to say he had the blazer, with my name inside it, and wanted me to autograph it.

Making the Olympic team wasn't about the uniform or the flag. It was about being an Olympian. You can represent your country regularly in various events and games, but the Olympics are something special. Some people compete in the Olympics only once in a lifetime. That was the greater significance to me: no matter what happened, for the rest of my life after LA, I would be an Olympian. If I lived until I was a hundred, I would still be an Olympian. It is an accomplishment never to be taken for granted. You are never an ex-Olympian. I didn't need any letter to tell me that.

chapter four

WHATEVER YOU DO, DON'T MENTION ANGOLA

SITTING through pre-game team meetings, it's easy to get distracted when you've heard the same thing a few times and seen the same tactical Xs and Os on the chalkboard. It's often easy to let concentration slip, knowing you are about to face an opponent your team should handle with few complications. Attentive as I was before the Boomers' 1986 World Championship game against Angola, I did a double-take to make sure I had heard coach Adrian Hurley correctly.

Without any warning, Hurley said he was sending me to the bench so he could start Ian Davies to try to run him into some form. A bit of a heads-up would have been nice, but the coach is the coach and he made the call. I just abided by it. As we headed out to the warm-up, Adrian called me aside to explain the situation. Ian tore a calf muscle at training in Verona, Italy, on the way to Spain for the world titles and had struggled with his form. An outside shooter who could knock the lights out at his best, Davies was leading scorer at the 1982 world titles in Colombia. But he was in a slump and Adrian and the Boomers needed him out of it. The rationale was simple. We were 1–1 after two games of our 1986 campaign in Spain, we would beat Angola, take care of Israel, run around with the USSR and be on our merry way like a bunch of basketball matadors to Madrid for the second phase of the tournament. It was the perfect chance to get Davies going for the finals in Madrid.

The reality was something else again. Davies went 2–12 from the field, I stayed on the bench for all but a few minutes and we lost to Angola, the rank underdogs from Africa, 74–69, in the worst loss the men's national team ever endured. It was a humiliation. Our campaign and reputations were ruined.

The north-western Spanish seaside town of Ferrol is an historic port with its roots based in the navy and its battleships. It is an idyllic retreat, yet we might as well have lived down a Welsh coal mine for the twenty-four hours after that loss to Angola. Nobody was game to put their heads up for fear of reprisal. We knew straightaway the loss would create a rumble that would remain an everlasting spike on Australian basketball's Richter scale. Interestingly, in researching this book, the AIS video library supplied several tapes of important games. The library had every game on the lengthy request list except one: the loss to Angola. Mention Angola and it's enough to send some of the local hoops community into facial tics and seizures. Why would you want any evidence of it?

I'll say one thing for Adrian Hurley in the aftermath of the Angolan defeat: he faced the Australian media and put his hand up straightaway to accept responsibility, totally and completely. As coach, he was compelled to do that. This was his first major tournament as Boomers coach and it turned into a nightmare with us finishing equal thirteenth. The coach had some help from the Boomers that night with a poor performance.

Who knows whether the result would have been different had I started and played more. I'd like to think it would have, given that I finished our five games in the tournament with a 16.0 ppg scoring average. What Adrian did in benching me was unusual, but I understood it. I'm sure Adrian mulled long and hard over the decision and maybe only decided at the last minute to pull the trigger on it. Such a change should not have affected our performance against Angola. No disrespect to the Africans, but the basketball community wasn't exactly building monuments to them coming into this game. While Davies was hobbled and we split games with a win over Cuba and a loss to Uruguay, Angola lost to the USSR by thirty-eight points and to Israel by twenty. After they beat Australia, the Angolans lost to Cuba by twenty-eight and lost to Uruguay by two in overtime. The Boomers were the only team Angola beat.

Even though Angola led the game for most of the forty minutes, there was always a feeling we would pull out the win we needed. So what if it wasn't convincing. We just needed the W, which we looked like getting when we led by five with about five minutes to go. Adrian kept faith with Ian and did not yank him in what might have been a sign of panic and it looked like we would steal it with our fingers burned at the tips. Then a skinny Angolan guard by the name of Manuel Sousa threw us into despair by repeatedly plunging a dagger through our hearts. Angola lost their two big men to fouls, but Sousa did the job from the perimeter, hitting seven three-pointers in the second half. By the time we doused his fire, the damage was done, the situation irretrievable. Just like it had been during the Watts riots in LA, this was a case of burn, baby, burn. We had been burned badly.

Back in the locker room where this chapter started, things were quiet. Shock, disappointment and anger permeated the room and there were some half-hearted attempts to buck ourselves up with the idea that we were still alive if other results went our way and we beat Israel in the next game and then took care of the powerhouse Soviet Union in the final pool game. But the main feeling among us all, players and coaches, was that we had royally screwed up.

If we played that Angolan team fifty times, we would have won forty-nine of them. It was just that World Championships are not where you want to have that freak loss. I was annoyed about it. I was annoyed because, given the way we had prepared and played, to change things for a game that was very important didn't make sense. My dad is fond of saying you should never give a sucker an even break. We did and, in a tournament where one unexpected result means you're stuffed, we learned the hard way. We were stuffed.

My anger and frustration over the Angola loss did not greatly diminish with a night's sleep. In fact, I'm not sure I slept too much. I was upset, confused, withdrawn and not in the mood for much of anything. At least by the time the next game against Israel rolled around, I was back in the mood to play basketball. Even though Adrian recalled me to the starting line-up, I was not placated. I seethed inside and that anger motivated me to whack up a few shots without too much concern for the result.

I finished with thirty-seven points and the Boomers beat Israel 98–91, but only after a mad minute and a half at the end when we overcame a one-point deficit, starting with my three-pointer and drive and capped by big Ray Borner's lay-up on the buzzer. For the sake of the calculations in splitting a possible tie in the standings, we had to win by five or more points. We won by seven, but, with the unlikely possibility of Angola beating Cuba to help us out, we still needed to beat the USSR. With giant centre Arvydas Sabonis at his peak, we never had a chance. We led 46–45 at the half, when someone suggested we take a photo of the scoreboard, but lost 122–92. Our tournament was over. Let the recriminations begin.

The fallout from the 1986 World Championships was substantial but Adrian Hurley kept the job as national team coach. It would have been unfair for him to be sacked. Hurley was assistant coach to my dad at the 1982 world titles and the 1984 Olympics, taking over when my dad stepped down. In a sense, this 1986 team really wasn't Adrian's because most of the players, especially the older blokes, had come through with my dad's system and Adrian was still finding the right blend of personnel and a system that would make the Boomers his team. That Hurley stayed in the job is perhaps an indication of how times and expectations have changed. When the Boomers lost to New Zealand in a three-game series and failed to qualify for the 2002 World Championships, Phil Smyth resigned as coach, though my take on it was that he was unfairly pushed.

There were factors that worked against Hurley and the Boomers in Spain. One was the team seemed fragmented from the start, coming together only for training and games. Cliques, if you like, formed and it didn't really help the group dynamic of getting twelve blokes on the same page at the same time. I hung around with Darryl Pearce and Paul Kuiper, then there was Brad Dalton and his younger brother Mark with Simon Cottrell and Ian Davies, while the veterans like Phil Smyth, Wayne Carroll, Larry Sengstock and Ray Borner were elsewhere. When we weren't playing, several different agendas were on the go and I'm not sure that was a good thing for the team. More than any hostility between individuals, it was a case of different ages and personalities and levels of desire as basketballers and competitors. There was no conflict, but there wasn't a lot of harmony and lovin', either.

That was soon evident once the team arrived home from Spain. Which was one other major problem of a trip that might have been doomed from the start. We couldn't get home.

Normally, if you don't qualify for the quarter finals of a major tournament, you are relegated to the minor classification rounds. In 1986 in Spain, the organisers scrapped the classification system, advancing only the top twelve of the twenty-four teams from the first phase to the finals in Madrid. So while we were booked to go to Madrid, we did not need to go. But nobody had assumed we would be leaving Spain so soon. There was no contingency travel plan and that caused a major problem.

We wanted to go home, albeit with our tails between our legs, as soon as possible. We had been on the road for a few weeks, away from family, from work and the NBL, which continued in our absence. That we were meant to be in Madrid for another week or so shouldn't have been a problem in arranging an early departure. Except that as soon as we stepped onto the plane at Ferrol airport to fly to Madrid, we might as well have stepped out the opposite side and started walking. We probably would have got home quicker.

When we reached Madrid, we found out we couldn't get home through all the connections we were booked on. Nor could we switch to another airline to get around the problem. Our return tickets were Australia–Ferrol–Australia, so as soon as we flew out of Ferrol, we were deemed to have started our return journey, eliminating the chance to swap airlines. While we could complete the next leg on what must have been a rock-bottom budget airfare from Madrid to Brussels, we had problems further on. The connection from Brussels to Singapore was the stumbling block in rescheduling our flights. That was where the situation became a case of every man for himself. We all wanted to get home and our NBL teams wanted us home, so the cashed-up clubs simply paid for new tickets for their players to fly home direct from Madrid.

Given that our clubs didn't have cash for a cab, let alone an airfare from Europe, Paul Kuiper, the Dalton brothers, Brad and Mark, Ian Davies, assistant coach Barry Barnes and I were left to fend for ourselves, while head coach Adrian Hurley and team manager Terry Charlton decided their best option was to head to England. As our immediate flight hadn't caused the delay, we decided to keep moving to Brussels. Then we stopped like a bug on a windscreen. There was no way of getting onto the next sector.

We booked into a hotel and I shared a room with Kuiper while we waited for help to arrive. Great though Kuips is as a bloke, two days in Brussels, regardless of the company, was plenty for me. In frustration, I picked up the local phone directory and flipped through the pages. Once I found the airline listings I started dialling and didn't stop until I was booked on a flight home. Finally, at about 1 a.m. and allowing for the fact Kuiper point-blank refused to fly with any airline he had never heard of, I managed to scrounge four seats on a flight home. Amazingly, after the milk run we faced getting to Ferrol and back, we snagged an upgrade to business class. At least we flew home to a breaking controversy in some comfort.

And at least we could say that we'd been warned. As I was having breakfast one morning in Brussels, Brad Dalton came into the dining room having just got off the phone to his wife. Already frustrated at being laid up in Brussels, Dalton had a new reason to be angry. Our captain, Phil Smyth, on his arrival home, had written a newspaper column that was critical of some of his world championship team-mates. 'The thing that hurt me most was the attitude of some of my team-mates,' Smyth wrote in the *Sunday Telegraph* column. 'That was even more disappointing than not qualifying for the next round.'

Smyth accused four un-named players of breaking curfew before the loss to Angola and repeating the breach the night before the loss to the USSR in the final game of our ill-fated campaign. There were two issues. Firstly, when Smyth spoke out of school in his column he was perceived to have broken not only ranks but the unwritten rule that what happens on the road stays on the road. Secondly, what he wrote carried more than an element of truth but all it did was create scapegoats. While this may have been a captain's attempt to take the heat off all of us as a team, it caused difficulties for the un-named players.

I knew some players had gone for a few beers to wind down and socialise with the locals. Ferrol was an encouraging atmosphere in which to enjoy the nightlife, if that was your go. In fact, a few blokes seemed to believe that to be the case in Verona and Menorca on the way to Ferrol, too. I didn't and don't condone big nights on the grog, and that's not what my team-mates indulged in. But 1986 was a different era in Australian basketball and there were different attitudes. There wasn't much money in the sport and some guys in Spain might have lost money being away from work. So for some people, going out for a few beers was perfectly reasonable. Nor were they causing any trouble with the police or getting out of control with their behaviour. These days, you just wouldn't get away with it and it wouldn't be tolerated. You would be found out in more ways than one.

Drinking's not my go, nor is it Phil's. Neither of us is Mr Party Animal. Like most of the team, Phil and I were intently focused on the job at hand, trying to make the most of the situation. With the exception of my father, there is nobody in Australian basketball who I have admired more. Phil was my hero when I was a teenager and my respect for him was further enhanced when I played alongside him with the Boomers. His dedication to the game and the way he prepared himself had a significant influence in shaping my attitude and approach to the sport. As a coach Phil is a professional and that's why he was so good as a player. He took his basketball seriously and he was a competitor, but it was unfortunate that his frustrations with the performance of some members of the team became public. Despite this, I endorsed his opinion that higher standards needed to be reached if we were ever going to have the chance to succeed at the top level. He was disappointed with our results and rightly so. Shortly afterwards, when our paths crossed in the NBL competition, I spoke to Phil about the article and he, too, expressed disappointment at the reaction to his comments in the newspaper. Of course, had we beaten Angola, there would never have been a problem.

The more I look back on the Boomers' 1986 World Championships campaign, the more I suspect the whole thing was doomed from the start. Certainly, there were signs as early as our first training session in Verona, Italy, when Ian Davies limped off the court with his torn calf muscle. It was as though the dominoes were set in place. Adrian Hurley, I think, sensed things weren't right when we got to Menorca for our final lead-in tournament. After getting belted by Brazil and Yugoslavia, Adrian gave us the rounds of the kitchen before our next training session. He gave us a real bake, telling us we needed to improve and apply ourselves in a more serious manner. Barry Barnes, as assistant coach, gave us a spray too, so we well and truly knew where we stood.

As soon as Hurley and Barnes cooked us, we put on our shoes for training. In a situation that tells you something about this team and trip, Simon Cottrell discovered he had brought two left shoes from the hotel. After the spray from the coaches, there was no way he would bring it to their attention and ask for somebody to go and fetch a righty. He laced up both left shoes and went out and trained. Everyone noticed it and even Adrian had a chuckle. Alas, there were too many times, especially against Angola, when we all played with two left feet.

Going home to Phil Smyth's comments probably epitomised the way our world championship had gone. There was never a sense of ease about the whole campaign from the start and that's just how it ended – uneasily. Eventually we got home, but this one was never going to go away. Never.

Angola. I'm twitching.

chapter five

THE COMMUNIST BLOCK

THERE was maybe three seconds left on the clock. Not enough time to boil the kettle, but an eternity in basketball as the might of the Soviet Union's Big Red basketball team clung to a three-point lead. Not a lot of time in the real world, but in basketball time enough to think, time enough to make a shot that might not be heard around the world but would be talked about for a long time anyway.

The Boomers had the ball out of bounds, with time to get a good shot. There was no play called by coach Adrian Hurley from the bench and we might not have heard it above the crowd anyway. With seven thousand people shoehorned into Melbourne's Glasshouse, it was engulfing and deafening but not distracting. As it was, we had come back from seven down with ninety seconds left, so we didn't have much to lose on the final play of the game.

The in-bounds pass came to me on a wing. As soon as I caught it, the clock started. The fuse had been lit on the bomb to eventually be launched. I passed the ball to big man Paul Kuiper, who was in the post. As my defender prepared to double-team Kuiper, I stepped back and was wide open outside the three-point arc on the left wing. The problem was Kuiper was looking the other way to pass to the opposite wing. I was screaming for the ball like a man freefalling without a parachute. Finally, even though it might have been half-a-second, I got Kuiper's attention. He passed the ball back out and I was set as I caught it.

The clock was as close to showing three zeros as you could get without it being there, so there was no question about whether I should shoot. It was only a matter of making it or missing it. As I shot the ball, a Soviet defender tried to close me out, but he was too late. The ball was in the air. The buzzer was sounding. I had gone for insurance and kicked out my legs on the follow through, hoping to draw a foul. No call. It was all up to the ball.

This was a moment I acted out as a kid at Albert Park, shooting around, pretending I was Eddie Palubinskas with the game on the line and no time on the clock. As the only person occupying any of the nine courts, it was usually quiet, except for the echo of the bouncing ball and the swish of the net. This was exactly the same, only I had a few thousand friends over and a television audience around the country riding the shot with me. I was in the zone during the game, hitting ten three-pointers before taking aim one last time. It was a moment that felt like everyone was drawing breath in anticipation, sucking the arena into a vacuum. Over time, you can draw out those last few seconds and the final split-second into the longest drama imaginable. The ending is always the same.

Bang! The bomb hit its target and the crowd exploded. The Glasshouse was in uproar. This was an atmosphere and experience that Australian basketball had never achieved. The Boomers, who twelve months earlier couldn't beat ramshackle Angola at the

World Championships, had just tied the superpower Soviet Union. In the first five games of the series, we lost by an average of seventeen points. Now we had tied the Big Red Machine 102–102. Playing the entire second half with four fouls and aware of my dad's advice from the night before about having good body language on court regardless of the situation, I finished with forty-four points.

That was the good news. The bad news was that we had to go back out and play overtime. Another five minutes seemed anti-climactic after the drama and thrill we had just endured. It *was* an anti-climax. We lost 110–108 and I finished on the bench, fouled out with a few minutes to go. To be in that moment, though, was enormous. As we left the court to a standing ovation, we had put to rest some ghosts of 1986. What we perhaps didn't realise was that we had also poured the foundations for the 1988 Olympics and a new era of international basketball for the Boomers.

There were several indicators of just how important the Soviet Union's tour to Australia was in 1987. For the sport at the elite level, it was huge as we played to sell-out crowds at major venues in capital cities, which was fitting for a team of the USSR's standing. The Soviets, with players like Sarunas Marciulionis, Aleksandr Volkov, Valerii Tikhonenko and Vladimir Tkachenko were massive, intimidating, well-drilled and bloody good basketballers. They were too much for the whole world to handle, let alone us Aussie battlers. The series gave the Boomers, the sport and me excellent exposure in the mainstream media and that meant a lot.

The other big indicator for me about the magnitude of our overtime loss to the Soviets was the reaction of my mum. Make no mistake, she was always my biggest and most staunch supporter. But sitting in the stands that day, even she couldn't hold it in. Word filtered back to me that mum was pretty emotional about me making the shot to tie it. I always knew she was there every time I played in Melbourne, and had been since I was a kid, but this was the first time I was aware of her being emotional with pride. My mum had been through plenty of international losses when my dad was Boomers coach, so she knew the history, she knew what that game meant to so many people. That's when I knew just how big it had been.

The series against the Soviet Union was a massive test for coach Adrian Hurley and the team after the embarrassment of the 1986 World Championships. We were twelve months out from the 1988 Olympics and anything but a competitive showing against the Soviets would have been unacceptable in many eyes. That we had possibly over-achieved against the best team to tour this country cracked the door to the future. Although we could not be sure, just as the weather forecasters are never certain, it looked like the peek through that crack was at blue skies replacing the heavy, dark clouds of Ferrol, scene of our disastrous loss to Angola.

There was no question in my mind that, after the shambles in Spain, Hurley decided that if the axe was going to fall, he would at least fashion the chopping block to put his own head on. In the six-game series against the Soviets, Hurley saw some new blokes against real international talent. Among the new faces in green and gold were John Dorge, David Graham, Mark Bradtke and Robert Sibley, while Damian Keogh was back after missing the Spain debacle. Significantly, with Bradtke getting his chance, a couple of other teenagers named Andrew Vlahov and Luc Longley would follow as controversial, yet excellent, selections.

After the heady finish to the 1987 tour, the Soviets returned to Australia as part of the build-up to the 1988 Olympics in Seoul. We were competitive against them again, and we lost by only one point in the opening match of the tour in Brisbane, but we still couldn't beat them. Mind you, not many teams could. But that 1988 tour, despite the lack of hype, got us ready for the Olympics.

The Boomers team for the 1988 Olympics had seven of the twelve players who suffered through the 1986 world championship fiasco and it was young, mainly because of three teenagers: Mark

Bradtke, Andrew Vlahov and Luc Longley. The trio came straight out of the Australian Institute of Sport and into the national team. Bradtke made his NBL debut with the Adelaide 36ers the year of the Olympics and Vlahov (Stanford University) and Longley (University of New Mexico) had played one season of college basketball in the United States. None of them was established at this level of competition, but they had all led Australia to fifth at the junior world titles in Bormio, Italy, in 1987 and Hurley must have felt pretty good about them and their futures, though you didn't need to be an atomic scientist to agree.

Comfortable as Hurley might have been about picking Bradtke, Vlahov and Longley for the Olympics, he still had to convince the critics. In fact, Adrian took the unusual step of penning a letter to one newspaper to counter criticism offered by a sportswriter. Hindsight says Hurley definitely got it right. While their selection might have been a nod to the future, it actually helped enormously with the Boomers' balance and rotations at the Olympics. Experience had proven we could not play all twelve players and be effective and it was like Adrian had decided to stick with his tried and trusted veterans in an eight-man rotation anyway. So it didn't matter so much who had spots ten, eleven and twelve. That helped the main core of guys, whose roles were much more defined and settled than two years previously. After the problems in Spain, we needed a happy and settled team and there was no question these three teenagers were happy to be along for the ride.

It turned out that Bradtke, Longley and Vlahov were promoted a spot up the order when we got to Seoul because forward Robert Sibley had a broken bone in his hand and did not play a minute of the tournament. It also turned out they were more than passengers, making contributions on a team bound to create Australian basketball history.

The Boomers drew a fairly tough pool for the Olympic tournament: Yugoslavia, the USSR, Puerto Rico, host South Korea and

Central Africa. The top four teams advanced to the quarter finals, which we figured we would do, but we needed to avoid finishing fourth, otherwise we would surely face the United States in the quarter finals ahead of the medal round. Just like in LA, our first game was crucial to that process. We had to beat Puerto Rico or our chances were in jeopardy.

My role on the team was much more prominent than my first Olympics in LA, so there was added responsibility and expectation on my shoulders. I picked up an eye infection just before leaving for Seoul, but thankfully, I (and the Boomers) got away to a good start, winning that crucial game against Puerto Rico 81–77, after the opposition ate up our fourteen-point half-time lead. With the danger game out of the way, the other contests went pretty much as expected, losing to the USSR (91–69), beating Central Africa (106–67), dropping one to Yugoslavia (98–78) and finishing on a high against South Korea (95–75). We finished third in our group and avoided the Americans in the crossover. But in the knockout quarter final we had to play Spain, a team we had never beaten in twenty-six years of trying.

When they write the definitive history of world basketball, the Boomers' 1988 Olympic quarter final against Spain may not figure prominently. But it will forever be etched in the minds, memories and hearts of the twelve players and the coaching staff who became pioneers as Australian men's basketball ventured into new territory.

The best the Boomers had ever done at an Olympic Games was seventh in 1984 and their best world championship finish was fifth in 1982. Now we stood on the brink of being the first Australian men's team to qualify for the Olympic medal rounds. We'd never beaten Spain, the silver medallist in LA four years earlier, and we'd never played for a medal, so this game was our grand final. It was basically a case of win and advance or lose and go home.

The historical nature of this quarter final was certainly not lost on the group, especially the coaching staff and the older players.

Even though I was only twenty-three, I knew how much this game meant. I knew we were on the verge of carrying the flag somewhere it had never been – not only for us but for those who had gone before us. Creating history quickly became the theme for the Spain game. It wasn't rammed down our throats, but you got a strong sense of it and enormous pressure built within individuals and the team.

One way of releasing tension is humour. In the apartment I shared in the athletes' village with Darryl Pearce, Ray Borner, Andrew Vlahov and Luc Longley, there was never much shortage of mirth. Olympic rookies Vlahov and Longley were always ready to pull some stunt like taping down the disposable sheets on my bed so that when I pulled them back for a snooze, they tore to shreds. Good one, guys. One of the key elements of good comedy is timing and the boys had yet to refine that aspect of their Abbott and Costello act. Which was what they learned a few hours before the quarter final against Spain.

As the team's leading scorer, I felt a bit of pressure to go with the natural nerves associated with such a big game, so I didn't need anything to disrupt my game-day routine in Seoul. After lunch, we had a quick hit of table tennis, then I returned to the apartment for my nap. But when I got to the apartment, my bed was missing. Gone. Call me slow, but I thought the cleaners must have removed the bed. I didn't give a hoot about the bed. I was just worried about how I would have my pre-game snooze. But the looks on a couple of young faces suggested something was up and, sure enough, my bed was out on the balcony. Longley and Vlahov had done it again.

While somewhat relieved that my bed's displacement was not due to a housekeeping snafu, I did not exactly slap my thigh and laugh along with Longley and Vlahov. Far from it. I went off like a box of Chinese firecrackers. I had a good hard crack, telling them it was a bullshit way to act and prepare for the most important game any of us might ever play. My reaction showed the anxiety and pressure I felt being so close to history, flirting with a moment and a chance you never get back. The message got through. While they didn't exactly scurry about like grovelling court jesters, they knew I was serious and replaced the bed exactly where it had been. These kids might have been planning a future in furniture removal, but my plans were for an Olympic medal.

We always knew Spain would be a tough opponent. We didn't need the record books or a scouting report to tell us that. We just needed to play our game and stay close, which was exactly what happened as the quarter final got to half-time with the Boomers ahead 41–40. This was good for us because there was always a chance the European temperament could become a factor when the pressure was on. Poke a stick at a wild animal enough and it will retaliate. We poked the Spaniards with baskets and they finally retaliated.

Early in the second half, I was in a rebounding contest at our offensive end. Just as the ball bounced away and Spain secured possession, 205 centimetre forward Andres Jimenez landed a blow that might have made Mike Tyson wince. It was the ultimate cheap shot: an elbow to the throat. I went down faster than bad shares. The referees called a foul and I scraped myself off the floor of the Chamsil Gymnasium, knowing louder and clearer than the ringing in my ears and the flashing lights in my eyes that the Spaniards were worried.

Naturally, I took the hit as I usually would. With all the calmness of a bloke who had lost his winning Tattslotto ticket. I was furious, but didn't really want the Spaniards to see they had upset me so much. I don't know if Jimenez understood English, but I gave him a few choice words of advice to take back to the Iberian Peninsula. Words were my initial retaliation because I remembered what my dad told me about physical payback: choose your time and place wisely. This was neither the time nor the place. Besides, I had something that would hurt Jimenez and his mates even more. The only way I could fight back, given my lack of pugilistic skill, was to score points, not throw weak-sister punches.

On the ensuing possession, I was buzzed with anger. My adrenalin gland was pumping harder than my heart and I was not backing down to Jimenez. I got the ball and I fired up an outrageous three-pointer. It went in. Next trip, same shot. Same result. Next trip, same story. I buried three straight three-pointers to give us a 56–52 lead, but I probably would not have taken those shots if Jimenez had not whacked me. I wouldn't have contemplated launching them, but I was in such a rage that I didn't even consider the consequences of missing. Also, I figured that under the circumstances the referees would give us a few calls, so I was almost playing with the bank's money. Those shots gave us a margin and we went on to win, 77–74. We had made history. Whether Senor Jimenez knew it or not, I could not have cared less.

Going back to the village that night was one of the greatest Olympic experiences I have had. Whenever an Australian medal arrived at the village or a significant Aussie performance was posted, there was a palpable buzz through the green and gold section. It was the same at all five Olympics I went to. This time, it was the Boomers providing the buzz. There was nothing worse than going back to the village after a loss. But we could answer all the enquiries of 'How did you go?' with 'We won. We're in the medal round.' There was a sense of relief and achievement all at once. There was a sense that finally, for everyone, including my dad, who had been trying since 1960 to get the Boomers into this position, we had helped Australian men's basketball come of age on the international stage.

Immediately after the Spain game, the locker room was an exciting place to be. We had created history, we were in the medal round, we had shown we could compete against and beat these powerful basketball nations. We had shown we mattered. But almost as soon as the celebrating had started, there was a realisation that we needed one more win to get a medal and that would not be easy, given that we were joined in the final four by the United States, the USSR and

Yugoslavia. If you ranked the three super powers of international basketball, they were the three. So with Australia qualified for the semi-final bracket, there was a feeling among some that the ride was as good as over and we would finish fourth. That was for some. For others, we felt we had a chance of snatching a medal.

The semi-final seedings panned out with the Boomers moving into the opposite group to play Yugoslavia, which had future NBA stars Toni Kukoc, Vlade Divac, Drazen Petrovic and Dino Radja in the line-up. The Soviets and the Americans, protagonists in a bitter basketball rivalry that was cranked up at Munich in 1972 when the USSR beat the US for gold in controversial circumstances, were in the other semi. The Americans, believing they were dudded by the Soviets' winning basket at the buzzer in Munich, refused to accept their silver medals. I knew if I had a chance for a silver or a bronze, I would walk backwards naked from Melbourne to Perth to get it. As it happened, we played for bronze after Yugoslavia outplayed us in the semi-final, turning a 44–31 half-time lead into a comprehensive 91–70 victory.

In the other semi-final, the Soviets didn't need any help from the officials, handing the Americans only their second loss in Olympic Games history. The USSR, with big man Arvydas Sabonis and guard Sarunas Marciulionis putting on a clinic, won 82–76 against a United States team that included future NBA superstars David Robinson, Dan Majerle, Mitch Richmond and Danny Manning. Indeed, there was some historical significance attached to these teams. By the time the next Olympics dawned, the Soviet Union had been dismantled and the Americans reacted to losing the semi in 1988 by keeping the collegians at home and sending the NBA Dream Team to Barcelona. Yet while we knew we were watching history, it was a bitter-sweet moment because, having played against and become so familiar with the USSR, we actually thought we had a better chance of beating the Soviets than the Americans and winning our first Olympic medal.

While the Boomers were going strong, so was the Australian women's team, then dubbed the Bloomers by ABC radio commentator Tim Lane in Seoul, but now known as the Opals. Pumped by South Korea in the opening game, the women hit back with excellent wins over Bulgaria and the Soviet Union to qualify for the semi-finals of the eight-team tournament. The Boomers felt the heat from the women and were keen to keep pace with them. So when they qualified for the semis, we had extra motivation to make it a double for Australia. They also lost to Yugoslavia in the semi-final, but in vastly different and heartbreaking circumstances.

I had committed to play the 1988–89 season with Seton Hall University in the United States. The night the Australian women played their semi-final, I was at the gym to meet Seton Hall athletic director Larry Keating. Because I had no transport back to the village, I asked women's coach Robbie Cadee if I could grab a ride on the bus after their semi. No problem, he said. Not with the transport, anyway. On the basketball court was another matter.

There is no other way to say it: Australia had the semi-final won and blew it. Australia had possession with time ticking down and a one-point lead. Michele Timms fired up a shot to beat the expiring thirty-second shot clock, but it missed. Yugoslavia rebounded and rushed down the other end, looking for a game winner. Yugoslav guard Andjelija Arbutina threw up a prayer, but it was short and bounced off the front of the rim. Nobody boxed her out, she got her own rebound and made the put-back as time expired. Yugoslavia 57, Australia 56.

Devastation is not too strong a word to use for the feelings of the Australian women. They were a snap of the fingers away from at least a silver medal. They would play for the bronze medal, just like the men. But the circumstances were as far apart as the north and south ridges of the Grand Canyon and walking between them with a rattlesnake in my pants would have been more pleasant than getting on the bus with the Australian women after that loss. I was stunned, so imagine how they felt. Nobody spoke. The only noise was some of the girls quietly crying. It was just the most dejected scene. It got worse, though. The women lost to the USSR in the bronze medal game. Their bravery deserved something, but they had to settle for history.

Once the Boomers knew we were playing the US for bronze, there was a feeling our chance of an Olympic medal might have gone. Even though we were one of the starters in a two-horse race, we had a feeling there was no way the thoroughbred superstar, beaten at its last start, would lose two straight. The Americans' anger at being relegated to the lowest Olympic finish in their history to that point had them looking for some Australian butts to haul back home as souvenirs complementary to the bronze medals.

If we were realistic, we were not disappointed. Having made the final four, anything else was a bonus. We were way ahead of what anyone ever expected. We had a crack against the Americans, but they were focused and driven and led by twenty-three at half-time. We pretty much played them break-even in the second half, which was little consolation as we got bumped to fourth with a 78–49 loss.

That was okay. We knew exactly where we stood with our performances. It was the Americans who would go home with explaining to do. Which was not lost on Boomers guard Damian Keogh, who passed the observation onto one of the Americans after the bronze medal game. 'We've lost and we're the happiest blokes in the world because this is our best finish,' Keogh said. 'You've won and got third and that's your worst performance.' Damian was pretty happy with himself. So he should have been. Like twelve months earlier against the Soviets at the Glasshouse, Australia had shown it belonged on the top shelf.

chapter six

A BASKETBALL EDUCATION

WHEN US college teams toured Australia during the 1970s and early 1980s, it was a pretty big deal. People would pack the old Albert Park Stadium, which was Melbourne's basketball Mecca, to see the overseas teams play the Boomers or one of the best local teams like the Melbourne Tigers or St Kilda Saints. Since I lived at the stadium, I saw just about every touring team that came through and I got autographs from the players and coaches. One autograph I still have is by the former University of Kentucky coach, Joe B Hall. Knowing I was the son of Lindsay Gaze, Coach Hall took some time with his autograph, which is on the back of his business card and includes a message:

'Dear Andrew,
When you're ready for college, look me up.
Joe B Hall.'

As a nine or ten year old, the message didn't mean that much. I hadn't graduated from primary school, so the idea of going to college in America was a dream if anything. Eddie Palubinskas was one of the first Aussies to play college basketball when he enrolled at Louisiana State University. And a couple of women – Maree Bennie, who became Lauren Jackson's mother, and Julie Gross – also blazed the trail at LSU. The closest I got to college basketball was watching touring teams, in my dreams and the occasional video or film my dad got from the United States.

Not long after that visit by Kentucky, my parents took me and Janet to the US and the Far West Classic tournament in Portland, Oregon. The tournament involved four college teams and this was more than just a few basketball games: this was an event. Well, it was to me, a wide-eyed kid, seeing maybe fifteen thousand people in the crowd for a basketball game when there might have been as many as ten people some nights at Albert Park. It reminded me of a footy match in Australia, with people swarming to the game. At least I didn't have to climb the fence or sneak in without paying, like I did for South Melbourne home games at the Lake Oval. It was a different basketball culture to the one in Australia and that was underlined again when my dad got hold of the video of the 1979 NCAA Championship game between Indiana State with Larry Bird and Michigan State with Magic Johnson. Some people have labelled it the greatest game ever. I remembered it because I had to pester my dad to bring the tape in from the car so we could watch it.

As a kid, the chances to see or read about college basketball were few and far between. There was the odd video or film and, if you were lucky and had enough pocket money, you would get a Street and Smith season preview magazine at the newsagency. The experience of college basketball, with its fervent support and massive media exposure in the US, was one I came to appreciate. It took a while to realise that the system of basketball in Australia, with its club-based competitions, was a lot different to that in the US, with its school-based system, but it made it an intriguing and attractive prospect.

It became more so on my first overseas trip as a player with the Australian team in 1983, playing US colleges. This was an excellent first-hand experience of college basketball with the crazy crowds and the death-or-glory attitudes of the players, coaches and fans. All those elements of the college game, not to mention the level of play, were attractive to me. By the time I was ready to go to college, Joe B Hall had been retired as Kentucky coach for a few seasons. Nonetheless, the running for my signature was taken up in earnest by an assistant coach from Seton Hall. The new name on the business card that I would never forget was John Carroll.

I signed to play college basketball with Seton Hall University for the 1988–89 NCAA season, but the pursuit by the Pirates had started a couple of years earlier when the Tigers toured the US with a schedule of games against teams from the Big East Conference. To be brutally honest, the Tigers of 1986 were horrible. We finished the NBL season second-last with a 6–20 record and we were matched on this tour against teams from the top-ranked conference in America. In fact, we were so bad, a few of us went over early to try to recruit a player to help us on the tour. The talent that turned up for the try-out on the campus of Loyola Marymount University in Los Angeles was a mixture of fat guys and shady looking characters from the 'hood. So we decided to pass and go with what we had. Better to be embarrassed than really embarrassed.

We started the tour against Boston College with a loss but came back to beat the University of Connecticut, which prompted UConn coach Jim Calhoun to call a practice for his team straight after the game. We thought it was remarkable that a coach would do such a thing with his team. To us, the punishment didn't fit the crime and we felt it was extreme. But it was an insight into college basketball that we otherwise might never have had. Either way, that win got us going and, while we were pretty much in holiday mode, we played hard. I put up some big numbers and got noticed by the time the tour made its final stop in New Jersey at Seton Hall University.

We beat Georgetown when I hit a three-pointer on a botched play at the buzzer and after the game against St John's in New York, Seton Hall coach PJ Carlesimo introduced himself, which was nice. As it was, his dad Pete knew my dad and they had worked together to organise this tour, so it wasn't like we were total strangers, even if we hadn't met before. We met again as we played the Pirates in the eighth and final game in thirteen arduous days and I made an impression with forty-six points. Decidedly less impressive were the facilities. We played Seton Hall off-campus at a community ice rink, which was by far the worst facility we endured on the tour. It was not a good recruiting tool, but at the post-game get-together, John Carroll, the assistant coach, introduced himself and started something of a sales pitch.

'We've been following your progress and no one puts up those numbers in the Big East,' John said. 'Some of the numbers you've put up are phenomenal. We think we've got a very good team, but we need some outside scoring. Have you considered coming and playing college basketball?'

A number of schools had chased me over the years, including Loyola Marymount, which was coached by team-mate Brian Goorjan's father Ed. In 1984, I was close to signing with the University of the Pacific, which is the alma mater of former Tigers players Bruce Palmer, Al Westover, Jim Stephens and Matt Waldron. On Waldron's recommendation to the coach, Pacific recruited me and I seriously thought about it, but the timing wasn't right, especially as I had just broken into the Australian team. I was keen to play in college and had I not made the 1984 Olympic team, I would have signed to play for and attend the University of the Pacific. Nor was the timing right in late 1986 after the approach from Seton Hall, which was keen to the point of waiting for me to become eligible after Christmas and missing about eight games of the season. It was an interesting proposition, but I had just come off the world championships with the Boomers and my major focus was the Tigers.

The other factor in turning down Seton Hall was the location of the school. While it was a great basketball opportunity, I just didn't really want to go there. After seeing schools like Connecticut, Syracuse, Villanova and Boston College, the facilities at Seton Hall were not flash by comparison, and the neighbourhood was also a big downer. South Orange, New Jersey, home to the Seton Hall campus, is, with all due respect to the residents, not among the world's most liveable cities. It was great they asked me to play but, at the time, they couldn't have paid me to live in that environment right on the border with Newark, which did not present itself as the most enticing destination. So I was very polite and said the timing was just not right, but that I might be interested down the track.

Giving a glimmer of hope that I would one day play for Seton Hall was enough for them to keep the bait on the fish hook and continue trying to reel me in. Not two months would pass without John Carroll calling, trying to recruit me to Seton Hall. He would be on the phone for at least an hour every time, talking about how college basketball would improve my game. He must have cost Seton Hall a fortune in phone calls. They tried to get me to go in 1986 and I said no. They said come for the 1987–88 season and I declined again, making the preparation for the Seoul Olympics the top priority. John Carroll was fine with my decisions, but he was relentless and made sure I completed all the formalities for enrolment just in case. Even so, I still doubted it would ever happen.

Either PJ Carlesimo and John Carroll were masters of the gentle art of persuasion or they were big fans of the Royal Canadian Mounted Police, working to the motto 'We always get our man'. In 1987, they had the chance to make another pitch when they came to Australia as coach and assistant coach respectively of the touring Big East All-Stars. The Boomers played them in a five-game series, so they had me face-to-face, every day of the tour, which might have been fate because the coaches were appointed to the Big East tours on a rotational basis and this was Seton Hall's turn. Finally, as the hoop gods' reward for their sheer persistence, everything fell into place. The dates of the 1988 and 1989 NBL seasons, the 1988 Olympics and the college season were all synchronised perfectly to allow me to commit to the Tigers, commit to the Boomers and commit to Seton Hall. Finally I said yes to a college basketball scholarship at Seton Hall University.

There was more to the decision than basketball. As a life experience, I would live in a different country and culture for six months. From a study point of view, I could catch up on my degree at Footscray Institute of Technology. Because of basketball commitments, especially with the Boomers overseas, my studies were up the creek, so I figured I would go to Seton Hall for two semesters, get some credits and have basketball help me with study for once.

As soon as the Seoul Olympics were finished, I was to fly home to Melbourne for a couple of days, pack my gear and fly to America for the start of school. But the longer the Olympics went, the greater the doubt in the back of my mind. I still wanted to go but by the time the Boomers reached the Olympic quarter-finals I had decided that there was no way I was going to Seton Hall if we won an Olympic medal. If we won a medal, I wanted to celebrate and to bask and share in the glory with my team-mates. Seton Hall could wait or whither – I wouldn't have cared. As it turned out, the Boomers lost to the United States in the bronze medal game and a few days later I was bound for Seton Hall.

The familiar voice was about to become a familiar face. John Carroll, the man who recruited me largely by telephone, was at Newark Liberty International Airport to collect me at 5 a.m. Perhaps wanting to ease me in, John took me to his house before we headed to the campus where I would live. Seton Hall is an enclosed campus with gates and brick walls all the way around. As I learned, this feature was not an architectural embellishment but a security necessity. One of the first things John Carroll explained to me was the nature of the location. Turn one way down South Orange Avenue and you're in an affluent, almost palatial, area. Turn the other, and you soon end up in Newark. The warning was stark: don't ever, ever go into that part of the community. It was a very dangerous place indeed. Think of the television mob show *The Sopranos*, then double or triple it. I knew I hadn't come to a lavish neighbourhood, but now it was clear that the school was the only safe haven around.

I did experience one nasty example of the neighbourhood dangers, though it was not with the humans. One day, I stopped at a petrol station and wandered into the service area looking for assistance. There was nobody around, but I heard the pitter-patter of approaching paws. Next thing I knew, a giant German Shepherd appeared through the door and sunk its teeth into my calf. My shouts quickly brought a response from the garage owner, who dragged the dog off me and apologised profusely. There was plenty of blood and not too much damage, but my Seton Hall team-mates reckoned I should have gone down, faked a major injury and got free car repairs. Which might have been a good idea, given the ramshackle vehicle I drove.

Being the big spender I am, I bought a small, four-door hatchback Dodge Omni that was advertised in the newspaper for $400. It was an absolute wreck and its reliability rating was close to zero. In fact, I always tried to time the traffic lights so I would get green and wouldn't have to stop and risk stalling. The other factor in not stopping was to do with safety. With the campus in a nasty part of town, I figured if I was always moving, I was less of a target for carjackers and muggers. Basically, when I got into my car to leave campus, the fewer stops I had to make, the better. That car lasted about three months before it gave up the ghost.

Another time, the Dodge Omni gave Melinda, my then girlfriend, some grief. Melinda had decided to come over for a few months, visit a friend, travel a bit and enjoy the experience of life in a big city. Thanks to the Dodge Omni, Melinda got more than an experience. One day when my mum and dad were visiting, Melinda took them into New York to see a Broadway show. On the way through the Lincoln Tunnel, the car started packing up and they pulled over to the side, only to be rescued by a tow truck with a sinister-looking skull on the dashboard. That Omni was also responsible for an elbow problem my dad still has. He was trying to wind up the window when the injury happened. To this day he carries a lump as a constant reminder of the Dodge Omni.

Aside from the car trouble, it was great to have Melinda there to eventually share in some of the events and successes of the season. Unfortunately, I was not able to offer her the accommodation I would have preferred, after some four years together. Following a week of sharing a small single bed in my dorm room, Melinda got her own apartment and organised work as a restaurant waitress. That allowed her some space and spending money, though her freedom was again restricted near the end of her stay. During the NCAA tournament, she moved back into my dorm room while the team was on the road. But as she didn't have a security pass to get in and out of the building, she stayed in the room like a recluse for a week. No wonder she decided to cut her losses and go home before my part in the season was through. None of us really believed we would be away right up until the ultimate day and defining game of the college basketball season.

The only player I knew of at Seton Hall was Ramon Ramos, who played for Puerto Rico at the Seoul Olympics. The second player I met was my room-mate, Trevor Crowley. I didn't need to get too acquainted with my team-mates immediately because the National Collegiate Athletic Association, the governing body of college sports, decreed we could not start official practice until 15 October. The other NCAA ruling that affected me was that you didn't have to attend the first semester of study if you had competed at the Seoul Olympics. But as I was there to study as well as play basketball I forewent the NCAA's generosity and hit the books.

After about a week of classes, it felt like what university was meant to be like. Coming from Victoria University's elite Physical Education program, I comfortably dealt with the workload and knew I was more than competent and able to get through. From being a borderline pass student in Australia, I looked pretty good in the PE program at Seton Hall, so that was a plus before a ball had even been tossed in the air.

However, there was a negative to even things out pretty quickly. When I took the physical examination to make sure I was good to go, I did some routine tests. The result of one test showed I had TB – tuberculosis. This was a shock to us all, but the staff told me it was possible to have the disease in a dormant form. I had more tests and X-rays and when they couldn't figure out the level or the source of the TB, they took it very seriously. There was a fear they'd have to manage it and work on it, but it turned out I wasn't sick at all. In high school I had been vaccinated against TB, which was why the test at Seton Hall showed up positive. Apparently, they didn't have that vaccination program in the US, so they didn't take that into consideration. After such a worrying false alarm, the start of the college basketball season couldn't arrive quickly enough.

The coaches were not allowed to work with the team until the start of the official training period in October, so I had had little more than a brief conversation with head coach PJ Carlesimo since I arrived in September. That soon changed as the clock struck midnight and 14 October became 15 October. The college basketball season was officially underway and pretty soon we'd had enough of PJ Carlesimo to choke a fat donkey.

The basketball season for Seton Hall, like many colleges, began with Midnight Madness, a training session that starts the very minute NCAA regulations allow. At many schools it has gone from a novelty to a tradition, even though it is more about media and marketing, as fans and media turn up to see the first official practice. About four thousand people packed into our little campus gym that night as the 1988–89 Pirates were introduced. We went through an informal, relaxed session with a few drills and dunks and a scrimmage, though I'm not sure how much I impressed the fans. While everyone else on the team seemed to be putting together a highlight reel of dunks and athletic moves, I was doing unexciting finger rolls and lay-ups. While we eased into the season that night, the next day, it all started for real.

The first dose of reality was from the coach. PJ Carlesimo suddenly transformed from this nice, mild-mannered, happy-go-lucky, fun guy who recruited me, to an intense, grumpy, yelling maniac who clearly sent a message about the high standards he expected us to follow and achieve. There was no reason for anybody not to get that message the first time, loud and clear. It was a shock for the new guys as we wondered how this transformation from funny, charming PJ to screaming, hard-nosed Coach Carlesimo happened. Nor was it just his criticism and demands. Training sessions went for three or three and a half hours and they were full-on. We were drilled in an intense environment where mistakes were not tolerated. Nor were slackers, which was quite a tall order given that we also had to attend 7 a.m. weights sessions every second day and we had study and classes between practice and weights. If you survived.

As I said, I was at Seton Hall partly to study and experience college life. When we trained, I competed and did my best, but I never carried or felt the expectation to be one of the primary contributors to the team. Given the intensity of the coaches and players and the way they go about it, I adapted to the environment, but it was vastly different from what I was used to. The level of input from the players was almost non-existent as the coach dominated the team and the way it played. It was a regimented situation without any grey area. Either you followed the coach's instructions or you didn't play on the team. The structure was not to be deviated from and the coach's authority was not to be questioned. Simple. There were elements of that in Australia, but because NBL coaches dealt with guys aged anywhere between sixteen and thirty-five who turned up for training after work, there was no dictatorship. NBL coaches were more willing to listen to their players, but that just didn't exist at college. It was hard sometimes, but I wanted to fit in, so I adjusted pretty quickly. I also bit my tongue a lot.

I was twenty-three, which was old to be starting college basketball in the US, I had been to two Olympic Games and had played five seasons in the NBL, so I had earned – and was used to – some on-court responsibility and flexibility. Initially, under PJ, I wasn't playing my natural game because of the system, which affected my confidence. There was also the fear factor. If you ever strayed from the offensive structure or attempted to offer input like I did with the Tigers, you would be berated by the coach. Being more mature and experienced, I knew I wasn't going to make that mistake. I also knew what PJ was looking for and I understood what he was trying to do.

PJ did not discriminate when it came to getting his message across and I definitely copped it a few times. But the guy who copped it the most was John Morton. John was a scorer and reminded me a bit of Lanard Copeland, my long-time Tigers teammate, with his perimeter shooting and ability to get to the basket on the drive. John was one of PJ's whipping boys. PJ rode him in games and at training and I'm surprised he didn't pop a vein screaming at him. There were constant digs at John – like when he bravely took a charge at training one day and slid across the floor after the collision. A team manager went to wipe up the sweat with a towel and PJ dismissed him, saying John didn't work hard enough to sweat, so there wouldn't be any sweat on the floor. John, who went on to play in the NBA with the Cleveland Cavaliers and Miami Heat, just kept putting his head down and working hard, accepting that was the way of college basketball. The coach was the boss, with a licence to abuse and teach; the player was there to learn and cope with the abuse. If he didn't cope, he would wither on the vine. Nobody ever rebelled against PJ during my season at Seton Hall. There might have been a few mutterings, but there was never a physical confrontation like when Latrell Sprewell attacked PJ during training when they were both with the NBA's Golden State Warriors. I can understand how players would get riled up at PJ. In Australia, blokes would eventually tell you to stick it and walk out. By contrast, the college kids accepted PJ because he was a good coach and, away from the basketball court, a great person. The players knew PJ's way was about making them and the team better.

The most memorable spray I received from PJ was after a game against Villanova. We were up by about twelve as the final seconds ticked off the clock and the ball came to me in the corner. I could have dribbled out the clock, but with about two seconds to go I chucked it up and hit a three. I didn't think anything of it, but a few team-mates warned I should brace for a blast from PJ. I innocently asked why and was told I shouldn't have taken that last shot because PJ was paranoid about being seen to rub it in to opponents, even though that wasn't my intention. Sure enough, we got to the locker room and PJ started. 'Fuck you, Gaze. When they beat us at their place, you remember that fuckin' shot.' PJ steadfastly believed I had given Villanova motivation to beat us next time we played and he had no qualms letting me know. That was my first lesson in ethics. In Australia it's really no big deal to whack up a shot at the buzzer. I was getting an education on and off the floor.

One thing I learned every day was how much pressure PJ was under, from himself and others. His job was on the line. There were times before I got there that the student body would greet the team on its return to campus with banners calling for PJ's sacking. It was a harsh business. Among the various pre-season media polls for the 1988–89 campaign, Seton Hall was picked to finish between seventh and ninth in the nine-team Big East Conference. Even though we had some reasonable talent and we were playing in a phenomenal competition, nobody thought we were any good. That was an affront to PJ Carlesimo.

After the physical exhaustion and verbal abuse of the gruelling pre-season sessions, we thanked whatever god we prayed to that we finally got to play a game. The first exhibition game was against Croatian club team Cibona and we waxed them. It was nice to just get a taste as we put training theories into game situations, establishing our roles and getting a handle on PJ's systems and expectations.

Our first games against college opposition were at the Great Alaska Shootout tournament in Anchorage, where the field was Seton Hall, Kentucky, Kansas, Utah, California, Iona, Florida and the local school, Alaska-Anchorage. We beat Utah in the opening game, then topped Kentucky and beat Kansas in the final. I top-scored with eighteen points against Kansas, but Pookey Wiggington, our 162 centimetre back-up guard, sparked the victory that gave us a national ranking and some prominence. It also gave those who predicted us to be lousy something to think about.

The team was humming along. We beat old rival St John's at St John's for the first time in seventy-five years and, at 8–0, we gave Seton Hall its best start to a season since 1952–53. But by the time we got to 10–0 with a win over Princeton, I had serious doubts about my place at Seton Hall. I had tried to find my role on the team but I was left wondering how I fitted in and how it all worked.

PJ played me as a forward rather than as a guard, as I was used to with the Tigers and Boomers. I had no ball-handling responsibilities and it was frowned upon to even contemplate dribbling the ball up the court. There was greater emphasis on my rebounding and defensive assignments, so PJ had obviously not tailored this role to what had been my strengths. It was just so foreign to what I was used to. I thought about it constantly and, regardless of what I brought to the table on game nights, the whole thing was like trying to put a square peg in a round hole. I'd played a long NBL season, I'd been to the Olympics and I wasn't feeling comfortable playing basketball at Seton Hall – in the sense that I felt like I couldn't contribute properly or my skills were not being properly utilised. As we headed towards Christmas, I thought, 'I don't know if I really need this. I don't know if I'm enjoying it.' I felt unfulfilled and I was ready to quit school and return home to Australia.

The only thing that kept me there was something close to a fluke. Seton Hall was going to New Orleans for the Sugar Bowl tournament a few days after Christmas, so mum, dad and Janet were going to meet me there as part of a holiday to America. Not that this was a major consideration as I went to see John Carroll and another assistant coach, Tom Sullivan, before we left for New Orleans. I told them: 'I've had enough. I'm not sure I want to keep going with this.' Because of my concerns about how PJ ran the team and his coaching personality, it wasn't a conversation I could have with PJ. I was worried he would just tell me to get out of the school and the country, only in much more colourful language. So I took the chicken's way and confronted John, Sully and two other assistant coaches, Rod Baker and Bruce Hamburger, in their office.

The coaches listened to me, but they were surprised because they felt I had been doing a good job. Then Sully spoke. He explained that PJ never introduced all his offensive patterns from the start and, as the season rolled on, I would get more comfortable and feel I was contributing more. The assistant coaches were positive, encouraging and complimentary and could not have been more supportive. They wanted to buy time and asked me to at least hold off until after we had been to New Orleans and I had talked to my parents. It was an emotional time and it was hard to talk to the assistant coaches because it felt like I was quitting. I had already spoken to my dad on the telephone and told him not to waste his money coming over because I was coming home. My dad's advice was similar to the assistant coaches': I should stick it out through New

Orleans because he, mum and Janet would be there regardless. It clinched the deal: I would go to New Orleans. I was still ready to pack it in, as I think was my room-mate Trevor Crowley. Trevor transferred to Seton Hall from a junior college in California, where he had been conference MVP and scored nearly 20 points per game. At Seton Hall, he hardly got to play, so our room was not exactly Disneyland, the happiest place in the world.

Fortunately, New Orleans had a positive effect on me, my season, my game and my outlook. Whether it was the hoop gods or whatever, I had a pretty good tournament and decided to keep that return portion of my airline ticket. Resigned to going home, I had gone onto the court with a nothing-to-lose attitude, did my thing and jacked up a few shots (and they dropped). The more shots I made, the more my attitude loosened and the more I kept shooting. It wasn't like I was just catching the ball and shooting from anywhere on the floor: I was just shooting more than normal, extending my licence. And the best thing about it, apart from the scoring, was that PJ didn't get on my case.

We beat Virginia in the first game and smashed DePaul in the final and I was named the tournament's Most Valuable Player (MVP). It was a pivotal moment. I still have the Dan Cornswith Snr memorial trophy for Most Outstanding Player of the Sugar Bowl tournament as a reminder of the weekend that saved my season with Seton Hall – even though, unfortunately, the little basketball player on top of the award has been snapped off. I owe a massive debt of gratitude to people like John Carroll (who moved on to the NBA and was interim coach of the Boston Celtics during the 2004 season) and Tom Sullivan (who was a pretty good college player at Fordham) for putting up with my sulking and not letting me quit. During one of my meetings with the assistant coaches, Sully said his piece and didn't mince words.

'Listen, things are going to come around,' Sully said. 'Andrew, you've got to understand, I've been around this a long time and from what I've seen of this team, nothing would be worse than you leaving and then seeing us in April playing for the national championship. I honestly believe we can win and do some good things. We can go to the NCAA tournament, anything can happen and we can win the championship.'

Sully was as sincere as he could be, but the inner cynic whispered in my mind. 'I hear you and you're saying the right things to try and pump me up, but do you think I'm an idiot? There's no way known we're going to win a national championship.'

Sully probably used that speech on every down-in-the-mouth, homesick, lovelorn, stuck-on-the-bench player that came into his office wanting to quit the Seton Hall basketball team. But I got the distinct impression he believed what he said. He believed we had a chance to do something special with this team. While I doubted them at the time, Sully's words turned out to be uncannily prophetic.

After winning the Sugar Bowl tournament and clearing the air with the assistant coaches, the season sailed by as the Pirates negotiated the usual highs and lows of a campaign. From the time we won the Sugar Bowl tournament, we never dropped out of the top twenty in the weekly national polls, which are based on the votes of media members and coaches. It was a big deal to be ranked and Seton Hall was becoming big time. A feeling started to materialise among the team that, as Sully had predicted, we were on the brink of something special. Our coach seemed to think so, too. We were 13–0 and ranked number 10 in the nation as we prepared to play the number 2 ranked Syracuse at Syracuse in upstate New York in early January. During a team meeting, PJ said to us: 'Listen, we're undefeated and, although we don't usually think of rankings, very, very few schools ever get to be ranked number 1 in the nation. If we beat Syracuse we have a chance to be ranked number 1 in the nation.' It was a pipe dream. Syracuse belted us, 90–66, at the Carrier Dome in front of 32,037 people. Just a small gathering, really.

After the Syracuse loss, we won four straight, but the competition in the Big East Conference got a lot stiffer as the season went on. We dropped a few games, but my game was coming together. I was playing my role, being efficient, hitting some shots, scoring some points and, believe it or not for those who reckon my name should be Anrew (no D), I was regarded as one of the team's better defensive players. Off the floor, things were pretty good, too. I had become accustomed to college life as a member of the Seton Hall basketball team.

For much of the time, we lived, worked, ate and slept as a team. It was a totally different situation to anything I was used to with the Melbourne Tigers, where we played Wednesday nights in the State League, played or trained Friday and/or the weekend in the NBL and had Tuesday and Thursday off. All that while blokes juggled work and study as best they could. In college, we had five coaches to oversee the regimented practice sessions and everyone had to be there on time or they would run laps until they vomited. It was a highly disciplined environment and new to me. In Australia we played for ten or eleven months of the year, but this was as intense a few months as I ever experienced.

It was pleasurable at times, with a few comforts thrown in on top of what we got with the Tigers, who were still pretty much an amateur organisation. One little extra was staying in a hotel the night before every game – even those home conference games at the Meadowlands (now Continental Airlines) Arena. A Sheraton Hotel was right across from the Meadowlands, so we would get a bus from school to the hotel at about 6 p.m., have dinner, then go to our rooms for a good night's sleep. The next morning we would watch some scouting film, have a pre-game shoot-around, play the game, get back on the bus and return to campus. It was regimented, unlike in Australia where you were left to your own devices and preparation. At Seton Hall, we ate, we practised, we lifted weights, we had meetings, we travelled, and it was all together and all scheduled and detailed. It was different from what I was used to with the Tigers, but at least I knew where and when I was supposed to be.

The place not many people thought Seton Hall would be was in the thick of the post-season action. By the end of the regular season we were 25–5 and tied for second in the Big East. That was good enough for the Pirates, picked to finish near the bottom of our conference, to be voted number 11 in the influential Associated Press national rankings. PJ Carlesimo was also recognised as Big East Coach of the Year, while our centre, Ramon Ramos, was named to the All-Big East first team and John Morton and I were picked on the third team.

They were mere entrees to what we really craved in terms of prizes. We wanted the Big East tournament title and we wanted a crack at the NCAA Championship. In the Big East, we lost by three in the semi-finals, going down to Syracuse for the third time that season and the sixteenth straight time under PJ. The Orangemen had our measure, even though we had our chances to win. Not that I could make any excuses. I was 0–5 on three-pointers in the semi-final and went 1–14 in the three games against Syracuse that season. We were disappointed because we felt we at least had the chance to make the final. We also knew our season wasn't finished. We still had the NCAA tournament to go. The NCAA Championship knockout tournament lasts a month, but it is the month seemingly all of America spends watching college basketball. We watched Georgetown beat Syracuse in the Big East final, then flicked on the television to see the draw for the NCAA tourney. We knew we would be in the 64-team field; we just didn't know against whom, or where, we would play our first game. Soon enough, we knew we were playing Southwest Missouri State at Tucson, Arizona.

We were heading west, not really knowing how long we would be gone. It turned out to be much longer than we all thought.

chapter seven

The Biggest Dance
of All

I was open, I was open, I was open. I was open and I didn't get the
ball. The clock said three seconds left. Plenty of time to make a play.
The only catch was we had the ball out of bounds on our defensive
baseline and had to go the length of the court for a score. After
thirty-seven games of the US college basketball season, after forty
minutes of regulation and another four minutes, fifty-seven seconds
of overtime, the last game of the NCAA tournament went down to
the very last second and Seton Hall had a chance to win it. I could
have had a chance to win it for the Pirates. Only I didn't get the
chance.

The 1989 NCAA Championship final against Michigan was not
my best game, nor was it my worst. Offensively, I did not see a lot of
the ball and did not score my first field goal until the overtime

period. Defensively, I had the tough job of guarding Michigan's lead-ing scorer Glen Rice. But I still thought I had a chance to win it for the Pirates after Rumeal Robinson emerged a hero by putting Michigan ahead from the free-throw line with just three seconds left. Robinson was a poor free-throw shooter, making just sixty-four per cent of his foul shots for the season. So, when he got the bene-fit of a referee's call to go to the line, we felt if anyone had to be up there we would take Robinson. Just to play a little on his mind, coach PJ Carlesimo called a time-out to let Robinson think about the magnitude of the situation. When we went back out onto the court, I wasn't so subtle.

I lined up in the position to block out Robinson and get good rebounding position if he missed. It was like one of those moments from the movies that are slowed down and the sound becomes all peripheral and weird. You look around at the 39,187 people in the Seattle Kingdome, with a live TV audience in the tens of millions and media all around the court. You just know these free-throws are for a lot more than a basketball game. So I said, 'Rumeal, hey, check out all those cameras there. Lot of cameras.' I had tried to psyche out Robinson and then I had a pang of guilt, realising what would hap-pen if he missed. Seton Hall would win the game, but Robinson would have lost it for Michigan. I almost felt I wouldn't want to be in his position. In one instance I was trying to get into his head and in the next I felt empathy for him. Eventually, I thought, 'I'm not going to be that unhappy if he makes the first and misses the second and we go to double-overtime.' Then it would be a neutral situation where Robinson wouldn't carry the burden of missing both shots and we wouldn't lose.

Sport, as in life, does not always turn out as you want. Robinson, the ordinary free-throw shooter with the weight of a two-storey house on his shoulders, made both free-throws to be nine of ten for the game and put Michigan ahead by one point. Now the onus and the pressure were back on Seton Hall. PJ Carlesimo called a time-out to set up one last play for one last chance to win the ultimate prize in US college basketball.

Although only three seconds remained to go the length of the court, we had a play we practised throughout the season that fitted the scenario perfectly. One of the big guys, usually Ramon Ramos, would take the ball behind the defensive baseline, John Morton and I would line-up either side of the basket at the other end, while Daryll Walker would go to the free-throw line as the prime target. The ball was to be thrown long and high for Daryll to catch and pass to me or John after we flared to the wings to get open. That was exactly how we ran the play against Michigan. Ramon Ramos threw the ball long and high to Daryll as John and I flared to the wings. I had just hit a three-pointer and I knew I was open again as I made position to receive the pass. Daryll caught the ball, landed, turned and shot under pressure from a couple of Michigan defenders. The shot was long and high and clunked off the backboard, missing the ring.

I was open and I was waiting for the ball. In my mind, I was probably open a lot longer than I really was. Daryll knew we needed to get a shot off and he made sure we did, so you can't blame him for that. If we didn't shoot, we couldn't win. But ever since that fateful moment, I've believed I would have made the shot. I felt good about taking the last shot. I wanted to get the shot. I really wanted the ball. It was one of those situations just made for a shooter. You've got no choice but to shoot and I just thought, 'This is it.' I did get open for a second, but it wasn't to be. From our regular practices I knew what the options were and that there was a big chance I would get that shot. The play was designed to go the length of the court and get a shot. We achieved that but missed out on the ultimate pay-off. As Daryll Walker's shot bounced off the backboard into the hands of Glen Rice, the game, the tournament, the season, the dream, the journey, the adventure was over.

Some feel the college basketball season starts with the NCAA tournament, the event known in the US as March Madness. It is a tournament that has grown enormously from humble beginnings into a massive and lucrative television-backed money spinner for the schools and the NCAA. It can also be an important launching pad for professional careers with its huge profile via the media. Michael Jordan, the greatest player of all time, gained an instant reputation as a clutch performer when he made the winning shot for North Carolina in the 1982 final against Georgetown. I sometimes wonder whether the legend of Jordan would have been so great had he not made that shot. One thing I do know is that the 1982 final was the game (after I saw it on video) that really made me want to play college basketball and maybe, just maybe, experience the NCAA tournament.

The tournament starts with sixty-five teams (there is one play-in game before the actual tournament tips off) and sixty-four teams go through a knock-out format until we get to the biggest weekend of college basketball, the Final Four, also known as the Big Dance. It takes just four wins to get to the Big Dance, now always played in one of the massive domed stadiums to maximise crowds and revenue, and six wins to take the championship. Seton Hall won five games in 1989, but what an experience it was just to get to the Big Dance.

The NCAA tournament started for Seton Hall in the West Regional at Tucson, Arizona, which was a bit of a bonus, with a few days in the warm weather. The added bonus was that, with the second round in Denver and the Final Four in Seattle, we had the incentive of staying out west as long as we kept winning, rather than commute to and from New Jersey. That meant no classrooms for as long as we could hold out. Not that it meant no work. Because school was still in, we had tutors on the road, but I'm not sure anyone was really able to concentrate on their studies. I was going well with school, so it was no drama for me, but the college system requires that everyone remain eligible to play by maintaining their grades to certain levels. Normally, we'd train, we'd eat as a team and every second day we had study hall with two tutors. It was a two-hour period in which we were forced to study. Not that too many of us were thinking of anything other than the NCAA tournament.

We stayed in resort-style accommodation in Arizona and we responded to the warm weather and surroundings by beating Southwest Missouri State in the first round and Evansville in the second to make the Sweet Sixteen in Denver. Making the Sweet Sixteen is a big deal, especially for a school like Seton Hall, because you will likely come up against a basketball powerhouse at that stage of the tournament. Which we did, drawing Indiana in the regional semi-final. Indiana has a rich basketball history due largely to former coach Bob Knight, who remains one of the most volatile, talented and winningest coaches in the sport's history. We beat Indiana by thirteen points, bringing about the Hoosiers' worst loss ever in NCAA tournament play.

It was an amazing achievement made even better when we beat the University of Nevada Las Vegas (UNLV) in the regional final to advance to the Final Four. Somehow, I was named Chevrolet Player of the Game in both of our Denver games and was awarded the MVP for the West Regional. But the most enduring memory of the game against UNLV was being on the wrong end of a nasty dunk by Stacey Augmon. It was a vicious dunk right over the top of me. I haven't seen video of that game and I'd like to, so long as somebody can edit out that dunk.

Making the Final Four might have been the biggest thing to happen to Seton Hall, the little school tucked away in South Orange, New Jersey. Seton Hall was founded in 1856 by Bishop James Roosevelt Bayley, the first bishop of Newark, who named the school for his aunty, Mother Elizabeth Ann Seton, a pioneer in Catholic education and the first American-born saint. The campus is about twenty-two kilometres south-west of New York City, sitting at the foot of South Mountain, which was where George Washington, the first president of the United States, surveyed his troops during the Battle of Connecticut Farms. From its humble and historical beginnings, Seton Hall grew from an enrolment of a few to a student body of about ten thousand drawn from across the US and around the world. But good though Seton Hall is as an education facility, not many people would know it existed if not for its basketball program, which is the school's main sport. Even fewer would have heard of the Pirates if not for our trip to the 1989 NCAA Final Four.

That just underlined the magnitude of the event. We thought it was a big deal to get an increase on our measly per diem as we progressed through the tournament and even better that we got to spend a few days in LA on the way from Denver to Seattle. But once we got to Seattle and experienced the Final Four, we would have paid our own way and given up LA every time. It was huge. Everything was huge – from the crowds to the Kingdome, from the locker rooms to the media attention. What made it bigger for us was that Seton Hall was the odd man out among the four teams. The other Final Four teams – Illinois, Duke and Michigan – were powerhouses with strong and proud basketball histories. Then there was Seton Hall.

The Seton Hall Pirates were the Cinderella story of the 1989 Final Four and we got plenty of media attention because of it. Some people just wanted to know where we were from. South Orange, New Jersey, is not exactly among the top ten cities of the world. The media coverage was intense. On arrival in Seattle, our five starters were required to attend media day, starting with an all-in media conference with about three hundred reporters, then we had individual interviews in allocated conference rooms, which added to the impression that this was pretty big and considered a major story for the city of Seattle and the nation. It was an event that demanded and received media coverage in every American city where a basketball ring existed. These days, people tune in on TV, too, with 17.5 million viewers watching North Carolina and Michigan State in one of the 2005 semi-finals. Just think about it: those 17.5 million viewers almost equal the population of Australia.

I got a fair amount of media attention for two reasons: first, I was a novelty; and second, I was playing okay. At that time international players in the US were still the exception rather than the rule, so for me to come from Australia, where some Americans still imagined kangaroos hopped down the streets, was like somebody coming out of the Amazon to play for the Melbourne Tigers. Winning the West Regional MVP helped my profile, as did being on the cover of *Sports Illustrated*. It's maybe every sports person's dream to be on the cover of *SI* and I pulled it off. But let me just clarify that. Banned baseballer Pete Rose was the main cover photo and my head was in a small square in the top right corner. Nor was my pic on every issue. Half the circulation had a photo of Danny Ferry of Duke and the other half had me. Either way, I was on the cover and people noticed.

Not that you couldn't be noticed as a player at the Final Four. Even the last man on the roster was of interest and had some kind of story to tell. The media were as insatiable as the public, which is what makes it such a big event. I'm no expert, but somebody told me that, outside the NFL Super Bowl, the NCAA Final Four is the biggest sporting event in America – bigger than the Olympics, which for Australians is the pinnacle. Certainly, the CBS television network thought it was a big event, shelling out US$6 billion for an eleven-year deal through to 2014. Whichever way you look at it, that's big bucks. As a kid watching tape of the finals between Georgetown and Villanova, and Indiana and Syracuse, I knew it was big. But it wasn't until I was actually in the middle of it that I realised just how big. It was one of those times that I actually muttered, 'Shit, I'm really here.'

And the media coverage wasn't confined to the US. Significant for Australian basketball and for me was the decision to show the Final Four on television at home. I hadn't realised the impact Seton Hall's march through the tournament had made in Australia until my dad told me Channel Seven was taking the Final Four live. I thought Channel Seven was showing it because it was basketball.

I never once assumed it was because I was playing in the game. I just never thought I would or could have that impact. Seton Hall Sports Information Director, John Paquette, got a lot of calls from Australian radio stations wanting to talk to me, too, and I put it down to the curiosity factor. I honestly thought I had a great story for dinner parties, but I gladly admit I grossly underestimated how much interest Seton Hall and I had generated back home in Australia during the tournament.

Duke was our semi-final opponent and it looked like the famous school from Durham, North Carolina, would be our semi-final conqueror, too. We were down by eighteen points, 26–8, in the first half and it seemed the ride was over. But to think that way was to underestimate our team and its heart. We gradually got going, pulled the margin into five at half-time and took over in the second half to win, 95–78. The final margin represented a 35-point turnaround. Those who had Duke as six-point favourites and Seton Hall at 8–1 outsiders for the Final Four got a harsh and fast lesson about the Pirates. Guard Gerald Greene got us going against Duke and, just before half-time, I made a couple of shots. In the second half, I hit a few threes and finished with twenty points, but the win for the team easily overshadowed any individual performances.

The final against Michigan is still considered one of the greatest NCAA finals. Which wasn't any great comfort after we lost in overtime. We had our chances to win, but we couldn't close it out. We came back from a twelve-point deficit in the second half to take a late lead as John Morton, often PJ's whipping boy, hit some big baskets. In fact, John's three-pointer with twenty-five seconds left tied it, 71–71, at the end of regulation. Glen Rice, the man I guarded and eventually *held* to thirty-one points, took a three-point shot to win with two seconds left. Having done everything but foul him, I was mighty glad to see the ball bounce off the rim.

That led to the fateful five-minute overtime period and, finally, I landed a field goal. If timing is everything, I was happy to wait for my chance providing it meant we would win. John Morton hit another three, giving him thirty-five points, to put us up by three with one minute, thirty-four seconds left. It was the last time we scored. John missed two shots on the next two possessions and Gerald Greene missed from the free-throw line. Terry Mills hit a jump shot for Michigan to cut our lead to one, then Rumeal Robinson stepped to the line with three seconds left to give the Wolverines the lead and, it turned out, the national championship when Daryll Walker's shot at the buzzer missed.

It was a bitter-sweet end to the season. We were all bitterly disappointed to lose the final in such heart-breaking fashion. But, in all honesty, after the hours of arduous work and training, I had looked forward to the end. I certainly didn't want to lose and I loved being at Seton Hall, but I was relieved it was over, that it was time to rest physically and mentally. Throughout our NCAA tournament run, we were always on tenterhooks, knowing that if we lost we were finished. Aside from knowing your season could finish abruptly, you didn't know when that would be. Nor did you want it to end. But I had played almost two years without a week off and I was glad it was over.

That said, the most immediate and overwhelming emotion was the shattering disappointment of losing the NCAA Championship game by one point in overtime. We could not have got any closer to actually winning it. Needless to say, the post-game locker room overflowed with emotion. There was the obvious disappointment, then reflection on the journey, then the realisation that this group had played its last game together – the realisation that a special relationship was over. Together we shed blood, sweat and tears trying to win a championship that seemed so remote at the start but was so attainable yet so elusive at the finish. The process of getting to that point was the most rewarding thing and now we were at the full stop. And not just for our college careers. For some guys on the team, that was their last game of official basketball. There were many reasons to spill tears that Monday night in Seattle.

The bloke who might have shed the biggest and most tears was our coach, PJ Carlesimo. The bloke who growled and bared his teeth like that German Shepherd I encountered at the petrol station just broke down and cried like a baby. Initially, PJ, upholding his role as coach through habit or the need to stave off his welling emotions, spoke analytically about the game and why we lost and what we could have done. He was measured in his tone and, frankly, my thought was, 'Who cares?' Then he started talking about the closure of the season, the achievement of the team and how proud he was. By then the change rooms were awash with tears and nobody bothered to try to hide them. It would have been impossible.

After a fairly rude introduction to PJ as a coach, I had gained more insight into PJ the person as the season wore on. We saw how much basketball meant to him, what it meant to his family, especially his late father, Pete, who played on Fordham University's football team with legendary gridiron coach Vince Lombardi. Pete coached a variety of sports, including basketball, at Scranton University, and returned to Fordham as athletic director before becoming executive director of the National Invitation Tournament. PJ had nine siblings, but none seemed to be as influenced by their dad, who died in 2003, as PJ.

After graduating from Fordham in 1971, PJ spent four years there as an assistant coach, was head coach at New Hampshire and Wagner, then moved to Seton Hall, where he spent twelve years. PJ was with the Pirates until 1994, when he got the call from the NBA. PJ coached the Portland Trail Blazers and Golden State Warriors, then became an assistant coach with the San Antonio Spurs. PJ was also a head coach or assistant of US teams at the Olympics, world championships and Goodwill Games. His only time out of a coaching job, between the Warriors and Spurs, was spent working as a television basketball analyst.

There was more to PJ than just being a basketball coach. Behind the massive CV and basketball brain and underneath the gruff and often profane exterior was a charming, charismatic man with a huge sense of humour and a big heart. Once you separated and recognised the two different personalities, you were fine. The first time I really saw PJ in another light was at the Sugar Bowl tournament in New Orleans just after Christmas. We were at a function for the teams and each of the coaches addressed the gathering. PJ's turn to speak became a comedy routine. On stage at the microphone, he was a brilliant, funny and entertaining speaker.

Near the end of the season, we had another glimpse at the other side of PJ. Before our last Big East regular-season game at Providence he spoke about our season and got emotional. Later, at a team dinner in the school food hall before we left for the NCAA tournament, PJ thanked the chef who cooked for us every day and described what his contribution meant to the team. It was enough for PJ to cry. The soft side of the hard disciplinarian was never far from the surface. So it was quite understandable on the biggest night of his life, when his dad and family could proudly see him in the national spotlight, that emotion readily broke the surface to show each and every player that PJ really cared about them.

With the basketball season over, the only thing left to do was go back to Seton Hall and pack my bags to return to Australia. There was a massive crowd at the airport to meet us when we flew in from Seattle and there were thousands back at the campus gym, where we were presented to the crowd. Each player was introduced and when it was my turn, the crowd chanted, 'One more year. One more year.' I desperately wanted to say I would be back, but I couldn't. I had seriously considered going back for another year, but circumstances simply did not allow it. It was a great feeling to be loved and wanted and respected and appreciated, but I knew I couldn't say I was coming back. So I told them I was not sure about the future and thanked them for the opportunity, support and unique experience in the school and community. The next day the celebrations continued, with the players paraded through the streets of South Orange in

Mercedes-Benz convertibles. Tens of thousands of fans came out to congratulate us, even though we had only finished second. I sometimes wonder what the response would have been had we won the title. Even so, I doubt that the accolades and recognition could have been any greater than what we received on our arrival home.

One of the reasons I couldn't play a second season at Seton Hall was to do with my eligibility. Under NCAA rules, foreign players lost a year of eligibility each year after they turned twenty-one. I was listed as a junior, but I would have been twenty-four by the start of the next season and out of eligibility. The school wanted to appeal on the grounds that I would have gone to Seton Hall a year earlier had I not been committed to the 1988 Olympics. But I don't think we would have won the appeal, anyway. Not after the furore that erupted in the media about my eligibility for the season just finished.

The NCAA was strict about two things: being academically eligible and being an amateur athlete. While I was academically eligible and held my own in the classroom at Seton Hall, there were question marks over my amateur status. Because I had played for Melbourne Tigers in the NBL, some people suggested I was a professional and a hired gun for Seton Hall. I had been home a few weeks and was getting ready to appear on Ray Martin's *Midday Show* on Channel Nine when I received a phone call in the green room. It was a reporter from the *New York Post*, who had tracked me down to ask about my time at Seton Hall and my eligibility. I certainly didn't leave the conversation thinking there was going to be controversy. But he had other information and was filling in the gaps for his column. This determined reporter obviously believed it was a very important story – otherwise he would not have gone to such lengths to track me down.

Now, if we hadn't got into the Final Four and the championship game, nobody would have cared about my eligibility and amateur status. But it became a fairly prominent story and the NCAA investigated my circumstances. What the NCAA – and anybody else who bothered to do some serious investigation – found was that, until 1988, I was not paid to play for the Tigers. There was some money placed in a trust fund for me, but it was minimal and I had declared it to Seton Hall.

There was also a belief that I didn't study at Seton Hall. One of the reasons I went there was to study to help my degree studies at Victoria University. I didn't have to go to class the first semester at Seton Hall, but I did, so in the second semester I only needed to study three subjects. Some people thought that, because I only studied three subjects in the second semester and left three weeks early to go home to play for the Tigers, I had just cruised until it was time to bail out. That was completely wrong. I discussed the situation with my lecturers at Seton Hall and they gave me assignments and projects to fulfil the criteria and pass the courses so I would receive credits towards my degree in Australia. In fact, when I left Seton Hall, I took with me twenty-four credits for my degree.

The NCAA's stance on eligibility, payments and direct or indirect assistance to athletes is quite laughable in some instances. As the National Collegiate Athletic Association it oversees sport in colleges, which really is a multi-million dollar industry, raking in revenue from ticket sales, merchandise and television rights fees. The athletes, aside from scholarships that include tuition, board and meals, get nothing and are banned from even the smallest leg up. For instance, if an athlete uses the telephone in the athletic department to make a long-distance call home to his mother, he has to pay for that call or he and the school would face sanctions. The NCAA looked into my situation and ruled that there was no case to answer.

This post-season controversy put a bit of a dampener on the Seton Hall experience. Then again, nothing could diminish the total experience – discovering college life, the atmosphere on campus and the adulation that comes with being on a successful college basketball team. I gained an appreciation for the history of the school and the basketball program and the bond between students, who have a real affinity with the school. While the street parade and presentation after the NCAA Final Four was big, there was one other night that probably summed up college life. It was the last home game of the season against little Brooklyn College, the lowest-ranked team in division one college basketball. But it was one of the most important nights of the season. It was Senior Night, when the seniors on the team are honoured in their last home game before graduation. Tradition requires that the seniors are presented at centre court and lauded for their contributions before they start the game, whether they are regular starters or the last man at the end of the bench. I started every game that season except on Senior Night, when I went to the bench so Khyiem Long could start. After the game, PJ talked about the seniors and how it was the end of an era. It got emotional, but it only served to strengthen the bond between players, team and school.

I did not experience Senior Night as a senior, but I kind of did about eighteen months later when the Tigers toured the US and played Seton Hall. I couldn't play because I was recovering from a blood clot in my shoulder, but I was on the bench. I was introduced to the crowd and they went nuts, with a standing ovation that went for an embarrassingly long time. I was stunned by this warmth and sincerity, especially as I had given the Pirates just one season of service. It was a special night made even more special when PJ Carlesimo met me on the court to present a Final Four ring. All the players had received one, but the school had held mine until I could return to receive it in person.

Simply, making the NCAA tournament final was an incredible result for the school, the team, the players and coaches. It was against the odds to go as far as we did. But stop and consider the odds of me being involved. The odds of one person from Australia going to one of the hundreds of colleges in America for one season and going all the way to the national final are phenomenal. To put it into perspective, there have been millions of college students throughout history and only a tiny handful have played in an NCAA Championship game. I had one year of college at a small school that was not considered a chance, not ranked in the pre-season, but through the good fortune of being in the right place at the right time, I got to share the most extraordinary experience. It was the longest of long shots. So perhaps asking to get the last, potential game-winning shot in the NCAA final might have been stretching the odds too far.

chapter eight

NOT SO SUPER SONIC

MEDICAL examinations before starting new jobs are routine and fairly standard. Even in the NBA, while the doctors might push and pull a few extra spots and limbs, snap a few more X-rays, it's still pretty standard. So I figured there was nothing to worry about as I stripped off and got ready to be given the all-clear to start my first NBA tryout with the Seattle SuperSonics.

The doctor chatted away as he poked, prodded, pushed and pulled. He was actually pretty cool and relaxed as he ticked off something on his chart and noticed my name on the sheet. 'Oh, Gaze,' the doc said. 'You're the guy from Australia. I saw you play for Seton Hall in the NCAA tournament.' It was nice to be recognised, so I complimented the doc on his memory and we talked about the championship game we lost to Michigan about six months earlier. But it wasn't my performances in college that were imbedded in his brain.

'I remember that game very well,' the doc said. 'I had a lot of money on you guys. You know what? You guys cost me a lot of money.' I quickly and nervously glanced over my shoulder only for my nervousness to turn to horror. The doc was slipping a rubber glove over his hand. 'Now,' he said with a smile as he remembered his lost bet, 'this is where I get some retribution.' Then, *zoop*. Welcome to Seattle. A visit to Starbucks for a caffe latte and a muffin would have been a nicer welcome to the city, but who was I to argue? This was the NBA and sometimes you just have to take some pain to try to make some gain.

After my one season at Seton Hall, I received letters from the New Jersey Nets, the Philadelphia 76ers and the Boston Celtics. It was flattering to get the letters, which carried the NBA and team logos and looked impressive, but they were basically generic invitations to see if I was interested in playing in the summer leagues or attending training camp. The NBL season with the Melbourne Tigers had started and as far as I was concerned my days of playing in the US were done. So I didn't really think too much about it – until I was approached by the Seattle SuperSonics.

Whether the Final Four being played in Seattle had anything to do with it, I'm not sure, but the Sonics made a solid offer for me to attend veterans' training camp later in the year. The approach came right out of the blue via my agent at Advantage International, Jeff Austin, whose sister is former world number 1 tennis player Tracy Austin. What made this approach so appealing was that it presented a good chance to make the team. I asked Jeff how realistic the Sonics' approach was and he said it was definitely an opportunity. They already had eleven guaranteed contracts for a twelve-man roster and they wanted to bring in five or six guys to try out for the last contract.

My interest increased when Seattle coach Bernie Bickerstaff phoned in September. He reiterated what Jeff Austin had told me, adding that they didn't know a lot about me but had seen me play at Seton Hall. Bickerstaff said all I needed to do was go to camp in October, do what I do best and if I did that well enough I would have a job in the NBA. The Sonics would pay my return airfare, but there were no other promises or commitments.

I signed a make-do contract, which would only be triggered if I made the final roster. That was fine by me. The only hitch in the whole situation was that the Tigers looked like going deep into the NBL play-offs, which we had not done before. If that was the case, I wasn't going anywhere near Seattle. Not that I told the Sonics that. I spoke to Jeff Austin and decided to accept the Sonics' invitation. If I pulled out at the last minute, so be it. I would not have one smidgen of guilt.

As the NBL regular-season wound down, the Tigers were considered a genuine chance to win the championship. We guaranteed a play-off spot a couple of weeks from the end of the season and finished fourth on the ladder. With four games left, we played the Eastside Melbourne Spectres and there was a bit of a dust-up in the last quarter as Tigers import Dave Simmons threw an absolute haymaker at the Spectres' Shane Froling. It was the quickest, most vicious, strongest punch I had ever seen, with Mike Tyson written all over it. Fortunately for Froling and Simmons, it missed, otherwise Sim might have been doing fifteen years for manslaughter.

Even so, Simmons was reported and suspended for the last three games of the regular season, which at least made him available for the opening game of the best-of-three play-off series against the Sydney Kings. We lost the last two games of the regular season, so we weren't flying into the play-offs, and even with Sim back in the line-up, we lost the first game in Sydney by twelve. That result was made worse when our other import, Dave Colbert, belted Kings tough guy Tim Morrissey with an elbow to the head. Colbert was suspended for two games, which meant the rest of the Kings series. Despite that, we won game two to level the series behind Dave Simmons' thirty-three points, only to lose the third and deciding game at the Glasshouse by two points. That ended our season, so I was off to Seattle for an NBA tryout.

I arrived in Seattle about two days before training camp started and ran straight into a familiar face. American Mike Champion had been with the Canberra Cannons in 1987, had played a couple of games with the Tigers in 1988 while we filled an import vacancy, then had gone home and was picked up by Seattle on a ten-day contract. Mike was trying out with the SuperSonics again, so we were competing for the same spot on the roster. I guess there's some advantage to knowing the opposition, but apart from Mike, I didn't know a soul when the players assembled for camp. All I knew was that five blokes were trying for one job and it wasn't going to be easy.

There were a couple of other astute observations that I made, with the help of Jack Hill the blind miner. The first day of training camp it struck me that the eleven players already contracted by the Sonics were black. Off-setting that, every player there for a tryout was white. It was fact. Now I'm not suggesting by any stretch of the imagination that race had anything to do with that last spot on the roster. I just thought it was a remarkable coincidence that all five of us were white. I couldn't shake the notion that, while all of us were players with a track record, the term *token white guy* would apply.

The other thing that hit me in the face like a Three Stooges' cream pie was the size of the players in for the tryout. I was a guard and the rest were all big men, centres and power forwards. That made one or two alarm bells ring. Clearly, in my mind at least, it didn't seem right that I was there.

Not that I was in Seattle too long. The team's owners were lobbying local politicians for a new arena and, in a move considered part of the bargaining process, we went south to San Diego for training camp. There was noise about the Sonics relocating, but while the climate in San Diego might be good all year-around, the facilities we encountered were a little dated. The six-day training camp was at San Diego University and, like the facility, the camp was about substance rather than show.

The four other players trying out were Chris Engler, who had had five years in the NBA, Scott Meents from University of Illinois, Wayne Tinkle, who played at Montana, and Mike Champion. These days, NBA teams usually carry fourteen players, with two on the injured reserve as insurance, but not many teams did so back in 1989 and the Sonics were committed to signing the NBA-mandated twelve. We scrimmaged when we arrived in San Diego and my first inclination was – call me a pessimist – that my chances were even slimmer than I had originally thought.

Despite that pessimistic streak, I was determined to give it my best shot. I might have shown that before we left Seattle, where we had to endure a fitness test when two players ran side by side on treadmills. I ran with one of the other uncontracted players, thinking, 'I might have to cough up blood, but I am not going to let this bloke beat me.' It was probably irrelevant to the whole selection process, but I wanted every advantage I could get. When the other guy had finished, I pushed myself a few seconds longer just to make sure I had an edge. I didn't have much left in me, but as long as I beat him that was the main thing right then and there.

The training camp in San Diego consisted of two training sessions a day, which was plenty of time to be awed by some of the athletes on the Sonics roster. I had played in two Olympics, but I was impressed by the sheer size of these blokes. There was Xavier McDaniel, Dana Barros, Sean Kemp, who was only nineteen and throwing down some incredible dunks, Dale Ellis, Olden Polynice, Nate McMillen, who eventually went on to coach the Sonics, Sedale Threatt and Avery Johnson, who I later hooked up with in San Antonio. This was early in AJ's NBA days when he was a minimum-salary player and on the first of the six teams he would eventually play for over sixteen seasons.

I shot the ball well in camp but always wondered what the

coaches thought. I found out one day when coach Bernie Bickerstaff and his assistant KC Jones were with me in the elevator. We exchanged small talk and Bernie said I was doing really well and had a good chance. That gave me some confidence, but every time I cast an eye around the court at practice the first five blokes I noticed were Nate McMillen, Sedale Threatt, Dana Barros, Avery Johnson and Dale Ellis – five contracted guards – and I didn't really think they'd add someone slower and less athletic to that mix.

Nor did I help myself one day at practice when there was a player ballot to decide which trialist to keep. Bernie Bickerstaff ended the session and picked two players to shoot two free-throws each. He chose Derrick McKey and me, with the challenge that if we made all four shots, the day was done. If we missed even one, then everyone had to run sprints. Derek made his two and you've never heard sixteen grown men cheer so loudly. I made my first shot, drew my breath for the second, cocked my elbow, released, snapped the wrist on the follow through, and missed. You've never heard sixteen grown men go so quiet so quickly.

The first pre-season exhibition game was against the Los Angeles Clippers in San Diego, which was interesting in itself. With talk of the Sonics moving to San Diego, the Clippers had returned to the southern Californian city they left behind. Bernie Bickerstaff indicated he would not make any cuts until we had played at least two pre-season games, which was fair enough, and Scott Meents and I got most court time among the free agents against the Clippers. We lost by eight, but I did okay without being spectacular.

Our next game was against the LA Lakers in St Louis. More than being against the Lakers, this was against Magic Johnson, one of the greatest basketball players ever to grace the court and still at his peak before being forced into retirement after contracting HIV in 1991. Most of the sixteen thousand people in the arena that night were there to see Magic, who showed just how good he was when he took over in the third quarter with a game-winning performance.

He hit three straight threes with sixteen points for the period. Magic was magic.

I'm going to take a little credit for Magic's third-quarter outburst because I might have spurred him on. With time running down in the first half, I found myself with the ball and defended by the one and only Earvin 'Magic' Johnson. I swallowed hard, tried to look composed, then launched up an absolute prayer of a shot I would not recommend you try in the backyard. It was all net. Money. Take that to the bank, suckers. Actually, I walked off trying to suppress the surprised look on my face. I can only imagine Magic was more surprised than me.

The big names kept coming and the next night we played the Detroit Pistons, who had picked up the nickname of Bad Boys while winning back-to-back NBA championships in 1989 and 1990. Needless to say, their nickname was not bestowed for delivering Meals on Wheels and manning school crossings. The Pistons were physical to the point of violence, so I wasn't all that unhappy to sit out the entire forty-eight minutes that night in Roanoke, Virginia. Except not playing would normally be a bad sign for a bloke battling to make a team. The only comfort was that neither Scott Meents nor Mike Champion played either. As we waited on the bus after the game, an equipment manager climbed on and told Wayne Tinkle and Chris Engler that the coach wanted to see them. That could only mean one thing: they were gone. 'The coach wants to see you' is coded warning to sportsmen on the fringes and we knew what it meant. But I'll say this for Bernie Bickerstaff: he played Tinkle and Engler against the Pistons to either give them a last chance to change his mind or as a farewell gesture. He didn't have to and I think those guys will appreciate that in time.

During the pre-season games I noticed a difference between the guys with guaranteed jobs, especially the superstars, and the guys on the selection bubble, who knew their NBA dream could burst any moment. Some guys cruised and others played for their lives. The coaches played the studs for maybe half of the game, just to get some court time and preparation but wary that they didn't need big minutes when they had eighty-two games in the regular season and, hopefully, the play-offs to come.

Even if the veterans and superstars cruised a little, you didn't get them angry or embarrass them. Sedale Threatt, who was on our team, should have known better. Sedale had some personality and spunk and wasn't beyond a challenge, even to the Pistons' Isiah Thomas, who was one of the best, quickest, smartest and toughest point guards in the NBA. As the clock ticked down to half-time in the exhibition game against the Pistons, Isiah had the ball, with Sedale guarding him. Sedale was also talking to him, baiting him, goading Isiah to 'Show me something.' Isiah, who had the face of an angel when he was a good boy rather than the leader of the Bad Boys, rolled his eyes and made a facial expression of 'Okay, you're making me play – let's play.' Isiah made a couple of crossover dribbles and had Sedale so off balance that he almost broke his ankles, then trotted in for a lay-up on the half-time buzzer. The boys reminded Sedale of what happened as soon as we got to the locker-room.

Sedale, who is good friends with my former Tigers team-mate Lanard Copeland, eventually moved to Australia. I spoke to him about this incident and he could not specifically recall it. It was a relatively mundane moment of a pre-season exhibition game for Sedale, but it was an indelible memory for me, as someone savouring every up-close encounter with the NBA superstars.

The exhibition season ended against the Sacramento Kings in Spokane, a city outside Seattle and the home town of legendary NBA point guard John Stockton. It was where my time with the Seattle SuperSonics ended, too. I didn't play and was in the locker-room when one of the team gofers delivered the message 'The coach wants to see you.'

Bernie Bickerstaff got straight down to business. He thanked me for my efforts and said I wasn't going to make the team. Bickerstaff said all the right things that you're supposed to say in those situations, including that he would follow my progress. I had no problem with all that. I wasn't looking for any explanation, so I thanked him for the opportunity and that was that. It was all straightforward and we moved on. Before the game against the Kings, I thought they would want the team set by the last exhibition game. I hoped they might have carried an extra player as insurance, which is common in the NBA now, but it never eventuated.

Going into that last game against the Kings, the one spot open was between me, Mike Champion and Scott Meents. The Sonics went with Scott Meents, which didn't surprise me. Scottie had been, and would be, around the NBA scene for a few years as a role player and he played in twenty-six games for the Sonics that season, averaging just 5.7 minutes per game and 2.1 points. I got the feeling in the last two exhibition games that Scott, who I roomed with in Seattle, was going to make it. I just felt and understood by looking around and asking myself, 'If I was coaching this team, what does the team need?' It was the twelfth-man spot, so they didn't need a superstar, but they needed a big guy. Much as they said they would take the best player, they needed a big guy. I felt, too, in the last week, in the way the coaches worked with other blokes, paying them more attention, that 'Gaze' was not about to be permanently stitched on the back of a Sonics jersey.

What hurt me most going into training camp was thinking it would be a good experience. Despite what happened on the treadmill when adrenalin and foolishness kicked in, I never had the mindset of being ruthless about doing whatever it took to make the team. I wanted to make the team, but it wasn't the be-all and end-all. Looking back, I might have done a couple of things differently from a playing point of view, but it was more an attitudinal thing of 'What is required to make the team here?' You need a level of commitment and determination as well as extraordinary skill to make the NBA. Shawn Kemp was a prime example of the athleticism and talent. He was only a skinny kid, but he was a dunking, athletic fool. In Australia and internationally we were conditioned to use the team structure with passing, screening and cutting to help you and the team. In the NBA, it's more individual, trying to break down someone one on one to exploit the skill, strength and athleticism. That wasn't my strength.

I was disappointed not to make the team after having gone so close, but I wasn't shattered. It was actually the first time in my basketball life that I failed in a tryout situation, but I didn't feel like I had failed. I went in with an open mind, looking for an experience, which I got. I hoped for the best, expected the worst and probably fell somewhere in between. The time with the Sonics did improve my game, without doubt. After being cut by the Sonics, I flew to Los Angeles and, having been selected pending the outcome of the Seattle tryout, I joined the Boomers, who were on tour and heading to Argentina. We played our first game against Loyola Marymount University in LA and it was an almost surreal experience. After playing and training at NBA level for a month, this was a step or two down and I was motoring in second gear but keeping pace with everyone else. It was like I had been trying to lift 120 kilograms for a month and then somebody gave me an 80-kilo barbell and I whacked it straight up over my head and held it for ten minutes. I had about forty points against Loyola Marymount, just because it felt so easy by comparison with what I had done with the Sonics.

The journey and experience that started with the Seattle SuperSonics continued with the Boomers on their tour through the US and Argentina and all came to an interesting end. After the return flight from Buenos Aires to LA, I struck problems with US Immigration officials. I didn't have the right visa to return to the US, even in transit. So while the Boomers waved me goodbye, I was left in LA to untangle red tape. When it was sorted out, my only route home to Melbourne was via Hong Kong. So I called Melinda and suggested she book a flight and meet me in Hong Kong for a holiday. We did the usual Hong Kong shopping and even picked up engagement and wedding rings for down the track. So I might be the only bloke in NBA history to end his first NBA tryout and his NBA career with rings! Even though that second ring was more than a decade and a highly improbable set of circumstances away.

chapter nine

A MATTER OF
PERSPECTIVE

WITH every weak breath, the excruciatingly sharp pain got worse. With every feeble cough, more blood flew from my mouth. It felt like somebody was ripping a 30-centimetre kitchen knife through my chest. There was no way I was going to survive this. No way. 'I'm going to die,' I thought. 'I'm going to die.'

Some things you just never allow yourself to say out loud. But in my mind, those words were louder than an AC/DC concert and the thought was running faster than Cathy Freeman. There was nothing I could do to silence or stop them. Lying in a hospital bed, I was in a full-blown panic, too scared to breathe, dreading the next searing, stabbing pain, fearing my next breath would be my last.

Never had my dad's philosophical line about absolutely needing to win only at surgery and war been so relevant to me. The rationale of that philosophy is that, if you lose at either of these, the chances are you'll be dead. Lying in that damned hospital bed, I knew what he meant. This was close enough to surgery and I was in one hell of a war, with a blood clot threatening my life.

The doctors had told me that as long as the thrombosis did not move from my right shoulder and upper arm, everything would be fine. If it moved, there could be problems. By now, the clot had moved and, given the pain I was in, I clearly had problems. I thought I was having a heart attack until it was diagnosed as the clot moving to my lungs. That did not ease my fears. Not with the pain ripping me apart.

It was my third night in the hospital for treatment for the clot and it was easily my worst. How much worse can it get when you think you're going to die? Every breath brought more unbearable pain, so I lay rigid, trying not to move, trying not to breathe. It was like when you're a kid in bed at night and can't sleep. If you lay still enough and quiet enough, the bogey man wouldn't come out of the dark to get you.

Then the blood started. I coughed and blood came with it. Every cough brought more blood. From where I was lying, it was the most vivid red blood I had ever seen and knowing it was mine certainly didn't help. I couldn't breathe, I was coughing up blood and I was panicking. In my mind, at just twenty-five, I was near death.

It was just a regular late Monday afternoon during the 1990 NBL season. The Melbourne Tigers had returned the day before from a road trip to Brisbane, where we got through a tight one to beat the Bullets, 133–132. That win made us 16–8, with two games to play and fairly secure in a play-off spot. So as we gathered for training at Albert Park to prepare for the next game against the Geelong Supercats, everyone felt pretty good.

Life, in fact, was good. I'd been to the World Championships in Argentina with the Boomers, I was playing well for the Tigers, averaging almost thirty-eight points a game, and I was renovating my house. Things weren't exactly a struggle as we headed into September, so to worry about a funny little feeling in my right arm was nonsensical. Nothing to worry about at all.

As I got off the flight home from Brisbane, I noticed my right hand looked more red than the left. It was part of the job to pick up lumps, bumps, bruises and scratches, so I didn't think much of it. Usually stuff like that came and went as I got on with life and basketball. What made me think more about it was that I felt very fatigued. I put that tiredness down to the fact that it was late in the NBL season and I had a big workload. Even when I turned up for training and still didn't feel a hundred per cent, I didn't think there was any drama. That was until we loosened up with a three-man weave drill and things started to happen. My arm felt really tight and within about ten minutes it was swollen from shoulder to wrist. It looked like I'd been doing curls in the gym for ten years. It was huge.

So I went over to my dad, who was coaching, and we looked at it. We thought I might have been bitten. The arm was tight, like the skin was stretched, and I had sharp pain in the armpit. There was no panic, but my dad said we should get it checked out. I called Peter Harcourt, who was the Boomers' team doctor. He wasn't at his surgery, but Karim Khan, the Opals' team doctor, was. He told me to come in and he'd have a look straightaway. It wasn't exactly encouraging when he mentioned he was worried because my arm condition seemed so unusual. It didn't get much better when he checked it further and pricked me with pins to see if the sensation was less acute in some areas than others. I must admit to some sense of panic when I wasn't feeling the pin prick all the time. Nor did it help my frame of mind when he said, 'Andrew, I don't want you to panic right now, but I've got to go to the textbook to check this.'

The textbook confirmed his suspected diagnosis: a thrombosis, more commonly known as a blood clot. His next words caught my attention. 'This can be very serious and I want to get it checked out right now.'

There was a sense of urgency as Dr Khan called a vascular surgeon, Dr Blombery, to ask if he could look at me. Within seconds we were in the car and off to Dr Blombery's office in Prahran. He looked at my arm and concurred with the thrombosis diagnosis. An ultrasound confirmed the doctors' suspicion when the vision on the screen showed a vein without blood flow. There, they explained, a blockage in the right auxiliary vein and they wanted to get on top of it immediately with a drug called Streptokinase. The drug dissipates the clot within a couple of days for most people and everything's fine, so I was admitted to the Alfred Hospital for the treatment.

That was the good news. The bad news, as had been mentioned a few times by the doctors, was that the situation still had the potential to be serious. I had caught the undertone of what 'serious' meant, but they explained it in more detail, telling me politely and calmly that if the clot moved to the heart, lungs or brain I could have some grave problems. The doctors tried to comfort me as they executed their duty of care to tell me the worst case scenario. It's not information I handle very well. All I knew was that I was being rushed to hospital and the doctors were talking about a potentially dangerous situation. I was thinking the worst. I thought I was in real trouble.

As the doctors arranged for me to check in to hospital I was still in my training gear and I suspected it was the last time I would wear it, at least for 1990 and maybe for a fair while. Maybe forever. I was shaken, but nobody else knew what was going on. My mum was working in the canteen at the Albert Park stadium and my dad was in a board meeting somewhere. I managed to raise mum on the phone and fill her in as best I could. She found my dad and they were at the hospital almost before me.

What made it tough was that every step of the process seemed to return more grim news. So I should have known what to expect as they injected me with dye to detect blood flow, or lack of it, and stuck me in front of the X-ray machine. The X-ray showed a nasty blockage about 25 centimetres long. I didn't need a doctor or specialist to tell me that was a substantial blood clot, but they did anyway, confirming that the vein from the shoulder into the arm was totally blocked. They decided to start the drug treatment straightaway in a bid to flush out the clot and return some blood flow to the vein. There were two catches: the drugs were so potent that I needed a nurse in my room around the clock to monitor me; and we had to hope the clot didn't move.

Once they discovered how big the clot was, I knew my season was over. That was my main thought at that stage: the season's gone; don't even contemplate playing again this season. Those thoughts were quickly overtaken by a bombardment of information about the course of treatment and drugs they were going to use. Streptokinase was only a short-term treatment that would fix the problem either in a couple of days or not at all. To stay on it too long was a dire health risk. There was another course of drugs after that and when I was discharged, I would be on medication for six to twelve months. One of the drugs was Warfarin, which keeps the blood thin and reduces the incidence of clotting but can cause serious internal bleeding. So they told me I needed to avoid stuff as simple as riding a bike or colliding with people, as would happen on the basketball court. To fall off a bike and get a cut or to bump someone and get a bruise would no longer be as simple as it once was. In either situation, if it was bad enough, you risked serious health problems.

I absorbed all this information but tried to stay calm and take it one step at a time. I knew I could be out of basketball for twelve months but it was the fear of the unknown that concerned me most. We still didn't know what caused the thrombosis and we still didn't know how it would respond to treatment. We didn't know if it would move and we didn't know if it would kill me. Talk about questions you need answers to.

My anxiety levels were high and I constantly analysed the doctors' words, delivery, facial expressions and body language, trying to read into what they told me rather than accepting the information as delivered. I was desperate and I needed a sign of hope. I needed to know more, but I was too afraid to ask because I didn't know what the answers would be.

The doctors explained that a clot in the arm was unusual; it was more common for clots to form in the legs. One thing they noticed when I was X-rayed was that I had something like an extra rib. It's not a bone, but it's similar to a calcification or cartilage. There was some talk of operating and cutting out this 'rib', but it never happened. At that stage, the idea of surgery on top of what I was going through was something I didn't need.

Lying in a hospital bed with a medical problem you don't know much about is not a good situation. Your mind starts to collate all the information being forwarded and often the mind's conclusions arrive at the worst. When you put together terms like *nasty, serious* and *potentially life-threatening*, there's really only one conclusion you can come to. When I did all that, the alarm bells start ringing. But I kept quiet about my fear and my mind played some horrendous games, like when I had pins and needles in my leg. I knew it was pins and needles, but I thought it could have been something serious. Maybe, I thought, I was developing blood clots all through my body. I was too afraid to tell the doctors or nurses because I just didn't want to hear any more bad news.

That Monday night seemed to go on forever, yet everything around me seemed to happen so quickly. Tuesday was a little slower and, at one stage, almost stopped completely. I had to have more tests and as I stood up for lung X-rays, I got instantly hot and light-headed and felt like I was going to pass out. I started vomiting so violently I expected to see to soles of my feet splash into the bucket. The emotion and drugs had started to kick in and, while the drugs were supposed to make me better, I certainly didn't feel too flash.

That night I started to feel some chest pain, but it was nothing too serious in the context of the situation.

Not until Big Wednesday rolled around, anyway. I was having a scan when the chest pain accelerated to the point where I honestly thought I was having a heart attack. Being fed into this massive claustrophobic machine to be scanned only increases the anxiety of wondering what it will reveal. By the time I was out of the machine and back in my room, the pain kicked up a couple of notches. You're not meant to have a heart attack at twenty-five, so another wave of panic swept over me. Soon enough Dr Blombery was with me and calmly explained that some of the clot had moved to my lungs, which was the cause of the chest pain. Straightaway, I remembered the early advice. If it moves ... I tried not to finish the sentence lurking with intent in my mind.

Calm and reassuring as Dr Blombery was, it didn't help when the chest pains became more frequent and more painful. By that night, every breath was agonising, like somebody was stabbing me in the chest. I didn't want to breathe, the pain was so bad. Then I started coughing up blood. I tried to cover my mouth with handkerchiefs, but they were soon soaked in red, and my mind was racing in a mad panic. I don't know that I had ever thought about how I wanted to, or would, die. I was too young to even think about that, let alone face the actual prospect. But I never imagined I would leave this earth in such pain, coughing up all the blood I had inside me.

Fortunately, I had a nurse with me and she told me what I was going through was a normal symptom of having blood clots in the lung. The blood I was coughing up was the clots themselves, which the lungs needed to be rid of. Much as I appreciated the support and care I got from all the nurses, I wanted to hear that from a doctor. I also wanted somebody to tell me I was going to be okay. But I was also too scared to ask.

The next day, the doctor confirmed what the nurse had told me. The horrible experience I had gone through was part of the healing process. He said the pain would eventually subside, I would cough up blood for two weeks to a month and the whole thing would probably reduce my lung capacity slightly. I had basically been through the worst on that Wednesday night: it was the low point of the ordeal physically. Had I known that, I might have handled it better and differently.

Mentally and emotionally, my low point didn't come till a couple of days later. I was overcome by a feeling of total helplessness. It was a horrible, horrible feeling that I was not geared up to deal with. Some people deal with a health crisis brilliantly and some patients control their minds to maintain a positive belief that they'll be right. But I couldn't seem to manage that. As I lay in the hospital bed, my mum sat in the room, supporting me, as she always seemed to do during a time of crisis. But I needed my dad. I needed reassurance and when I was growing up it had always been my old man who had the answer. Most boys think their dad knows all and if he says it's going to be all right, then it's going to be all right. That was what I needed to hear. I needed my dad to tell me everything would be fine. I wanted him to give me positive feedback and help explain, rationalise and interpret just what was going on inside my body.

My dad shuttled between the hospital and his work and coaching commitments, so he was under the pump from several angles but soon after mum phoned him he arrived at my bedside. Even though I had bottomed out physically a couple of days earlier, I was still a bit jittery and just wanted to know what was going on. My dad talked to me, then got the doctor in and, between them, they tried to alleviate my anxieties and fears. I couldn't articulate all those fears and anxieties, partly because I was embarrassed, wondering if I was overreacting. That said, it was a traumatic time.

Having my dad beside me did the trick. I calmed down and my anxieties were eased. Now that Melinda and I have our own four beautiful, precious children, I would like to think that, if any of them ever has to go through something like that, I could provide them with the reassurance and calmness I got from my dad.

I was in hospital for nine days, but the blockage in the vein never cleared and I am on daily medication for the rest of my life. We never ever found out conclusively what caused the blood clot, either. There was a theory about that extra rib. I had been renovating my house, doing a lot of painting, and they thought that, because I had my arm up for extended periods, the extra rib might have pinched the vein and blocked it, causing the clot to form and grow.

It was not lost on me that my biggest health problem, ironically, had not been caused by basketball. Among sportspeople, a group typically dogged by injury, I guess I was unusual in that regard. Throughout my twenty-five years' playing basketball at a high level, I was extremely lucky with injuries. There were always a few niggles to carry, I've had a couple of arthroscopes and a broken bone in my foot, and there was an ankle injury that needed two operations and kept me out of a bunch of games during the 2003 NBL season. But that's about it. Probably the most eventful basketball-incurred injury was one we think started as a scratch on the right knee and developed very quickly into a full-blown infection that put me in hospital feeling like I had been slugged by a baseball bat.

The Tigers had played the Wollongong Hawks at home on the Saturday night and training on Monday and Tuesday was no problem. After training on Tuesday, I called in to the Australian Basketball Resources office to see Nigel Purchase, my business partner and brother-in-law, and it was then that I noticed my knee getting sore. I didn't think anything of it, other than that age might have been creeping up on me, and I went to the MCG to shoot a promotional video for the 2006 Commonwealth Games. The knee was sorer and more swollen and I got cold, irritable and tired waiting around for this shoot to get going. I thought I might have been coming down with the flu, so while the camera crew got organised,

I went down to the change rooms and had a snooze on a massage bench. But by the time we had finished the shoot, I was in a bit of strife.

Instead of going home, I drove to see the Tigers physio, Paul Visentini, and told him to turn the heater up. It was early December, so it was no wonder he looked at me strangely, but I was shivering and freezing. Paul examined my knee and straightaway diagnosed an infection. Visser dashed next door to the doctor to get a prescription for antibiotics and then I hobbled to the car and headed home. I telephoned Melinda and asked her to run a boiling bath to help get me warm, but by the time I got home, the leg was useless. It was blown up like the Hindenburg and I couldn't move a millimetre without being in severe pain.

The next course of action was to get Tigers doctor Andrew Garnham to come around. Straight off a flight from Canberra, he dropped in, gave me a jab of penicillin and then drained some of the infection from the knee. It was Doc Garnham's belief that the antibiotics would kick in and I would be right in a couple of days. But pretty soon I was throwing up every half-hour. I couldn't even keep down water. I couldn't get out of bed, I could lift the leg, I couldn't put it down. I clearly was not getting any better.

By the next day, I was prepared to do whatever it took to get this problem solved. So Doc Garnham called renowned surgeon David Young, who told me to get to hospital. But I couldn't move and Melinda couldn't move me, either. She phoned my Tigers team-mate Mark Bradtke (known to everyone as Hogey) for help and it was a struggle even for him, at 209 centimetres tall and weighing 129 kilograms, to get me to his car to head for the hospital. I don't know why we didn't just call an ambulance, but Hogey was the designated driver and every small ridge in the road caused excruciating pain to shoot through my leg. By the time we got to The Avenue hospital, the air in Hogey's car was as blue as a cloudless sky and I was begging the docs to knock me out and do whatever was needed.

They put me on a drip that night and the next day David Young saw me and said I would need minor surgery to get on top of it. All he planned to do was make a little cut in the knee and drain the infection. He was so confident, he didn't even reckon he would need a stitch to close the cut. I was as sick as a dog, but it sounded good. The next morning when I woke up after the surgery and found the knee heavily bandaged, I wondered if I had dreamt that conversation. It turned out that the infection was much worse than anybody had thought, so they had to keep opening the cut to suction all the pus. When they finished, they decided to leave the wound unstitched so it could air and aid the healing process.

The only problem was that I didn't know the cut had been left unstitched. At least I didn't know until my mum and I were driving to the Alfred Hospital for hyperbaric treatment to speed the recovery process. Fortunately, mum was driving when I lifted the edge of the bandage to give my knee a scratch and looked down to the sight of a wound the length and width of the Grand Canyon. I swear I could have placed my finger in it like a hot dog. It was so long and deep, I thought I spotted my ankle bone. I experienced an instant hot flush, which produced a thick lather of sweat. I pulled that bandage back into place and stared out the car window for the rest of the journey. I was trying to overcome my feeling of horror and at the same time wondering whether the surgeon had been called away to a more important operation.

I needed a second go in surgery to drain the rest of the infection – and this time, thankfully, they stitched up the wound. Apart from the scar, I was left with some telltale signs of the infection. Like my right leg glowing bright red from hip to toe and a body covered in red blotches as a reaction to the penicillin. I eventually found out it actually could have been far worse than glowing, blotchy skin.

The analysis of the infection showed I had a serious case of streptococcal A. An expert microbiologist came to see me and explain the situation. He had been a Melbourne Tigers season-ticket holder for twelve years, so I knew I was in good hands. He told me it was a nasty infection but it had been caught in time. With the penicillin and other drugs they could get on top of it. Which was good news because in the 1950s, apparently, they either amputated your leg or you died. When they did the initial analysis of my infection, the reading was off the scale at about four hundred. Every day, the readings dropped and one day I asked what the normal level should be. Nine. David Young had never seen a reading so high and so potent as mine.

I was out of action for four and a half weeks and lost ten kilograms. The last time I had been eighty-three kilograms was when I was fourteen. But at least I was on the way back from a nasty experience. During this episode I never thought my life was in danger, but there was a certain amount of anxiety dealing with an uncertain situation that seemed to get worse before it got better. That was where my pessimism kicked in and certainly did not help the situation. People say, 'It couldn't happen to me.' But I know it will happen to me, which is unusual because I've had a lot of good things happen to me. But I don't take the good things for granted because I know the bad things that can happen. I've seen them up too close and too personally.

When you're lying in a hospital bed, believing you are going to die, that's when you find out about yourself. That's when you find out about the strength of your self-preservation. I am not a religious man by any stretch of the imagination, but when I thought I was going to die from the blood clot in my lungs, I made deals with God that could never be upheld. When I was being torn apart with chest pain and I was coughing up blood, I was prepared to give anything to get peace of mind, to get rid of the uncertainty. If someone had said, 'This is as bad as it gets, suck it up for a few days and in a week's time you'll be one hundred per cent guaranteed of being fine', no problem, I could have dealt with that. But when the news keeps getting worse and you believe the Grim Reaper is on his way, you'd better find something within to hang onto.

I don't recommend anyone try it, but as a life experience, dealing with that blood clot and the fear that I was going to die was as big a challenge as I'll ever have. I had been to two Olympic Games, I was playing well, the Tigers were on the up, and I guess I had got caught up and become obsessed with winning and losing. When nothing else provides perspective, winning becomes more euphoric, losing is more disappointing than it should be and plenty gets taken for granted. Your entire well-being and existence depends on whether you win or you lose. You win and life's great. You lose and life sucks. But, in very quick fashion, winning and losing meant absolutely nothing to me. When you're lying there struggling for a breath and wondering what you'd give to not be in this situation, being so bitterly disappointed after losing a game of basketball is stupid. When you're faced with making a deal with God or the devil, you would no doubt accept being an all-time loser on the basketball court if it meant living.

The late Green Bay Packers football coach Vince Lombardi and his colleague across the Atlantic at Liverpool, the legendary Bill Shankly, were famous for proclaiming that winning and losing involved a life-and-death struggle. But being in a real life-or-death situation gives you perspective and, I can tell you, life and death have nothing to do with winning or losing sporting contests. What being in a life-threatening situation does is bring a relativity to all things. What used to be an awkward situation is not so awkward any more. Anyone can imagine being in such a crisis situation, but believe me, you do not want to go there just to experience the bleakest of reality checks. I came out of it with tangible evidence that when you think you are doing it tough, things can always be tougher.

On the basketball court, there are lots of decisions to make. Some turn out to be right, some turn out to be wrong. Some cause a loss, some prompt a victory. But not one of them is ever about life and death.

chapter ten

THE ITALIAN JOB

LEGEND has it that the Castle Hill overlooking the small north-eastern Italian city of Udine was built by the foot soldiers of Attila the Hun, the king and warlord who rode his run-and-gun game for all it was worth through Europe in the fifth century. The story goes that Attila ordered his soldiers to fill their helmets with dirt and keep dumping it until he had a hill high enough to observe the burning city of Aquileia in the distance.

In a nutshell, you could say Attila was into inflicting pain. From what I understand, he was a take-no-prisoners kind of bloke who earned the nickname of the Scourge of God for his ransacking of several European countries. Anyway, I'm pretty sure I ran into one of ATH's ancestors during my time playing for Udine. In fact, he just happened to be the doctor attached to the basketball team – and pain, it seemed to these people, did not matter unless they were suffering.

During a home game one night I copped an opposition elbow in the eye just before half-time. There was blood everywhere and my white playing top more or less looked like a barber shop pole. Attila would have lusted at the sight. As there was no blood rule in 1991, I played the rest of the first half before seeking treatment. The good news was that the doctor was keen to treat me and stitch the wound closed. The bad news was that the doctor wanted to do it without anaesthetic.

Now you can call me soft and a wimp, but I usually prefer a painkilling injection before someone starts a bit of needlepoint on my noggin. So as the doctor was about to start sewing, I was compelled to stop him and ask, 'Where's the painkiller?' Something might have got lost in the translation because as his eyes rolled and eyebrows lifted, I got the distinct impression he thought it was no big deal. But I persisted. 'Hang on a minute, mate. Whack a little something in there, mate, because I assume that's probably going to hurt a little bit.'

The doc was more concerned about getting me stitched up quickly so I'd be out on the floor for the start of the second half. Normally I'd agree that was the way to go because I was the last person to sit out a minute if I didn't have to. But on this occasion I thought it would be worth sacrificing a little playing time for the sake of a pain-free experience. Even so, the doc still wasn't reaching for the anaesthesia, so I reluctantly agreed to give it a try. Wrong decision. He did one stitch and it was killing me. I was almost in tears, which I don't think Attila would condone. So I stood on my digs and I told the doc, 'Either whack something in it or we don't do it.'

Again he looked at me like I was a weak sister. He agreed to put in a little painkiller and when he said 'a little', he did mean only a little. When he put the next stitch in, the pain was a bit more tolerable, but only just, so I said that was it, two's enough. The doc protested that he needed to do more stitching. I replied he should have been a tailor. We compromised by putting some tape on my head to cover the gash. If my brain oozed out, I'd take responsibility, but I wasn't having any more stitches without anaesthetic. I mean, I've had a lot of stitches in my life, but only once without a painkiller. Later on, I thought: surely these Italian doctors don't go around just stitching blokes up without any anaesthetic. It seems they do. I just had to wonder whether it was one of those cultural things in Italian basketball or whether it was a normal part of every-day Italian life. As I found out, the Italians do a lot of things differently. My season with Udine proved that.

The call to join Udine came just as the Melbourne Tigers were dumped from the 1991 NBL play-offs by the Adelaide 36ers. We lost in two straight games in the best-of-three first round, making for an unexpected and unfulfilling end to the season. We had made the play-offs three years straight but had never got through the first round. So I had been brooding over that for a couple of weeks when the phone rang.

It wasn't unusual for my agent to call with an offer from overseas. There was always plenty of interest and sometimes he didn't even bother to pass on the offers that weren't worth it or wouldn't inter-est me. This offer from Udine, though, ticked all the boxes. The timing was right, the money was good, they needed a perimeter shooter. What was I going to do during the NBL off-season? Play golf and renovate my house? No, sir. I was going to Italy to play bas-ketball.

I knew Udine was in trouble – that's why I received the call in the first place. I knew Udine had started the season 0–2, that I was replacing one of the team's two imports, Terry Tyler, and that the coach didn't speak a lot of English, although it was debatable how long he would be around anyway. But I wasn't sure how the Udine officials decided I was the man to help arrest a poor start to the Italian A2 (second division) season. I suspect my efforts at the Goodwill Games the year before might have had something to do with it. On the way to the World Championships in Argentina, the

Boomers stopped at the Goodwill Games in Seattle and I ended up averaging 35.6 ppg for the tournament. Included in that lot was forty-four points against Puerto Rico and fifty against Italy as we smashed the Azzuri 106–78. I shot at seventy-six per cent from the field and hit nine three-pointers. People tend to remember nights like that. If I sold the Italians on my game that night, they didn't need to do much selling to me. I'd heard a lot about Italy, knew it was a basketball-mad country and thought I would love to go there. Everything fitted, so why not? I decided to have a crack – and, bang, we ran with it.

There was one problem about going to play in Europe: getting there. I started in Melbourne with a direct flight to Rome and a connection to Trieste, followed by a two-hour drive to Udine, which is tucked neatly into the north-east of Italy near the Austrian and Slovenian borders. If only it had been all that straightforward. I flew business class with Alitalia, which was nice – except that it seemed every other passenger smoked non-stop for the entire flight. I might as well have asked the stewards for a carton of duty-free Marlboro and lit up myself.

As for the drive from Trieste to Udine, the man behind the wheel might not have been related to Attila the Hun but he sure thought he was the reincarnation of Juan Manuel Fangio, the F1 champion, who once drove for Ferrari. When he met me at the airport, it struck me that he didn't even look old enough to drive. He was maybe eighteen and, from what I could glean, he was the Udine go-fer. So we jumped into his car and he just planted it. We were on the autostrada and I could tell by the whining noise coming from the little Italian engine that 'Fangio' had his machine wound up. I plucked up the courage to casually sneak a peek at the speedometer and the needle was touching 150 kilometres per hour. Not that other drivers discouraged him. As I brought my eyes back to the road ahead, a BMW screamed by like we were standing still. I wanted to tell Fangio to ease back on the throttle, but I decided the best action was to just sit there, shut up and hold on tight to whatever provided the best grip.

The driver's orders, it turned out, were to take me straight to my hotel in Udine. When we arrived, I met the Udine general manager Carlos Fabriciatore. The colour had only just returned to my fingers after the white-knuckle ride and when we shook hands, I suspect my sweating palms suggested I had just been through an interesting ordeal. It was only an introduction.

A couple of days after I arrived, Udine had a road game against Rimini. I didn't know what the rules were relating to import changes, but the team officials indicated that I would sit this one out and they would release Terry Tyler after the game. Before the game, I attended a training session, which presented an awkward situation. As soon as I walked into the gym, Terry and the other American on the team, John Devereaux, knew one of them was about to lose their job. The problem was that neither of them had a clue who it would be.

I joined the team for the four-hour bus ride to Rimini, a beautiful town on the Adriatic coast, with a team that featured former NBA guard Darnell Valentine and an up-and-coming Italian named Carlton Myers, who went on to captain Italy and carried the flag at the Sydney Olympics. On arrival in Rimini, I found out about one of the perks of being an import in Italy: you got a hotel room to yourself on the road. The local players still had to share, which was the case in the NBL for everyone. In Italy, it was a small privilege for risky job security.

Watching the game with the general manager and team president, I was introduced to basketball Italian style. The arena held about four thousand people and it must have been compulsory to light a new cigarette before stubbing out the old one. The game was played in a permanent haze, which might have been good for Udine if it wanted to disguise its problems. The team did not look disastrous, but it was clearly not going to frighten too many others, either. When Udine lost, staying winless, the president looked at me quite forlornly and said, 'Andrew, you must help us.' I smiled at the president, but thought to myself, 'What the hell can I do?' As we climbed on the bus to head for a restaurant before the drive home, I noticed a couple of shady figures loitering near the bus. On closer inspection, they were two Udine players getting in one or two last cigarettes before hopping aboard and into one of the few places in Italy where smoking really was banned.

After arriving back at my miniature hotel room in the middle of the night, I was still none the wiser about when I would officially join the team. Not too much had been communicated, but I wasn't worried. I learned quickly that the Italians do things in their own time and their own way.

At training the next morning, the first person I saw was Terry Tyler. Instead of packing his bags, Terry was dressed ready for training. I thought Terry was supposed to be gone, but I wasn't going to tell him. When training started a few minutes later and John Devereaux wasn't there, it was clear the Italians had changed their minds at the last minute about which import to sack. One of the Udine players, Paolo Nobile, spoke five languages, including English, so he was my unofficial translator. The trainer, Gigi, also spoke English, but I don't think either would have had an explanation for the sudden change of mind. All I knew was with Devereaux gone, I was definitely in and ready to play the next game, which was on the road against Montecatini.

The stadium at Montecatini was magnificent and the team was one of the best in A2, so we had our work cut out. Not surprisingly, we lost, 98–78, but I played all right and hit thirty points in thirty-five minutes on the court. I was happy to play so much rather than be eased in, and from there I barely sat down for the rest of the season. There was only one game in which I played less than I did the first night and, of the twenty-six games I played for Udine, I played every minute in eighteen of them. The Italians certainly believed in making the hired help work for their lire.

The bottom line after the Montecatini game was that we were 0–5 and there was unmistakable dejection among the administrators and players. The fact that I thought I did all right was obviously irrelevant. Lorenzo Bettarini, the Udine captain, told me I did a good job and tried to reassure me that I was not the reason for the team's woes. After one game, I'm glad he came to that conclusion.

My first home game was to be a few days later against Fabriano. Our home stadium seated about 4500 fans, which was not bad for a city with a population similar in size to Ballarat. Udine is not a big city but it is steeped in history and its citizens are proud of their sporting teams, especially soccer and basketball. They like to see results, so there was a little bit of extra pressure in this game for me and the team. You just knew something was going to give and, with one import already sacked, all I could do was hope I wouldn't be next.

The day after the Montecatini game, I was working out, taking some extra shots when Carlos the GM walked into the gym with another bloke, whom I recognised. It was Radisav Curcic, a 208 centimetre Yugoslav, who had played at the 1990 World Championships in Argentina. Clearly, Curcic wasn't calling through on his vacation. Carlos (who spoke little English) introduced me (who spoke minimal Italian and no Serbian) to Curcic (who spoke neither Italian nor English). The conversation was brief, but before the handshakes were through, I wondered whether I would be going home as an expendable import.

We trained later that day and the answer to my concerns became apparent. I was there, Curcic was there, but Terry Tyler was not. While Curcic added a big body to the mix, he also added to the complication and confusion, given that Curcic, the coach and I were all speaking different languages and didn't really understand each other. But the three of us might as well have been conversing in the Queen's English while sipping tea and eating cucumber sandwiches. It would have made more sense than what was to come.

We were getting ready to play Fabriano in the usual Sunday timeslot of 6 p.m. when the locker room door swung open and in walked Terry Tyler, the bloke who had been sacked so Udine could sign Curcic, and started to get changed. Being the inquisitive type, I asked Terry what was going on. It turned out the club could not get Curcic's clearance and paper work completed in time, so they asked Terry to play one more game. Terry was still in Italy because he and his wife had planned a holiday before going back to America.

There was another reason not to skip the country too soon. As an import in Europe, you want to make sure you've got your payments before you leave, otherwise there's a good chance you'll never see the money. Terry knew that, which was partly why he was filling in for Curcic. The team still held his registration and contract and he helped his own cause by playing for Udine even after being sacked. It was a goodwill gesture and it was insurance because his contract had still to be paid out. If he refused to play, the club could sack him for breach of contract and not have to pay him. Terry was about thirty-six, had been around and knew the drill.

While I was surprised to see Terry walk in, I was not surprised he had come back to play. He is a good guy and was one of the finest professional basketballers in every sense. Terry played eleven seasons in the NBA before capping a distinguished career in Italy, where he was revered. One night Terry and I went to a Euroleague game to see Terry's former team, Trieste, play Real Madrid, which had Arvydas Sabonis, the giant Lithuanian centre. Terry had helped Trieste gain promotion to A1, which was a big deal, and the fans appreciated what he had done for them. We arrived late at the game, got our tickets and had to walk courtside to our seats. It is no exaggeration to say that, on seeing Terry, every person in the 5000-strong crowd broke into applause that quickly escalated into a standing ovation, with some sections chanting his name. If you wanted an experience to make goose bumps rise on your arms, that was it.

Unfortunately, Terry's return to the Udine line-up against Fabriano was not so romantic. We lost again. I hit thirty-five points at a pretty good percentage and, near the end of the game, I made a shot that prompted the crowd to rise and acknowledge me. It was encouraging, to say the least. But having dropped to 0–6, you could sense the natives were restless. Actually, it was obvious. A bad call by the referee down the stretch sparked a hailstorm of coins, rubbish and anything the Udine fans could throw on the court to vent their anger and frustration. While I was a little taken aback by this action, the Italian players merely shrugged their shoulders. Just another day at the office for them.

After the game, Terry was gone again and Curcic was back in with his papers stamped and finally ready to play. Not that he looked like it. Curcic was a big bloke, but he looked solid, lumpy and overweight. If the Udine officials reckoned Curcic was the man, then he'd better be able to play. Otherwise, they might find themselves on the end of some Attila the Hun treatment from the fans. As might have been predictable, it was the players who felt the sharp end ... the coach even sharper.

Even with Curcic in the line-up, our fortunes did not change, and I was called to a meeting with Carlos the GM. The way things worked, I half-expected to be handed my return ticket to Melbourne. Carlos confided that the club was thinking of replacing Paolo Bosini as coach and he wanted my thoughts. I pretty much sat on the fence, saying, 'Listen, boys, I'm new here and I want nothing to do with that. I think we've got more problems than the coach.' I never thought he was a bad coach and I certainly didn't want to bag him.

When we arrived for training the next day, Bosini was still calling the shots, but he was gone within twenty-four hours. His replacement was Rudy D'Amico, who had coached in Italy for several years but was a hundred-per-cent American from New York. For me and some of the other players the beauty of Rudy's appointment was that, while fluent in Italian, he was an English-speaking coach. Rudy was a nice guy, was level headed and, importantly, understood the Italian culture. The first day, Rudy just watched us scrimmage while the assistant coach took charge of training. Rudy had been back to America studying the backdoor passing game made famous by Princeton University and he wanted to incorporate some of that into our game. That was fine by me because we were clearly terrible and not much else had worked.

The Udine bosses also decided to change their plan of attack and called a team meeting. Carlos the GM and the club president fronted the players and laid down the law. They were speaking Italian, but I didn't need a translator to know this was serious. The president was never around unless it was serious. Having lost seven or eight games in a row might best be called a crisis, so this was where we were. Anyway, amid the flowing Italian words, flailing arms and gesticulating hands, my translating team-mate Paolo Nobile conveyed the president's message: no players would be paid until we won a game. Withholding payment from foreigners was not allowed, but it was (and probably still is) common practice for the locals to have their money suspended as motivation or an incentive to get a win. It's a dubious tactic, but it happens in Europe.

There was no immediate payoff, or pay, from the president's scheme, but eventually Udine hit gold with a win. After losing ten straight games, we beat Reggio Emilia 96–89 at home and the boys popped a cork at the buzzer. It was like we had won the championship. In reality, we were 1–10, but why let that get in the way? We had won a game, the monkey was off our backs and the boys would be getting paid. I hit thirty-seven points in the win and Curcic had twenty-five points and seventeen rebounds, so the imports had done the job and the heat was off us for a while.

Amazingly, we won the next game, too, beating Sardegna Sassari. But after we lost the next weekend to Brescia, we also lost Curcic. The big bloke had trouble with a knee, only managed to play twenty-eight minutes against Brescia and needed arthroscopic surgery. Which meant yet another import change. And *that* meant another return for Terry Tyler. Under the import rules, teams were restricted to a number of changes and players. If they brought in someone new as a short-term replacement for Curcic, then Curcic could not return when fit. Hence Terry's return. As it turned out, it didn't matter because Curcic, who eventually became an Israeli citizen after playing there and marrying a local woman, was done for the season. In some ways that was unfortunate, because he could play and was a serious inside presence. Otherwise, I wasn't that unhappy to see him leave.

I was still living in the hotel when Curcic had arrived at Udine and had taken a room at the same place. So we shared a car to training. Actually, because it was his car I couldn't really ask the big bloke if he wouldn't mind butting out the cigarette that was filling the vehicle with smoke. Curcic couldn't speak a lick of English, so there was no communication except for the odd, raspy cough between puffs. But while the plumes of smoke were almost bearable for the short journey to training, worse was yet to come.

One weekend, the local soccer team Udinese, which played in Serie A, had a big home game and all the hotels were packed. Our hotel offered to squeeze in a few extra punters, so I had to give up my room and share with Curcic. Talk about up close and personal. The hotel rooms were so small I had to be careful not to bang my elbows putting on a T-shirt, and here I was cooped up in one of those rooms with a second bloke. As a host, Curcic did not exactly go out of his way to spruce up the place. The first thing I noticed was the cigarette between his lips. It never seemed to disappear the entire weekend, taking chain-smoking to a new level. The amount of smoke billowing out of his body made it feel like I lived next door to a small factory that showed no regard for pollution levels. The second thing that hit me was the smell. Either he had the worst body odour, his aftershave was long past its use-by date or something had died in that room. Just to add to the aroma, Curcic had hung his training gear around the room and by the open window, which meant the breeze blew the stench back inside the room. Fantastic.

So there we were for the weekend. He couldn't speak English and I didn't speak Serbian. I couldn't even escape into the television because Curcic had commandeered the remote control and had on Yugoslavian programs that were beamed across the border. If I even looked like reaching for the remote control, he grunted in a way that suggested I would play basketball better without a couple of broken fingers. It was a torture test. I had no car, there was nowhere to go for a walk because we were out of the city centre and the notion of entertainment was zero. I'll say one thing for Curcic: he was polite. Every time he lit up a smoke, he always offered me one. It got to the stage where I knocked him back so often that I started to feel guilty.

For a while cars and accommodation were as much a problem as winning. I was supposed to get one of the cars used by Terry Tyler or John Devereaux. They had driven a BMW and an Audi. I was driving a Fiat Uno. It was a butter box. There was no radio and I got the feeling the engine and wheels might have been extras. But I eventually got a decent car and I eventually got some accommodation away from the hotel.

After that weekend with Curcic, and with Melinda, my wife-to-be, having joined me, I told the club I needed an apartment. The club found me a great place in the downtown area of the city, right near where Terry Tyler lived. It had two bedrooms and a big living area. I took it on the spot, raced back to the hotel and told Melinda to pack. But our first night there was our last night. The apartment was on what must have been the busiest street in Udine. When I inspected it, I hadn't noticed the noise. But that night, as I tried to sleep, I figured I might as well have been camping on the median strip of the Hume Highway. Trucks, cars, buses, motorbikes – hundreds, thousands of them, and none with a muffler – seemed to be driving through the living room. Melinda sleeps like a bear in winter, but I need the cone of silence and was going loopy unable to sleep. I actually took a blanket and pillow and tried to curl up in the kitchen pantry to avoid the noise. It was impossible.

Somehow, maybe through exhaustion, I eventually nodded off. But not for long. At about 7 a.m. I was woken by a high-pitched whining. It sounded familiar and, soon enough, I recognised the sound of a dentist's drill. Our apartment was next door to a dental surgery. During the night we could listen to trucks and during the day we could listen to cavities being filled. I marched into the bedroom and we started to pack our bags. We were going back to the hotel.

After a week, the club found us a one-bedroom apartment in a quiet area near the stadium. The kitchen was smaller than my car's glove box and the apartment consisted of a living room, a bedroom and a bathroom with no bath. I didn't care. After sticking my head out the window to gauge traffic levels, we took it. We just wanted to get out of the hotel. Our first night's sleep was blissful . . . until about 6 a.m., when a dog started barking and didn't stop for the next four hours. At least it wasn't the middle of the night. But it happened the following morning and the next. So we wrote a letter to the dog's owner, but the dog never shut up and, perhaps being more Italian than we thought, we just shrugged our shoulders and learned to live with it.

Living in a foreign country is always an exciting experience and I was determined to enjoy it and get immersed in the culture, see the cities, soak up some history and try to learn the language. We always had the day off after a game, so Melinda and I would usually go somewhere. If we were on the road and it wasn't too far, Melinda would drive to the game, we would stay the night and do the tourist thing the next day. Udine was only about a ninety-minute drive from Venice, or a short drive from Trieste and some of the bigger cities. The history of Italy and some of the historically significant buildings that are thousands of years old were mind-boggling. It certainly hits home when you think the white man only set foot on

Australian soil not much more than two hundred years ago. The other city we liked to visit was Klagenfurt in Austria. It amazed me how you could get in the car, drive two hundred kilometres up the road, cross the border and find everything in a different language and being lived according to a different culture. Not that the culture was why we were in Klagenfurt. Except for modern culture, maybe. Klagenfurt had a McDonald's.

For me, trying to learn the Italian language was a little tricky. In fact, beyond *buongiorno*, *arrivederci* and *grazie*, it got downright shaky at times. Although I got a few things horribly wrong at the supermarket, I could go to a restaurant and get what I wanted, mainly because a lot of Italian people spoke English. But I was determined to grasp the language and the culture, sometimes to my detriment and embarrassment. Like the night I attended a dinner party at the house of Carlos, the Udine general manager. I was seated beside Carlos's wife during dinner, which would have been a talking point for a few of my team-mates, who reckoned she was quite attractive and rather provocative. I can't say I noticed. But I was keen to try out some of my Italian on Signora Fabriciatore, so I started telling her about my new apartment and she nodded her head politely. Pretty soon the confused and affronted look on her face indicated something was amiss. I forged ahead, telling her how big and beautiful my house was and she probably needed to see it to believe it.

It was at about this stage that Carlos interrupted and told me I could speak English and everyone would understand. What was wrong with my Italian? My Italian pronunciation had let me down. Badly. While I thought I was saying 'casa', the Italian word for home, I had been saying 'catso' which is a term I had heard the Italian players use at training when they were upset and admonishing themselves. Basically, I had told Signora Fabriciatore she should come and see my magnificent and very large penis. No wonder she looked at me funny and Carlos tried to get me to speak English. *Casa. Catso.* Sounded close enough to me.

No matter where you play in the world, game day is always the best day. In Italy, there was a familiar pattern, given that every game was played at 6.15 p.m. on Sundays. Don't ask me how they decided that was game time; they just did. The preparation would start at about one o'clock with the pre-game meal. Being Italy, pasta was a given, but the Italians also would tuck into a big juicy steak and wash it down with a glass of red wine. At least they weren't lighting up post-meal cigars and sipping cognac.

The real action was always at the arenas, where smoking was compulsory, even though the signs everywhere said '*Non fumare!*'. It was just part of the deal that we would play in a haze. Just as it was part of the deal that every player on the court was a target for physical or verbal abuse if he or his team failed to live up to the fans' expectations. The fans could be very aggressive and often seemed on the brink of a riot.

Safety flares, with their bright red or orange smoke, were not uncommon at games, but we played on through the dense, choking stuff. Actually, not much ever stopped a game in Italy. During one game, coins were pelted onto the court and I asked the ref if he was going to stop play and clear the floor. Basically, his response was that it wasn't his job. We kept playing.

The one time we did stop showed just how farcical things could get in Italy. It was a home game late in the season and a harmless missile, like a scrunched up ball of paper, came out of the stands. It hit the visiting team's trainer in the head and he went down quicker than a skydiver without a parachute. The blow would have surprised or stunned him, but this bloke turned it into a re-enactment of the Kennedy assassination, with him playing the part of the President. They brought out a stretcher and carried him to the locker room and the game finished without further incident. But there was uproar the next week when Udine was banned from playing at home for two games. Our next two home games were played at Treviso in this big, beautiful stadium that normally held about six thousand rabid fans.

It's just that these two games were the exception: we had to play behind closed doors, with no fans. The joint was empty except for the players, coaches, team officials, referees and score bench officials. The loudest sounds were those of the referees' whistles and the squeak of sneakers on the floor. Chalk it up as just another Italian experience.

At least the fans back in Udine would have seen the two games. A local television station covered most of our games to replay them late at night and they had the attitude of whatever it took, they would get the job done. It certainly wasn't a high-tech outfit and they weren't fussy about job qualifications. Which might explain why on a road trip to Naples, the bus driver doubled up as the TV cameraman, recording the game with a handheld video camera.

If the bus driver could do the camera work for TV, by the time I got to the dentist with a screaming toothache, I wondered what qualifications the man in white did or didn't have. My confidence was shaken further when I entered the surgery to take the chair and was greeted by a dentist with a cigarette in his mouth.

It was around the time Magic Johnson revealed that he was HIV positive and there was still a lot to learn about AIDS, so I was certainly wary of health issues and what a rusty old dental implement could do. Next thing, the dentist was telling me to open up so he could have a look in my mouth – with the cigarette still dangling from his lips. I was in so much pain, I didn't really care too much and in a way it was a handy distraction. Looking up at this bloke, I got a mental image of a mechanic with a smoke in his mouth, leaning over the car engine for a bit of a tinker. The other mental picture I got was the cigarette ash falling straight into my gob. There he was, working away with the smoke going and holding a conversation all at the same time. Anyway, I don't know what he did in there or how he did it, but he fixed the toothache.

I also made a visit to the hospital at Udine, as a consequence of being knocked out and concussed at training one night. After

I eventually got up off the floor, I wobbled to the side of the court and threw up, which sent the team officials into enough panic to call an ambulance. I was tossed onto a stretcher and taken to hospital, which was disconcerting enough in a strange place, but even worse when I didn't speak the language and didn't know what was going on. Gigi, the trainer, was with me and explained that they wanted to do X-rays and keep me in overnight. I felt a bit groggy as they wheeled me into a ward with five other blokes. It was about 11 p.m. and it was clear I was going to sleep there. Or I was supposed to sleep there. The other five blokes were out to it and competing for the snoring world championship, while I stared at the ceiling. The next morning, I overcame the language barrier and made it quite clear I was going home. The Italian health system might have got the job done, but you wouldn't want your life to depend on it.

The season with Udine was one long struggle and well before the end of the thirty-game schedule we were doomed to a lowly spot on the ladder and relegation to the third division. Udine played in a good competition with some big-name American imports, but we were just not good enough and that 0–10 start did a lot more harm than good. Actually, we were terrible, but there were circumstances that didn't help, like the changing of imports and coach. We got better when Rudy D'Amico took over as coach and we played some decent basketball, but we'd dug such a huge hole, there was no way of climbing out of it.

Being relegated was a big disappointment for the fans, who had such a strong sense of community and made a real emotional investment in the team. They were very supportive towards me, mainly because I put up some big numbers and finished the season averaging 30.9 ppg over forty-minute games. They had an appreciation for individual performances, but they followed the team and wanted their team to win. When we won, everyone was a king, and when we lost, everyone was a pauper. There was not a lot of grey area.

There was and is a civic pride connected with basketball in Italy.

There was also a lot of pride within the club at Udine, which was why they wouldn't let me leave early for the start of the 1992 NBL season. Udine had one more game to play and I wanted to get back to Melbourne for the Tigers' first game at their new home at Melbourne Park. It was a big deal for the Tigers and I really wanted to be there and felt I needed to be there. So I asked Udine, given that we had already been relegated, to let me skip the last game of the season. They refused. I offered to sacrifice salary to get away early, which would have meant giving up about $10,000, but still Udine management wouldn't budge. It was about saving face, finishing the season strongly and showing that the club was not a sinking ship. So I stayed in Udine, played the last game of the Italian season on a Thursday night, hopped on a plane on the Friday and was back in Melbourne and the NBL by the weekend, having missed the first game.

As with all my overseas ventures, Italy and Udine were a worthwhile experience. I got to see a different country, got to experience a different style of play and got to mix with different personalities. And the season in Italy helped my game. In Australia we like to get up and down the floor, but in Italy it was a much more controlled tempo, more regimented and structured. Certain elements of the game in Italy were very physical. Off the ball, they held you and the referees let the players belt the numbers off your singlet in a rebounding contest. Everyone in Australia reckoned I was a protected species because I got a lot of calls and got to the free-throw line. But the fact is: I got to the line a lot more often and a lot more easily in Italy because of the way the referees called the games. They looked after the shooters and even light contact on the perimeter drew a whistle from the refs. Of course, there were times when I couldn't get a call and felt like I had a couple of bouncers twisting my arm up my back. If the ball wasn't in the area, the defenders could get away with murder. Which might just have been the legacy left to Italian basketball by Attila the Hun.

chapter eleven

NO REIGN IN SPAIN

THERE were at least three personal relationships formed during the Barcelona Olympics. Two of them became long-term, hopefully life-long, partnerships. The third I can't be sure of. In fact, the boys from the Boomers only got wind of it when they peered over their balconies into the park adjoining the athletes' village to see one of the rides moving fairly vigorously. Closer inspection showed it was two members of the greater Australian Olympic team getting amorous. Actually, they were more than amorous, if you know what I mean, but we'll leave it at that.

Barcelona was where my Boomers and Melbourne Tigers team-mate Mark Bradtke discovered tennis had some obvious attractions, like the woman who was to eventually become his wife, Nicole Provis. Hogey and Nicole seemed to spend a fair amount of time watching sunsets in that infamous park by the beach. Not that they were the couple on the ride and not that Nicole was so nice to me on one embarrassing visit to the Olympic tennis courts. Nicole invited Hogey, Shane Heal and me for a hit one day, but I don't think I got near a single ball. I certainly gained instant respect for Nicole and her tennis game. Not that I didn't go unnoticed on the tennis court. South African Wayne Ferreira wandered past and asked Nicole who was the lily white streak of pelican poo with his shirt off at the other end. I suppose that would have been me.

The one relationship I can speak of with the most authority is my friendship with Shane Heal, known pretty much to everyone as Hammer. Although Shane had been on Boomers squads and teams before, the 1992 Olympics were his first (my third) and, whoever organised the room allocations for Barcelona plonked us together. It was the first time we had roomed and there were few subsequent trips overseas with the Boomers that we didn't share quarters and get up to plenty of boyish no-good.

The thing about our friendship that a lot of people can't understand, and which puzzles even me, is that we are two opposites. We are diametrically opposed in some respects. He's good looking, I'm not. He's very volatile and I'm fairly placid. It's just one of those things that while we seem opposites, we also have a lot in common. These differences probably qualified us as basketball's 'Odd Couple', with me as nerdy Felix Unger and Shane as grouchy Oscar Madison. Despite our opposite personality traits, we are very good friends. In some ways, it's not unlike the friendship between Phil Smyth and Steve Breheny, who played for the Boomers at the 1980 Moscow Olympics. They are opposite personalities but are closest mates. In fact, they went so far as to make a pact that, when they were both retired from playing, if one had an NBL head coaching job, the other would be his assistant. Which is what they have done for three championships with the Adelaide 36ers. I don't see Hammer and me going into a coaching partnership, but if we did, there would be no lack of loyalty or mutual support. That's because loyalty is probably Hammer's best quality, and he expects it in return.

I suppose if you looked for a clichéd description of Hammer, it would be that he is a man's man. He's personable, he's attractive to women, he's knockabout, he's a good sportsman, he has made good money, he doesn't mind a blue, he has a level of notoriety and fame among the general public, he has the confidence to wear a diamond stud in his ear and bleach his hair, he has travelled the world and he has a beautiful wife and three kids. If you offered that to any young bloke as his lot in life between the ages of eighteen and thirty-three, he'd be stupid not to take it. Let's face it, it's what almost every Australian bloke would love his life to be. The difference is that Hammer has lived it and he has been clever about it.

Hammer doesn't have a university degree but he's street smart and a switched-on individual with a good radar that cuts through the bullshit pretty quickly. He might have done silly things on the basketball court now and then, but he has also acknowledged, when the temperature cooled, that those things were silly. Mind you, if Hammer belted you on the basketball court it was because he reckoned you deserved it and you probably did. Like when he took on Charles Barkley, chesting and abusing the American superstar during a pre-Olympic game between the Boomers and the US in 1996. Hammer, who retired after the 2004 Athens Olympics, could always be so respectful, polite and charming, but put him on the basketball court and it was him against the world. Sometimes he let his emotions get the better of him, but he was a fighter in the sense that he'd get the job done.

It was that determined, fighting make-up that enabled him to be the successful basketballer that he was, playing in Europe and the NBA and being a big part of the Boomers for more than ten years. I mean, look at him. He's not big, he wasn't super quick, his shooting technique was not in any textbook I've read, but he got to the top on will, determination and smarts. He's a lot smarter than people give him credit for and he was also more than just a shooter. He's got baby hands, but his reading of the game and his passing ability was such he could usually get the ball where it had to go.

Apart from scoring, passing and leadership, Hammer brought personality to a team. He's a fun guy to be around because he's a practical joker. Sometimes that was construed as good fun and sometimes people saw it differently, but in the team environment he was a take-charge guy who wasn't afraid to back his ability. Some basketball fans have found Shane to be cocky. Other people don't like him because he has never been afraid to speak his mind or stand up for team-mates and what he thinks is right. But if you're lucky enough to get to know him you love him. It's a bit like the public's attitude to tennis player Lleyton Hewitt. We all agree he's a great tennis player, but sometimes he goes over the top with his emotions, which is what splits public opinion.

One thing about Hammer's street-wise persona is that it's not fake. He grew up in the tough outer Melbourne suburb of Lilydale and copped a few beatings in his day, but that only made him stronger and more determined to handle himself. I learned the rules of street fighting from Hammer, not that I've needed to apply them, and I'd have to say that you would back him into a corner at your own peril. Put it this way, if Mike Tyson and Shane Heal were in a street fight, I would not be putting all my money on Tyson. Hammer will find a way to get the job done or he'll go close to dying while he tries.

Like the night I thought he was trying to kill me. I had sustained a scratch on the eyeball during the first game of the Olympic tournament against Puerto Rico and was in excruciating pain, so the doctors gave me some drops to numb the eye. The drops had to go in every few hours, which was not ideal in the middle of the night. Shane played the role of dedicated nurse, squeezing the drops in while I held my eyelid open. In fact, we became so good at the routine that we didn't even bother turning the lights on, operating like clockwork in the dark so we could get back to sleep faster. That night, after the three hours between treatments ticked over, Shane's reached out, grabbed the bottle and squeezed, but nothing came out. After a few misfires, we turned on the light and saw he was holding a container of nasal spray. We eventually whacked in the eye drops, but I'd hate to think what would have happened had he squirted the nasal spray into my eye. I suppose I wouldn't have had a blocked or stuffy pupil.

At least Hammer was on his best behaviour in Barcelona. That will happen when you're a wide-eyed Olympic rookie who doesn't get to play much. As a back-up guard for the Boomers that year, in some ways he represented the changing face of the team as we emerged from the Phil Smyth–Larry Sengstock era of leadership into the Andrew Gaze–Andrew Vlahov–Shane Heal era of leadership. Barcelona was fairly uneventful in terms of our placing, but it was, in hindsight, a transitional period for the Boomers. With the experience and success of finishing fourth at Seoul in 1988, we assumed our time had arrived and Barcelona would be our platform. Clearly, it didn't work out that way.

While our preparation wasn't ideal, given that we were in the midst of an NBL season and had to break for the Games, we still had a very good team. Lame as it sounds, things in Barcelona just didn't go our way. We weren't shockingly bad on the court, but I felt that the make-up of the team, the rotations and the roles of the players weren't always quite right and we weren't always on the same page. The intangibles and the edge you need to be successful weren't there in Barcelona. It was a difficult time with the group, mainly because of the individual desires of wanting to do well. In Seoul four years earlier, the team and the roles were clearly defined, mainly because of a delineation between the senior players who were established and played and the young guys who were just happy to be there and be part of the Olympics.

With a twelve-man roster, it can be almost impossible to play everybody in every game, so unless everybody buys into the team aspect and is prepared to sacrifice and sit on the bench when necessary, there's going to be some friction. That worked well in Seoul, but in Barcelona, it didn't. We had a lot of players who were worthy of playing, but throughout our preparation we didn't identify the players' roles early enough, so it was difficult for the coaching staff and the players because the roles and playing time issue was not clear-cut. Our roles were more about adapting to a situation and planning it on the run, which is often not a bad approach. But because we didn't have a lot of preparation, players' ideas of what they should be doing and were supposed to be doing sometimes differed. Playing time was split, the intangibles needed for a good team were missing and we never really got the best out of everyone at the same time.

The Barcelona Olympics were without doubt the most difficult of the five Olympics I played at. During the NBL season, I hurt my knee, tweaking the cartilage in a game against the North Melbourne Giants at the Glasshouse about six weeks before the Games, and I didn't have time to get it fixed. I played with the injury, which continued to bother me. I did okay in Spain and was able to get by, but I was never at my best.

My own circumstances were reflective of the team's. On ability we were right there and had what it took, but as a team we didn't quite get there and finished sixth after losing to Brazil in the playoff for fifth and sixth. We started the tournament with wins over Puerto Rico and Venezuela, dropped one to the Commonwealth of Independent States (the remains of the just-splintered Soviet Union), beat China and lost to Lithuania, which placed us in a sudden-death quarter final against Croatia. Just split from communist Yugoslavia, Croatia had a rich basketball history and some excellent talent with players like Toni Kukoc, Drazen Petrovic, Zan Tabak, Stojko Vrankovic and Dino Radja but I still thought we were a big chance to win. The game turned into the greatest disappointment of the Olympics for me as we lost 98–65. We were spanked and put in our place by the Croatians and it was a big blow.

Again, it was probably the expectations we had built after Seoul that caused us to be so disappointed by that loss, even though

Croatia went on to play in the gold medal game, where it was beaten by the United States, otherwise known as the original Dream Team. The Boomers had Luc Longley in the team, with his size and growing NBA experience; Andrew Vlahov and Mark Bradtke were maturing as players; and NBL legend Leroy Loggins was in the team after taking Australian citizenship, which gave me a real thrill as Leroy, a role model for any aspiring professional basketballer, was one of my heroes. We were friends, but we had also been opponents for a long time, so it was nice to team up alongside one of the NBL's all-time greats. In other words, there were signs to suggest that we were ready to make the next step. That we didn't take that step would normally mean fingers would be pointed at the coach.

Adrian Hurley was an interesting bloke and an astute coach. I was lucky that I took something good from all my coaches, Adrian included, and I'm grateful for the opportunities he gave me, picking me in two Olympic teams. I'm just not sure that, in the later phases of his Boomers tenure, he got the right response from the players. That's not being critical of Adrian, who, during his seven years as coach, experienced the greatest low and the greatest high the Boomers ever had.

Adrian took over from my dad as Boomers coach after the 1984 Olympics and in 1986 oversaw the disaster that was the loss to Angola and failure to qualify for the final stages of the 1986 World Championships in Spain. So he was right under the pump in 1988 as we headed to the Seoul Olympics and a campaign that took on the attitude that if he was going down, he was going down his way. That 1986 team wasn't really Adrian's team. It was still pretty much my dad's team and Adrian, even though he had been the assistant coach, had inherited players who were used to a different system and a different way of doing things. So with his neck on the chopping block in 1988, he went his way. Some people were critical of the selections of teenagers Mark Bradtke, Andrew Vlahov and Luc Longley, but Doc Hurley had the courage of his convictions, we had an excellent warm-up series against the USSR, we had a brilliant Olympic tournament and we finished fourth for our best ever international finish.

At Barcelona, I thought Adrian did as much as he could in light of the team's limited preparation. The Olympics were held in the middle of the NBL season and, while we may have been physically prepared, we did not have enough time to refine roles and make sure everyone had an intimate understanding of what we wanted to execute on the court and how. Adrian was a student of the game and his coaching style was very academic. Everyone's different in their coaching and at the elite level I don't think there is any right or wrong way. Adrian was good with the Xs and Os, in terms of tactics, and he liked to be well structured. If people wanted to find a criticism of Adrian they could say he hadn't coached a lot in the mainstream, which was true. He coached for many years at the AIS and was very sound in his teachings. You need players to understand and buy into the philosophy and program; otherwise any coach in the world will have difficulties. After leaving the Boomers program Adrian coached the Perth Wildcats to an NBL championship, but they eventually parted company amid whispers of personality conflicts between coach and players. That should not reflect on Adrian as a person or a coach. He is a very good person and a very good coach and I enjoyed playing for him. The personality of the team and the connection with the coach can vary over time and there certainly seemed to be change in that regard in the four years between Seoul and Barcelona.

The most significant aspect of the Barcelona Olympics was the United States fielding its first NBA-supplied team: the original and, as far as I'm concerned, only Dream Team. After finishing with the bronze medal in Seoul (the only time before Athens 2004 that the US had not won gold or silver at the Olympics) it was decided to bring on the big boys to make sure the US – the creator, nurturer, basketball missionary to the world and all-conquering power – never again suffered such an international embarrassment. At least until the 2002 World Championships, anyway, when the Americans slumped to a shocking sixth place and then struggled to a bronze medal at Athens. The rest of the basketball world was catching up to the United States.

While the introduction of the Dream Team – with Michael Jordan, Magic Johnson, Larry Bird, Patrick Ewing, Charles Barkley, Scottie Pippen, Karl Malone, John Stockton and others – meant everyone else played for silver and bronze, that was fine by me. Rising to the level of a rock-star phenomenon, the Dream Team brought basketball to the forefront of the sporting world in Barcelona. I supported this one hundred per cent and made sure I watched as many of their games as possible in Barcelona. It was exactly the right time for the NBA players to represent the US, simply because of the quality and integrity of the line-up, the effect it had on the Olympics and basketball worldwide and the fact that it underlined the ideal that competing at the Olympics meant you were competing at the pinnacle of your sport.

Even though we didn't play the United States in Barcelona, the Boomers were inexorably linked with the first Dream Team and were not looked at all that favourably by some because of it. Controversy flared when Boomers captain Phil Smyth publicly conceded he had concerns about playing against Magic Johnson, who had tested HIV positive in late 1991. At that stage, as I have said, there was still not a huge amount known about HIV, which could lead to AIDS, and how it could and couldn't be contracted. That was partly Phil's point: who was going to guarantee the safety of opposition players if Magic suffered a cut and came into contact with them? Phil expressed a concern that many people silently held and it made headlines around the world. I was playing in Italy with Udine when news of Magic's HIV broke and it was shocking. It was world news involving a much-loved and admired superstar and now some Australian was questioning whether Magic should be playing at the Olympics and whether he was a health risk on the basketball court!

In Italy I had plenty of time on my hands, so I read a lot about Magic's situation and the virus and came to understand it a little. I had zero problem playing against Magic. What the Boomers wondered was whether Magic and the Dream Team minded playing against us. PJ Carlesimo, my college coach at Seton Hall, was one of the Dream Team assistant coaches in Barcelona and Shane Heal and I ran into him during the tournament. Then we spotted Charles Barkley approaching us. Wanting to know the lie of the land, we asked PJ whether these guys were going to belt us because we'd upset their superstar. You never knew what was going to happen with Charles, who had provoked controversy in Barcelona by elbowing a hapless Angolan and explaining to the media that he didn't know whether he had a spear. Charles came up and chatted and was as friendly as you like, which was a big relief. There was no animosity. In the NBA world these guys deal with issues and controversies all the time and understand it's not always a case of people being nasty and vindictive.

I was disappointed we never played the original Dream Team. We might have taken our punishment like the other teams in Barcelona, but it still would have been nice to say we played against them. So we left Barcelona without any up-close, on-court Dream Team experiences and we still hadn't done enough to win an Olympic medal. But it wasn't all a dead loss. The boys had enjoyed a two-minute thrill out the window, Mark Bradtke had met his future wife and I had been to life's hardware store and found a Hammer that would be a mate without a use-by date.

chapter twelve

My Country's Captain

MODERN technology means it's possible to screen in-coming telephone calls and avoid those people you're not too keen on talking to. When Boomers coach Barry Barnes telephoned me in early 1993, it certainly turned out to be a call I would never want to dodge. Far from it. After some initial small talk, Barnesy cut to the chase. He basically said: 'I've decided it's time for a new leader and you're going to be the captain.' My appointment as the captain of the Australian men's basketball team was almost a part of the conversation rather than a formal invitation or command. Then again, it wasn't like I was going to say I didn't want to be captain.

To me, it was as if Barnesy, who took over as Boomers coach when Adrian Hurley stepped down after the 1992 Barcelona Olympics, considered my appointment a fait accompli and presumed I would be the captain after Phil Smyth. I had been on the national team for about ten years, so in terms of seniority, experience and on-court role, it was a job that almost naturally evolved. Even so, I'd never really contemplated being the Boomers captain. But it was a big thrill to be afforded the honour of leading one of Australia's sporting teams. The funny thing was that once I was captain I started to think: 'What does the captain do?' Till then I'd just played and was probably considered one of the team's unofficial leaders. Now I wondered what I should be doing as captain. Once I figured it out, there wasn't a whole lot to it on the basketball court.

Probably the most poignant aspect of my appointment was that I took over from Phil Smyth, who was one of my basketball heroes. That probably dates The General a bit, but, as his nickname indicated, he had been a leader, officially and unofficially, of the Boomers for almost as long as I can remember. When I first made the Boomers squad, Phil was the leader and for a while (including the Barcelona Olympics) Phil and Larry Sengstock were co-captains. So I was actually following a couple of legends into the role.

It turned out I needed to do more than uphold my on-court form, be a morale-booster and media spokesman. I became more conscious of my responsibilities as a link between the coaching staff and players and as the one who reported to Basketball Australia (BA) on behalf of the players. In one guise I was the on-floor leader of the Boomers, while in another I was a union rep and diplomat sometimes trying to juggle a few tricky balls. Towards the end of Phil's and Larry's time as co-captains came a more professional era and I needed to be more involved in negotiations over conditions for tours and training camps. The political stuff probably took up more of my attention than I would have liked, but it couldn't be avoided. When it came to dealing with BA over our workplace agreement, the players expected me to go in to bat for them. While more often than not I understood why and what BA proposed, sometimes there were issues and proposals I knew the players would not go for and my obligation and duty was to them. That said, I also tried to negotiate a compromise with the group if I felt that was the fair and reasonable thing to do.

I wanted to make the role mean something – not just to me, but to those I led and represented. I was conscious of representing the players well off the court because on the court it came naturally. Off the court, I was determined for them to know I would look out for them and communicate their wishes and desires. As a group, we did a pretty good job of keeping any grievances in-house. We didn't rant and rave, even though such actions seemed justified on a few occasions, because everyone was aware of the big picture. We wanted what we believed was fair and reasonable and what we had been promised in some cases. I was sometimes loud and aggressive in dealing with some BA officials because I wanted to make sure they understood our stance and I wanted to show the players I had the necessary passion and bravado to represent and support them. Unfortunately, I had very few wins at the negotiating table. Fortunately, I was often able to offset my inability to be a tough union negotiator with a few good games here and there. Though I doubt that I would have been so bold in my dealings with officialdom had I been unsure about my form.

Taking over as Boomers captain was a little awkward in some respects, given that my predecessor, Phil Smyth, was still in the team. Phil was someone for whom my dad, as the national coach, had enormous respect and they achieved a lot together, with Phil being something of a basketball icon in this country. When Adrian Hurley took over from my dad as Boomers coach, it was a foregone conclusion that Phil would remain captain, albeit sharing the job with Larry Sengstock at the 1992 Olympics. So I felt honoured and a bit uncomfortable, especially when I had to give my first pre-game talk to the players. That was Phil's job, and had been ever since I first played for the Boomers ten years earlier, and I actually felt a bit embarrassed but Phil was great about it. He was getting to the end of his brilliant international career and the 1994 World

Championships were his last major international tournament as a player. During my time as Phil's team-mate I had never seen him touch a drop of alcohol. But as we rode the bus back to the hotel after the Boomers' last game in Toronto, Phil joined in the celebrations and skolled a can of beer.

One thing that did help my development as Boomers captain was the evolution of the team and a new generation of core players and leaders. By the time we arrived in Toronto for the 1994 World Championships, the Boomers had become a different team. The young guys of what seemed only a few years earlier were now the foundation and the guys who seemed like they would play forever had moved on. There is always a turnover of players from Olympics to Olympics and world titles to world titles, but this time it seemed a bit more poignant. Larry Sengstock had gone, Wayne Carroll had gone and influential veterans like Phil Smyth, Damian Keogh and Ray Borner were edging to the end of their international careers. They were Boomers when I started internationally and it felt a little strange, even though guys like Mark Bradtke and Andrew Vlahov had been on the team for a while, to be playing with a new set of group dynamics. The old guard had gone or was going and the new guard, including coach Barry Barnes after doing his international apprenticeship as assistant coach, was coming in.

What made my first major event as Boomers captain even better was the fact that the 1994 World Championships were most enjoyable I went to. I played at four world championships, but Toronto returned the best result for Australia and the greatest memories. The Boomers finished fifth, equalling the best Australian men's effort at Colombia in 1982, I finished as the leading scorer, the tournament was well-attended (which was certainly not a given at World Championships) and Toronto was a great city to be in. It was a really enjoyable experience all round.

Perhaps the most satisfying thing about the 1994 worlds was that we finished fifth with a team that didn't look great on paper but worked well together with an all-for-one, blue-collar attitude. With all due respect, you would not normally see guys like Greg Hubbard and Paul Rees on an Australian team for the world titles, while Tony Ronaldson and Pat Reidy were still young in terms of international experience. Nor did we have big men Luc Longley and John Dorge banging the boards in the middle, so it shaped up as an interesting adventure.

After negotiating the group games, with wins over South Korea and Cuba and losses to Croatia and the United States, we were served up Russia in the elimination quarter final and were belted. We were humbled by twenty-seven points, 103–76. Russia was a very good team and eventually lost the gold medal game to the United States. The disappointment for us wasn't so much that we lost the game, but how we lost. If we had beaten Russia we would have played for a medal. It was a simple scenario and we barely turned up, which was the most disappointing thing of all. Take away that one performance, and forget the big loss to the NBA-laced US team, and we did a pretty good job.

When we finished, it was a satisfying, if pleasantly surprising, result. The disappointing thing about finishing fifth was to come home and find that people thought we had failed. After finishing fourth at the Seoul Olympics in 1988 and sixth at Barcelona in 1992, people expected the Boomers to win medals at major events. While we did extremely well at major events, maybe the best we could do, that wasn't good enough for the people who failed to grasp the reality while building grandiose, if not false, expectations. Then when those expectations, which did not come from the Boomers themselves, were not met, we were held accountable. Sure, we went into tournaments wanting to win a medal and thinking we could win a medal, but we never expected to win a medal and that's a big difference. So this time, it hurt that we didn't get the recognition we deserved for a good performance. I felt we were unfairly dealt with by people saying we *only* finished fifth. Think about that statement.

Fifth in the *world*. That's fifth in the world of basketball, which is played in probably every country around the globe by hundreds of millions of people. So when you feel good and you've done well to finish fifth against some excellent talent in a prestigious world event and you get canned, it's hard to accept. It also brought home to me that there are a lot of people who have no idea how big and important basketball is on the world stage. Instead of being congratulated for finishing fifth behind basketball powers USA, Russia, Croatia and Greece, people wanted to know what went wrong. That was disappointing because I thought we'd done something special that deserved credit rather than criticism.

Basketball had grown in popularity in Australia and so had the expectations of the Boomers after Seoul and Barcelona. But go back to when my dad was coaching the Boomers and they finished fifth at the 1982 world titles in Colombia. That was a phenomenal performance and one that was probably not given the respect and credit it deserved. We had gone through the late 1970s and early 1980s as undersized overachievers, where finishing seventh or eighth was expected and accepted. By the 1990s, we were considered by some to be talented underachievers, where medals were expected and anything else was unacceptable. I don't think that was a fair reflection of where we were on the international stage, but it was the perception we had created, if only by playing so well in the big tournaments. We created a rod for our own backs and people used it to whip us.

Finishing fifth at the world championships is probably a better achievement than finishing fifth at the Olympics. People will scoff at that because they hold up the Olympics as the pinnacle of sport. But, in terms of how the basketball tournaments are run, the world championships are more difficult because there are sixteen teams (twenty-four from 2006) compared with twelve at the Olympics, so there is more quality opposition, and you need to go through two pool groups in the preliminary stages to reach the quarter finals. Simply, I reckon the worlds are harder to do well at, but the Olympics get more recognition because they are the Olympics when the once-every-four-years basketball fans and critics take some interest.

My first world championships, in Spain in 1986, were a disaster, with the infamous loss to Angola and the failure to qualify for the second phase. It certainly wasn't a pleasant introduction to the senior world championships, but it taught Australian basketball some valuable lessons. So we weren't about to treat anybody lightly when we got to Argentina for the 1990 world titles. Then again, after finishing fourth at the 1988 Olympic Games, none of the other teams was going to treat the Boomers lightly, either.

We prepared for the worlds with a stop at the Goodwill Games in Seattle on the way to Argentina, I had a couple of fifty-point games and we did well, so things looked okay for our group games against China, Brazil and Italy. We knew we could handle China, but Brazil and Italy were always going to be difficult. No matter how many times we played Brazil and Italy, we were never sure of beating them, which was how it panned out. We beat China by twenty-one, lost to Italy by five after beating them at the Goodwill Games, then got over Brazil by one in a game we absolutely needed to win. Oscar Schmidt, the legendary Brazilian scoring machine, was on fire, but Andrew Vlahov shut him down and played a significant defensive role. It was arguably the most important defensive job in Boomers' history, helping us to victory and through to the final stages.

We had a chance for a big finish at the worlds in 1990 and we didn't take advantage of it. We lost to Puerto Rico by ten when we should have got closer, then we missed a golden opportunity to beat the United States, losing by one. We were up by four points with only a couple of minutes to go and had it in the bag. Or should have had. We threw a couple of errant passes, they scored a couple of baskets and we lost. After the game, coach Adrian Hurley was irate and vented his frustration in a way I had never seen from him. We had to wait outside the change room because the door was locked and, whether it was the loss or because the key was taking too long to arrive, Adrian decided to smash the whiteboard he used to diagram plays during time-outs. The only problem was, the more he tried to smash it, the more it wouldn't break. Eventually, he put one end on the ground, held the other in his hands and snapped it under his foot. His frustration was understandable. We should have won a game that might have meant our campaign turned out quite differently.

A one-point win here or a one-point loss there at the Olympic Games or world championships can mean the difference between playing for medals and playing for minor placings. We beat Brazil by one, we lost to the US by one. If either result had gone the other way, so would the Boomers' world championships. If we had lost to Brazil we would have been sent to the bush to play for places nine to sixteen. If we beat the US, we might have been in the medals.

The 1990 World Championships were not memorable in the sense of a great team achievement, given that we finished seventh after beating Argentina in the play-off for seventh and eighth. But back-up guard David Graham gave everyone something to remember with what must have been a moment of brain-lock. As we warmed up, I noticed David's singlet was a different colour to mine. We wore either a gold uniform or a green uniform, depending on the opposition colours and which teams were designated home and away. Immediately, I went into a panic, thinking I had put on the wrong colour. So I quietly asked Damian Keogh what colour we were wearing and double-checked with somebody else. I breathed a sigh of relief, then thought somebody had better break the news to David. So I told David he was wearing the wrong gear, he told the team manager and that sparked a mad scramble back to the team hotel then back to the venue, all the while negotiating Buenos Aires traffic. Clearly, having the correct uniform before tip-off wasn't going to happen. David spent a lot of time on the bench in Argentina and coach Adrian Hurley decided to have some fun. As Adrian called us into the huddle before tip-off he announced: 'Oh, David, you're starting.' I don't think David saw the funny side of it, but his uniform arrived and he was in the same colour as everyone else, even if his face was still a little red.

Stuff like that was not all that unusual. One time when we played New Zealand, Shane Heal was told by the coach to check into the game. So Hammer whipped off his tracksuit pants and reported to the score bench, only to be told he had his shorts on back-to-front. Being the shrinking violet he is, Hammer just yanked them down in front of the crowd, turned them around, pulled them back up and checked into the game for the last few minutes. No problem.

After finishing fifth at the 1994 World Championships and fourth at the 1996 Olympics, there was some expectation that the 1998 world titles in Athens would bring another satisfying performance. It turned out to be neither the Boomers' finest hour nor the most enjoyable tournament. The Boomers finished ninth, which was our worst finish at a major event since the disaster of the 1986 worlds in Spain and not at all in keeping with the program's reputation and achievement over the previous ten years. The tournament itself was poorly attended, except for the Greek games and the last three days from the quarter finals on, which meant one of the two venues always lacked atmosphere, with fans dotted around the cavernous arena. Part of the reason for that was the non-attendance of NBA players for the United States because of a labour dispute, so some of the attraction for spectators and demand for tickets was diminished.

Another reason for disappointment was the fact that the Boomers were in a labour dispute of their own with Basketball Australia, which neither made for a happy camp nor helped generate good performances. The dispute was about prize money that the players believed they were entitled to from the Goodwill Games in New York, where we finished second on the way to Athens. BA believed we were not entitled to the money, enmity developed, the players felt they were being treated unfairly and, as a result, I believe, the dispute affected how we played in Athens. That was reflected in a ninth-place finish. The players took responsibility for finishing ninth without question, but the testy atmosphere surrounding the stand-off did not help our performance.

Politics and sport are not supposed to mix, but in the modern age there seems to be no way of avoiding that, certainly when it comes to negotiations between players and the establishment. In the early 1990s, some of the senior players in the Boomers worked with BA to establish a workplace agreement that covered travel conditions, payments for games and training camps and other related issues. From time to time BA would come to us and say they had to reduce payments or costs for certain trips or camps and most of the time, while there might have been some grumbling, the players would accommodate the request. In the lead-up to the 1998 world titles, the players were asked to take a fairly hefty reduction on their payments, which were calculated on how many days we were with the team in camp or on tour. As a compromise, we struck a deal that the players would share some of the prize money from the Goodwill Games, where we eventually finished second, losing the final to the United States in overtime.

The compromise deal sounded good. If the players performed, they got paid. The better we performed, the more we got in a deal that was a fifty-fifty split between BA and the team. But when we got to New York, we found out BA had already received a guaranteed payment in the form of an advance on any prize money. In other words, BA was paid an appearance fee for us to play in the Goodwill Games, so the prize money to be divided at the end of the tournament was less than it should have been. For example, the prize money for finishing second was US$75,000, so the team should have got $37,500 to share. Because BA had received an advance, say $22,500, which was the minimum prize money, that meant the team would only get $26,250 from the $52,500 left. In this instance, the team would be $11,250 down on the deal because of the guaranteed money given to BA.

The situation got worse and more confused when we queried BA officials about what the deal actually was. At one stage, it looked like we wouldn't get any money, but we got a little windfall compensation when we made the final. It was not a good situation because the players, with the chance to pick up about $4000 per man, were not happy about how they were treated. As captain, I was sent to negotiate with BA president John Maddock and high-performance manager Gary Evans. I assured the players we would sort it out, but it wasn't resolved to the players' satisfaction and the affair carried over from New York to Athens.

This might sound like a cop-out and I know people don't like hearing professional athletes complain about not being paid enough, but in the end the situation wasn't about the money. It started out that way, but the players felt we weren't respected and BA had broken an agreement. BA was doing it hard financially and we were happy to help when asked. But when we had a compromise deal in place that struck pay dirt and we never got the rewards, it upset the team. It created an us-and-them mentality, with the players believing BA was not fully with us. I believe it had an impact on our attitude in Athens and it was a distraction. It also diminished the level of goodwill that existed between officialdom and the players. While all the players were disappointed, some were resentful; they felt they were being screwed by BA, plain and simple.

If BA was looking at the big picture, settling that dispute quickly by stumping up some cash and having the players feel appreciated would have been a small price to pay heading into the world championships and a small price to pay to maintain goodwill between players and officials and to make sure the Boomers went into the tournament in a positive frame of mind. Ultimately, we got some money, but nowhere near what the players believed was due. The worst thing was that neither the players nor BA won. The dispute affected our performance at the world titles and it affected relations between the team and BA. While we were never going to go on strike or boycott the world titles, we just wanted a show of support and faith from BA. It never came. People perform better when there's a good atmosphere and BA did not help by taking its stance over the prize money.

After losing to the United States in overtime in the final of the Goodwill Games in New York, there was a perception that things were on track for a successful world championships. Perhaps too much was read into that performance, because there was a counter feeling that something, aside from the prize money dispute, was a bit awry as we headed to Athens. That was borne out in a bad start to the tournament, with losses to Argentina by four and Spain by one in the first two games. We had chances to win or at least tie both games, and we actually blew a seven-point lead against Spain, which made us 0–2 and put us behind the eight ball. Even though we beat Nigeria to advance to the next round of group games and beat Lithuania and Brazil, we were relegated to the consolation round by a loss to the United States. We didn't play well against the US, which was a team of mainly European-based players because of the NBA labour dispute lockout, but our tournament was decided in those first two games against Argentina and Spain. After the second round, the Boomers and Argentina were tied with 3–3 win–loss records, but the South Americans took the last quarter-final place because of the opening-night win over Australia. The first game of the tournament was the killer.

The frustration of the dispute and our performance against Argentina overflowed on the way back to the locker room when Chris Anstey booted a rubbish bin and sent the contents to all points of the compass. It was an understandable, but not an ideal, reaction. Scott Fisher calmly picked up all the rubbish and placed it back in the bin. Then as soon as the locker room door closed behind him, he launched into Anstey. Fisher, as proud an Australian as there is despite the fact he was an American for the first thirty-odd years of his life, lectured Anstey in no uncertain terms about appropriate behaviour for someone wearing the national uniform and what was expected when playing for Australia. It caused a few people, including Chris, to sit up and take notice. I was impressed with Fisher's sentiment. It showed great leadership qualities and it showed that, no matter the circumstances, when you're representing your country you do so to the highest possible standards.

There was a little twist in the equation of trying to reach the quarter-finals in Athens. The curtain raiser to our game against the US at the Peace and Friendship Stadium down by the docks of Piraeus was between Brazil and Argentina. If Brazil beat Argentina, the Boomers would advance to the quarter-finals regardless of our result against the Americans. So read into this what you will. Remembering the seven-point game between Italy and Cuba that eliminated Australia from the medal round at the 1980 Olympics, a little monkey did laps of my brain as I watched a lacklustre Brazil play Argentina. Brazil had nothing to gain by winning. It could not make the quarter-finals; nor would Argentina if Brazil won. Which meant no South American team in the quarters, and this could affect the number of qualifying spots available for that region at the next Olympics. It sounds convoluted and maybe I was jumping at shadows, but desperate men think desperate thoughts and at that stage of the tournament, I was part of a desperate team. Not that we played like desperate men against the US. We should have been at least competitive, but we were terrible and didn't deserve to have Brazil bail us out of trouble. We just didn't perform and were out of the contest before half-time. We were out of the quarter-finals and out of the medals. Again.

It was a lesson in not taking anything lightly or for granted in international basketball. The final standings after the two group rounds were so tight that, had the Boomers beaten the US, we could have finished as high as second and cruised to the quarters. The other indicator about winning the games-that-matter was that the Boomers eventually finished ninth with a 5–3 record. We had had an identical win–loss record two years earlier at the Atlanta Olympics and finished fourth. The quarter-final teams at the 1998 worlds were Yugoslavia, Greece, Russia, the US, Lithuania, Spain, Argentina and Italy. If you substituted Australia for Argentina, the regular order of world basketball would have been maintained and nobody would have raised an eyebrow about our performance, even though our two best big men, Mark Bradtke and Luc Longley, were absent and we fielded a fairly inexperienced team. We beat Brazil to close the tournament, but ninth was simply not good enough.

For me, there was one historical note about the 1998 World Championships in Athens. During the consolation round game against Canada, I moved into second place on the list of all-time world championship scorers, but still a long way behind legendary Brazilian Oscar Schmidt. I added to my tally in the game for ninth and tenth against Brazil, which was more historical in some ways. It was my last game for the Boomers at the World Championships. Thankfully, I still had a few more to go as captain.

chapter thirteen

TITLE TIME

I don't know what it is about me and trophy presentations, but the crowd was booing me like I was a crooked politician. Frankly, I couldn't have cared less, either. All that mattered was that I was raising the Dr John Raschke trophy, which could mean just one thing: Melbourne Tigers had finally won the NBL Championship.

The Perth Wildcats fans did not exactly endear themselves to the rest of Australia when they booed during the trophy presentation after game three of the 1993 grand final series. But after ten seasons of the Tigers trying to win an NBL title, they could boo all they liked. Across the other side of the country in Melbourne, every Tigers fan was cheering. Some of them were crying. I admit I even got a little choked up about things myself.

From among the post-game scenes that followed the booing and subsequent controversy, the memory most people have is of me gripping my father/coach Lindsay in a headlock that seemed to get tighter the more he tried to ease out of it. At the time, it was a very emotional moment and experience. We had achieved our goal of winning the title after surviving the pressures and expectations of a long season and to share that with team-mates was exciting. To share it with my dad was something extra. After the horn sounded, we were buzzed by the immediate euphoria, but I finally found my dad and just grabbed him. That headlock was partly in celebration and partly me trying to hide my emotion, trying to shield it by burying my head into his neck and shoulder. It was a great moment for our club and our family. God knows, the Tigers and the Gazes had paid their dues.

A lot of people only recognise the Melbourne Tigers' history from 1984, when we entered the NBL. But that's only one part of it, albeit a decent portion. It's the same as my own history. I started in the NBL the same time as the Tigers, but had played senior basketball for a few seasons before in what was an interesting and educational experience.

The first of my two biggest pre-NBL moments happened while I was playing for the Tigers' second team, Auburn, which was coached by the legendary Ken Watson, who coached Australia at two Olympics and was considered the father of basketball in Victoria. I was only a kid of about fifteen or sixteen, but I'll never forget the Sunday afternoon we played the Geelong Cats in a VBA summer comp game at the Corio Leisure Centre in Geelong. I'll never forget it because we played against blokes like Cal Bruton and James Crawford and I did all right and scored some points. All the way back to Melbourne I sat in Ken's car with a silly grin on my face, thinking I had hit the big time. Ken dropped me at Albert Park Stadium where the Tigers were training with my dad. I was just busting for somebody to ask me how the game went, so I could tell them how *I* went. It never happened and I had to keep my joy to myself.

My second big pre-NBL moment was more than a memory. It was actually recorded for posterity by the *Herald*, Melbourne's now defunct afternoon newspaper, with the headline 'YOUNG ANDY LIFTS TIGERS'. It was a 1981 VBA final that thrust me into the headlines purely by circumstance rather than good management, but it was a key moment nonetheless. I was coming off the bench for the Tigers' state league team as a sixteen year old, making some impact here and there but not expecting any time during the finals, which were fiercely contested in the best competition in Australia, even during the early days of the NBL.

We played Geelong at Albert Park and were cruising with a lead of twenty-one points. Then Geelong went on a run and we hit the wall. When Brian Goorjian fouled out and Al Westover was tossed out, leaving us short of experienced guards, my dad moved Bruce Palmer to the point to carry the ball, but Bruce struggled. So my dad bit the bullet and gave me the responsibility of being the main ball carrier for the last ten minutes. I scored only seven points, but I was able to help the Tigers home in a fairly pressure-packed situation after Geelong had got to within three. Cal Bruton, one of the NBL's all-time great players, still talks about that game, surely believing his Cats would take advantage of the dorky kid and get the win.

I often wonder how crucial that game was to my development. They say necessity is the mother of invention and I was thrown into a situation that normally would not even be contemplated. I survived and got a boost to my confidence, knowing I could perform at a high level. I played more minutes and started a few games the next year and by 1983 I was a starter on the team that would go on to win the South East Conference (SEC), which involved teams mainly from Victoria, South Australia and New South Wales and continues today under the guise of the SEABL. It was basically considered the poor man's NBL and is still a second-tier competition. The VBA state league was always the top competition in Australia through the 1970s and early 80s and a lot of players moved to Melbourne just to play in the comp, even after the NBL's inception in 1979. The Nunawading Spectres and St Kilda Saints joined the NBL for its first season and the Coburg Giants followed in 1980. The Tigers had to wait until 1984 to join the NBL, biding our time in the SEC.

The SEC dated back to the 1960s when the teams from New South Wales and South Australia wanted to play the Victorian teams to get better regular competition. But when Melbourne kept winning, the Victorian teams decided not to waste time and money and the league folded. That caused resentment among the New South Wales and South Australian factions, so in 1978, when the plan to launch the NBL was hatched, the Melbourne Tigers were not invited to the meetings as retribution. Politics in sport is not a new phenomenon.

So with the reformed SEC in action, there was a path into the NBL. Geelong won the SEC title in 1981 and went to the NBL in 1982. The Tigers and Frankston Bears indicated a desire in 1982 to step up to the NBL in 1983, but the league didn't want two new teams and decided the winner of a best-of-three play-off would be promoted. The Tigers won the last regular-season game against Frankston and the Bears won the SEC grand final in overtime at Albert Park, then won the deciding game and a spot in the NBL on a neutral court at Nunawading.

We won the SEC Championship in 1983 and were accepted into the NBL for the 1984 season. I became a starter with the Tigers in 1983 and had a good season and put up some decent numbers. I lived off Brian Goorjian, who, with Al Westover, was a veteran head and an excellent passer who created a lot of scoring opportunities for me. That's how I developed my game of constant running, movement and working off the ball. I'd run backdoor cuts and Brian would find me with a pass. I found a little toy to play with and it grew from there. I knew it was a way of picking up cheap baskets, especially if I was prepared to outwork people off the ball to get those opportunities. Not to mention the unselfish passing of Brian and Al, the guys who once played while I just watched.

The Tigers' NBL debut on 4 February 1984 was against the Brisbane Bullets at Albert Park. I don't remember a whole lot about the game except that Leroy Loggins, one of the NBL's all-time greats and a legend even then for his scoring exploits, played for the Bullets, that we lost and that I had sixteen points. The Tigers actually started the season poorly and we were 1–8 and in all sorts of bother. Brian Goorjian wasn't going to play that season, but my dad talked him into it and once Brian, a major key to our team, found his legs, the Tigers starting winning a few. We did recover from our 1–8 start to finish 11–13, but as my dad likes to say, it was a case of operation successful, patient died. The competition was split into two eight-team conferences and, despite winning six of our last seven games, we missed the play-offs by two wins.

Perhaps the most notable thing about 1984 was that the NBL had started to become more professional and players were getting paid more money. But while the Adelaide 36ers, Brisbane Bullets and Canberra Cannons had picked up the level of professionalism in their programs, the Tigers were still a fair way off. In fact, we were pretty much rank amateurs. Our administration was one person: my dad. We did pick up ANA health insurance as our major sponsor because we had an insider in the upper levels at ANA who helped swing the deal. I think it was a $20,000 sponsorship and that pretty much covered our costs for the season. These days, $20,000 is the minimum player salary in the NBL. So our first NBL campaign was encouraging.

It turned out to be a false dawn. For the next three seasons, we were terrible and won a total of fourteen games out of seventy-eight. We just did not have the horses to compete with the best teams in the competition and we couldn't beat the others, either. We went 5–21, 6–20, 3–23, which were excellent bowling figures but terrible win–loss records for an NBL team.

I suppose the softener for me was that I had started to emerge as a player in my own right. I went to the Olympics in 1984 with the Boomers and had a reasonable season in 1985, although I broke my foot and missed some games. There was some natural progression and development involved, but the jump in my scoring and profile was more an unfortunate reflection of our team. We weren't very good and I became more of an offensive focus and simply got more scoring opportunities. My role and responsibilities in our structure had grown and evolved to put me in a position, with the help of my team-mates, to score more. There was still a matter of trying to win games, but we didn't have much luck in that area.

I led the NBL in scoring (36.9 ppg) for the first time in 1986 and my Tigers team-mate Paul Stanley (33.8 ppg) finished second. Any team with two players combining for about 70 points per game should win plenty of games. We won six. The offence was structured around me and Paul and our big man was Dave Clement, who was just 198 centimetres tall but had to play the post position. Dave was a wonderful human being and worked his heart out, but he was small for the position and we got exploited by bigger and better teams.

Stanley, an American, was a great left-handed shooter, who never met a shot he didn't like. He was much more of a gunner than me and was very good at creating his own shot. I relied more on the offence to get open and on my team-mates to get me the ball, which usually presented higher-percentage opportunities. Off the court, Stanley was a nice guy, but on it he was highly competitive and fiery. Stanley was a real white-line fever candidate and 1986 was his only season with the Tigers before going to the Hobart Tassie Devils.

Stanley's departure certainly didn't help the Tigers. About the only thing it helped was my scoring average, which jumped to 44.1 ppg in 1987, beating Stanley for the scoring title again. It was one of the few victories the Tigers had for the whole season, but it was slim consolation for our poor on-court efforts. We were so bad that our imports didn't even finish the season, which is perhaps not unusual given that imports get sacked regularly. It was just that our imports, Matt Fleming and Paul Kapturkiewicz, left of their own accord. One had a European deal to go to and the other just couldn't hack the losing. Nor were they getting paid much, so you couldn't blame them. By the end of the season, we were down to an all-Australian line-up. We were a bunch of keen youngsters, basically, but we produced one of the greatest wins in club history.

Coming into the last round of the season, the play-off spots were still up for grabs, with the North Melbourne Giants and Eastside Melbourne Spectres both trying to make the post-season. The scenario was that the Giants needed to win one game against the Tigers or the Spectres to make the finals but the Spectres needed the Giants to lose both. As we had won only twice and were on a then NBL record seventeen-game losing streak, it seemed a foregone conclusion that the Giants would beat us to make the finals. Which was exactly what Spectres coach Barry Barnes thought. Barnesy was so sure the Giants would beat us that the Spectres didn't even bother training that week. You only had to look at the stacked Giants roster – Scott Fisher, Wayne Carroll, Bennie Lewis, Ray Shirley, Willie Simmons, Dave Graham and Ray Gordon – to see we had no chance. Well, we had some chance. The game was on SBS, to be shown on replay, and it turned out Barry Barnes was doing special comments on the telecast. What he saw was his worst nightmare. I had fifty-two points, Nigel Purchase had thirty-odd and we won a remarkable game. That meant the winner of the Giants–Spectres game the next day would make the play-offs. Even though the Giants weren't rested, the Spectres weren't ready. The Giants won and went to the finals, but they lost in the first round.

It was a big finish to a low season. While my scoring was up, it was almost a collection of irrelevant points. I had six games of fifty or more points but I didn't even think about it at the time. We lost so much and I felt almost embarrassed because there was a perception that I was just out there to get my own. It wasn't that. We were trying to win, but we never had a lot of talent. I was just battling away doing whatever I could to try to get a win for us.

In those days we had no obligations to anyone but ourselves because we weren't paid a cent. But it still hurt to lose. We were young, we weren't a good team and it was very disheartening. Every Monday I had to go to university and talk through another loss – or two if we had a double-header. In the big picture it was tolerable in the sense that we weren't very good, we had no resources or no money, we didn't train full-time, not everybody could make training anyway, and if we got two hundred people to a game we thought we had had a big night. So what could anyone expect? On an individual basis I was young and, while I derived some satisfaction from my performances, it was frustrating. We just had to be realistic. That didn't mean we had to enjoy and accept losing in the NBL. Fortunately, we still won enough games in the VBA state league to maintain some semblance of self-belief and know that we could compete. In fact, those Wednesday night wins were pretty important for the fabric and psyche of the team.

By 1988 we were starting to feel pressure, even if it was only self-generated, to win more games. The club came good with some excellent sponsors through the work of Peter Sheahan, who was in the corporate world and had a son playing juniors with the Tigers. We still didn't have any corporate boxes, but Sheahan was able to generate a significant sponsorship total of about $250,000 for the season. It sounds minuscule now, but in those days it was like getting the keys to Fort Knox after the Tigers had lived a hand-to-mouth existence. We had money, which improved our resources, which in turn allowed us to get paid a little, increasing our commitment and need to win. Simply, we didn't want to let anyone down for fear of this windfall disappearing. In fact, the way the NBL had improved and evolved, I don't know what would have happened if the Tigers didn't get that financial support.

The fresh injection of funds meant we could go shopping for a couple of good imports. We needed a few superstars who could help get us to the play-offs for the first time. At the end of the 1987 season, I accompanied my dad to the United States on a scouting mission to find the players who could help the Tigers in their play-off quest. An agent in Los Angeles gave us two names: James Bullock and Frank Smith. Both players lived in Indiana, so we flew from LA to Chicago and then drove to Gary, Indiana, to work them out and see if they were suitable. We wanted to see them in a scrimmage, but there was nobody else available, so I got kitted up and we ran some drills. Bullock looked a bit undersized for what we wanted but his skills were impressive and his college record at the University of Purdue indicated that he could be a good player in the NBL. Smith was a string-bean 208 centimetres who had gone to college at Arizona, been picked by Portland in the eighth round of the 1983 NBA draft and played professionally in New Zealand. Both were decent players, but we passed on Smith and made our big offer to James Bullock. The offer was something like $20,000 and use of a car and an apartment. He accepted and we moved on to New York searching for one more player.

We went to a New York Knicks NBA game, met some agents and, eventually through the help of John Carroll and PJ Carlesimo from Seton Hall, organised six blokes for a tryout. It was a real hotchpotch collection of bodies and talent and there was nobody we were absolutely convinced was appropriate. Then in walked this guy who was about 208 centimetres and with talent as raw as uncooked carrot. He said he was from the Caribbean and had played a little bit, so we figured we had nothing to lose by having a look at him. He was impressive in the sense that he was tall, athletic and could dunk. It turned out Rowan Gomes, who went to a small school called Hampton Institute, had been taken by the Denver Nuggets in the seventh round of the 1987 NBA draft but hadn't played pro. We decided to go with him as the Tigers' second import for 1988.

Bullock and Gomes arrived in January 1988, and it was Gomes who made the first big impression. It was the height of summer, so we had a team barbecue at my nanna's house down near Chelsea. Naturally, we got out the bat and ball for some backyard cricket, which needed some explanation for James, but Rowan said he knew all about it. We were a bit sceptical, but if we had listened closely to his mixed American–Caribbean accent, we might have twigged. I was batting when Rowan took the ball and stormed in on a long run in the textbook style of a West Indies fast bowler. He zinged the first ball around my ears and then proceeded to send down a stream of bullets like he should have been in the Test team.

Unfortunately, that was as good as it got for Rowan. The first weekend of the new season, we played the Hobart Tassie Devils and the Westside Melbourne Saints on the road. We led by about twenty against Hobart and lost, but thought we could get one back against the Saints the next day at Keilor. It was a tight game and scores were level with about twenty seconds to go. We made a steal and Gomes got out on the break for a lay-up to put us in front. As he jumped, his knee gave way, he missed the lay-up and crashed to the floor in a painful pile. We lost the game and he needed a knee reconstruction. We had lost two winnable games and one import in two days. Already, there was a feeling that we couldn't take a trick.

We picked up Mike Champion, who had played the season before with the Canberra Cannons, to fill in for a couple of games, and then we signed broad and beefy big man Alvis Rogers from Wake Forest University. Rogers, who was taken by the Kansas City Kings in the sixth round of the 1983 NBA draft, was good for us, but we regularly found ourselves coming up short without the talent to get over the line. We went 8–16 and were more competitive than our win–loss record indicated. We certainly weren't in the same class as the 0–24 Geelong Supercats, but we still finished only one place above them on the ladder. While we thought we had two good imports, we needed more talent, Australian and American, to improve.

In the quest to beef up our roster, the Tigers took Warrick Giddey, who had split with the Wollongong Hawks, on our 1988 post-season trip to the United States and we picked up naturalised centre Brad Pineau and another big-bodied American workhorse, Dave

Simmons. Giddey never played much with the Hawks but he went on the tour after a recommendation by Phil Smyth, who coached Wozza at the AIS. It turned out Woz and Simm would be with us for quite a while. We picked up Simm about half-way through the trip at Oklahoma and it was an easy decision to sign him. We also had an eye on another import to replace James Bullock, who never gave the club a clear indication about re-signing, and we ended up going with Dave Colbert. We also got back Ray Gordon, a close boyhood friend and one of my junior Tigers team-mates, after two seasons with the North Melbourne Giants. There was no question we had recruited, it was just a matter of finding out how well.

I had spent the off-season playing at Seton Hall and only got home about a month before the 1989 season, keen to see our revamped team. I knew there was a chance we would be decent and that was how it panned out. We won our first four games and went 16–8 to make the NBL play-offs for the first time. We only missed top spot by a couple of wins, so there was some justification in believing we could do something in the play-offs. That justification never came to pass against the Sydney Kings in the first round after a messy finish to the season.

Dave Simmons got reported for taking a swing at Shane Froling and was suspended for the last two games of the regular season. Unfortunately, his lead was followed by Dave Colbert in the first game of the best-of-three play-off series against the Kings. Colbert gave Tim Morrissey a forearm to the back of the head and was suspended for two games. After losing that first game, we swamped them in game two against the odds at home to force a deciding game, which we lost by two, 85–83. This was a pretty big effort and it goes without saying that if Dave Colbert had played we would have had a better chance of going to the next round. To do that, we would have to wait at least a year.

We improved to 17–9 in 1990 but still had a reputation as play-off pushovers. Near the end of the regular season, I was struck down by the thrombosis that started in my right shoulder and fragmented into my lungs. I didn't play again that season and the Tigers got waxed in the first round of the play-offs by the Perth Wildcats. It was a similar scenario in 1991 when we went 16–10. We played the Geelong Supercats in the last game of the regular season, needing to win to finish second. We lost and finished fifth, then went out of the play-offs in two straight games to the Adelaide 36ers. It was an embarrassing end to the season. Dave Colbert spat the dummy and had some off-court issues and that game-two loss to the Sixers was his last game for the Tigers.

Disastrously as the 1991 season finished for the Tigers, there was a little cream to come for me individually. After the NBL season closed, I signed to play in Italy with Udine. While I got accustomed to my Italian surroundings, news came from home via my dad: I had won the NBL MVP award for the first time. For the previous two seasons I had been runner-up and, while it was a huge honour and nice to win the MVP, it hadn't ever been a major goal so I was pretty calm about the award. I guess being on the other side of the world lessened the impact and it certainly meant I couldn't be at the NBL awards dinner. But that didn't stop me appearing at the World Congress Centre in Melbourne – via a satellite hook-up. TV commentator Bruce McAvaney was the MC for the evening and interviewed me live. I'm tipping Bruce had an easier trip to the interview than I did. My dad told me the NBL wanted to do the live cross, which was fair enough. The only hitch was that I had to drive from Udine to Trieste, which was about two and a half hours away, all on the wrong side of the road as far as I was concerned. Channel Seven, which organised the feed, gave me directions to the studio in Trieste, but having no Italian language skills to ask the way if I got lost, I had little margin for error. Fortunately, I got there on time, Bruce told me I'd won, I tried to look as though he had broken the news, and everyone was happy.

What didn't make me happy was the day I called home to find out about the Tigers' new import, only to be left thinking he was a dud. At that stage, I didn't think I would be home in time to meet, let alone play with, Lanard Copeland.

After releasing Dave Colbert, the Tigers put feelers out for an import forward. We found a guy named Barry Mitchell, but the deal fell through. As my dad kept calling agents he asked one about a certain player, then casually mentioned he'd also been given another name: Lanard Copeland. The agent told my dad to forget the other guy and go for Copes, who had played in the NBA and was playing in the minor league CBA. It was worth a shot and Copes basically agreed to a deal on the spot. After his first training session, though, some guys suspected why this bloke with thirty-three NBA games for the Philadelphia 76ers and LA Clippers to his credit had so readily agreed to come to Australia.

When I phoned from Udine to check on Copes's first training session the alarm bells rang as soon as they said he was a guard and not a forward. He wasn't what we were looking for, but the feeling was that he would eventually be okay. Maybe. The first session had been so dismal that Melbourne was almost in a state of emergency, the reason for the concern being that Copes had been taken apart by Dean Vickerman, one of our backups. Vickerman, by all accounts, absolutely lit up Copeland and destroyed him. The concern and general consensus was that we had been sold a dud. How wrong we were, given that Copes stayed to clock up fourteen NBL seasons with the Tigers. All these years later, Copes still maintains that his poor showing was because our then general manager Bruce Ward welcomed him to town with lunch and a few beers before going to training. Whatever.

Within a few more training sessions, the concerns eased considerably and the Tigers felt good about Copes. He caught attention with a few dunks and my dad was impressed with his athleticism, even though his shot was apparently a bit shaky. When they got to the K-Mart Classic pre-season tournament, Copes started to showcase his package. He executed some spectacular dunks and had people buzzing. I made one of my regular calls for an update and my dad said that while Copes was a little slow picking up the structure of our offence and the way we wanted to play, he was one heck of an athlete who could jump out of the gym. Apparently, at the K-Mart Classic, he tried one dunk where he took off from the foul line, only for the ball to bounce off the ring. By then, he showed he was capable of thirty-five points a game. He was going to be a player.

The Tigers' first game of the NBL season was our first game at Melbourne Park and it was on TV, so it was to be a perfect opening for the new campaign and a new era in a 15,000-seat stadium. And a perfect opening for Copes. On the very first play of the game against the Canberra Cannons, Copes took the ball from the tip-off and dunked it. It was the first of thirty-eight points for the night as he grabbed the hearts of Tigers fans to start a long and happy relationship.

My first NBL game with Copes, on my return from Udine, was the next Saturday night against the Perth Wildcats. But first we played on the Wednesday night in a VBA game at Albert Park. I'd only had two training sessions since arriving home from Italy, but I'd heard a lot about his incredible jumping ability and I wanted to test him. So I threw up some alley-oop passes for Copes to catch and dunk. He was just amazing, doing stuff we'd never seen before with his freakish athleticism, helping his reputation and our partnership to grow quickly. This bloke was certainly no dud. We had found the class import we craved for a shot at the NBL title.

It should be mentioned that we also signed forward Robert Sibley from the Brisbane Bullets. Sibs was one of the funniest blokes going around and certainly added plenty of life on and off the court during an amazing season. We had a bit of a hiccup to start, but we finished third on the ladder (15–9) behind the South East Melbourne Magic (which was in its first season after a merger between the Spectres and the Saints) and the Sydney Kings. We still hadn't won a finals series and had to play the Perth Wildcats in the first round, which was something of a short straw because they were a better team than their regular season placing indicated. We lost in Perth to open the best-of-three series but came home to win both – by a point when we survived a Wildcats shot to win it, and by sixteen. We finally had the play-off monkey off our backs and were rolling.

We played the Sydney Kings in the semi-finals and stepped up to a different level in front of some big crowds. There was a feeling from the basketball pundits throughout the season that the Magic and the Kings had us covered and this was the Kings' year to win it all. We forced a rethink after winning game one, but we were carrying injuries. I had a crook knee and Sibley was hurt, too. Even so, we were elated to win the opening game and were jumping up and down celebrating at the buzzer. The Kings considered our post-game celebration premature for a best-of-three series and they slapped us by winning game two to level the series as Kings import Dwayne McClain went to work.

There was a real sense that the series had swung irretrievably Sydney's way. I had rolled my ankle to match my bung knee, we were banged up and some must have wondered just how much we would lose the deciding game by. I had carried the injury since mid-season, taking it into the Barcelona Olympics and through the NBL resumption, not having time to fix the torn cartilage. When knee surgeon David Young examined the knee after I hurt it, he also drained some fluid from it. As he whacked in the syringe, I thought I was going to faint. I'm the first admit my trophy cabinet has no awards for bravery in it. But from then on, the knee was drained and painkillers injected on a regular basis to get me through the Olympics and the rest of the NBL season. At half-time of game two against the Kings, I had a jab in the ankle that I'd rolled and another in the knee. At the time, I didn't worry about what this could do to me long-term. It was just about being able to get back on the floor. That was in vain given the result and, after losing game two on the

Friday night, our season was on the line on the Sunday afternoon. It was a brilliant Sunday to be a Tiger.

The Sydney Entertainment Centre was sold out for the deciding game and we shocked the home fans by taking a good lead. Due to all our injuries, we played a zone defence for most of the game, stifling the one-on-one brilliance of import Dwayyne McClain and forcing the Kings to shoot from the perimeter. Predictably, the Kings made a run at us and brought the margin back to two points, which got the crowd going and placed the whole season on a knife edge. As the Kings charged, we lost Lanard Copeland to an ankle injury with a few minutes left, so we weren't exactly feeling like Tattslotto winners. We were playing for survival over the last few minutes as we went up and down the floor, knowing that every possession and every shot was precious and could determine the season's fate. Young forward Stephen Whitehead was in the game for Copeland, so the Kings targeted him to send him to the free-throw line, hoping he would miss and they could cash in at the other end. With about eight seconds left, the kid we called Rookie stepped to the line and made two free-throws to seal the game and the series. We were drained physically and mentally, but we had won and we were on our way to an all-Victorian grand final against the Magic.

The Magic, which was coached by former Tiger Brian Goorjian, went 20–4 in the regular season and swept both their play-off series against the Canberra Cannons and North Melbourne Giants. We certainly seemed to have a daunting task ahead of us, considering the team's size, talent and depth and the fact that several Magic players were looking for redemption after losing the previous season's grand final to the Perth Wildcats when they were with the Spectres.

Somehow, even though the Tigers were bruised and battered from the semi-finals, we won the first game of the grand final series, 116–98. It was as convincing as you could have hoped. But there was an incident during the game that might have unwittingly turned the series the Magic's way. Darren Perry, the Magic's starting point guard, went down with an Achilles tendon injury and was done for the rest of the series. On the surface, it was a massive blow for Darren and the Magic. It also possibly won the title for them. With Perry in the line-up, we had a distinct height advantage that Copes or I could exploit. When they brought in Scott Ninnis, who was taller and more athletic, as Perry's replacement, that changed the way we played, too. Ninnis took Copeland as his prime defensive assignment and I was stuck with Darren Lucas as usual. Life wasn't so easy after that.

Renowned for his meticulous preparation, Brian Goorjian went to work salvaging the wreck of game one to have it re-sprayed, polished and fine-tuned for game two. Whatever he did, it worked a treat for the Magic as they smashed us, 115–93, to level the series and set up a third and deciding game inside a seething Melbourne Park two days later. The momentum was clearly with the Magic and it was our turn to scramble, make adjustments and recover from the beating. We fronted up and took the game right to the Magic, keeping it close down to the final minutes. I did not have a great game, fighting a losing fight with my outside shot, but the rest of the Tigers dragged us along to have a chance of winning. There was one specific play from the deciding game that I reckon was pivotal. We were making a run at the Magic and were in offensive transition, running up the floor looking for a quick basket to maintain pressure. I threw the ball ahead to Stephen Whitehead, who pulled up for a three. If he made it, the Magic might sag with doubt about their ability to hold us off. If he missed it, they were off the hook and we were looking for a miracle. He missed. We lost. It had been close, 95–88, but not close enough for the Tigers.

The championship series was a spectacular success for the NBL with two crowds of more than 15,000 and one of more than 13,000, and it was a crowning moment for Brian Goorjian and the Magic. It was a bitter-sweet experience for the Tigers: we lost the grand final but were considered overachievers for getting further than anybody

Showing speed some never knew I had.

My dad with his castle and his car. We lived in the little brick cottage attached to the Albert Park basketball stadium.

First day of high school. Fortunately my sister Janet was ahead of me and helped me out.

Proof that my head wasn't always bigger than a ball.

Head and shoulders above my classmates physically, but maybe not academically.

Given the environment I grew up in, family, basketball and education were constant and important influences.

HWT

HWT

HWT/Colleen Petch

Opposite page: (top) the Gaze clan – or part of it. My dad (centre) and his brother Tony (behind me at left) with their families; (bottom left) just a young man playing the game; (bottom right) my first state team, coached by Ron Anderson. David Graham, a Boomers team-mate at the 1990 World Championships, is wearing No. 8.

This page: (top left) going to the basket for Seton Hall during the 1988–89 US college season and doing the same for the Tigers in the NBL; (top right) at the old Albert Park stadium; (left) education was always important, even if did take me eleven years to graduate from Victoria University.

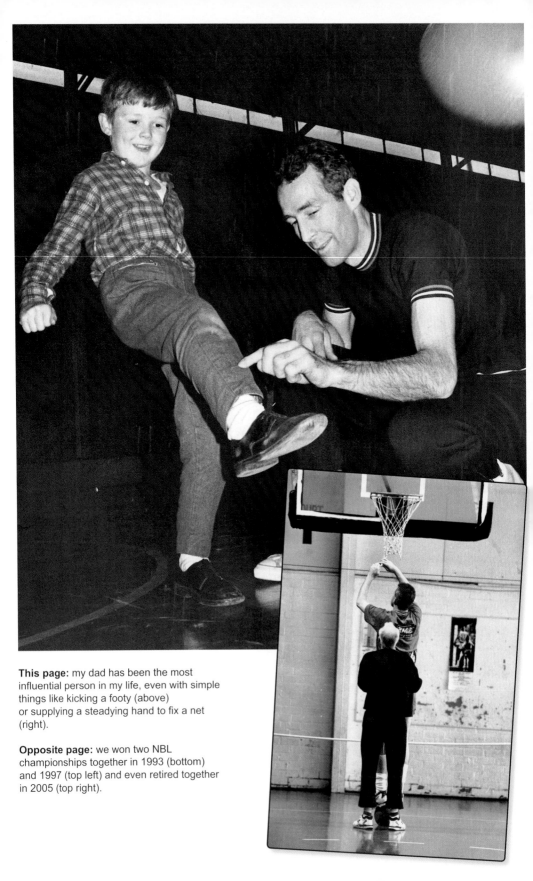

This page: my dad has been the most influential person in my life, even with simple things like kicking a footy (above) or supplying a steadying hand to fix a net (right).

Opposite page: we won two NBL championships together in 1993 (bottom) and 1997 (top left) and even retired together in 2005 (top right).

HWT/Michael Klein

Sport the Library

Sport the Library

HWT/Colleen Petch

Newspix

HWT/Colleen Petch

HWT/Wayne Ludbey

Undeniable proof I wasn't always a prisoner of gravity – I did get off the ground and above the ring once or twice during my career.

This page: playing for Australia was an honour, a privilege and a buzz, especially when I got to share the experience with mates like Shane Heal (top left).

Opposite page: Lanard Copeland reckoned he carried me for much of my career. Here (main pic) he gets a hand from Daryl Corletto after my 600th NBL game. We celebrated many wins, including the 1997 NBL championship (inset).

HWT/Colleen Petch

HWT/Michael Klein

I always had a special relationship with my opponents, including US guard Gary Payton (top) and seemingly all the NBL referees.

KODAK COLOUR 0 6 7 5 4 1 0 0 4 HWT/Colleen Petch

Newspix

MITSUBISHI

HWT

HWT

17 17A 18 18A 19 19A

HWT/Colleen Petch

Newspix

I learned over five Olympic Games that fashions never stay the same. My dad and I heading to LA in 1984 (top left) and me at the opening ceremony (top right); leading the Australian Olympic team at Sydney 2000 (bottom left) and sharing our win over Italy (centre); (bottom right) losing to Lithuania in the bronze medal game was a low point.

Getty Images/NBA

HWT

HWT

Sport the Library

Sport the Library/NBL

Top: NBA champion San Antonio Spurs and an Aussie wearing No. 10. Middle, from left to right: my mate Wayne Peterson shared the spoils of the Spurs' win with Will Perdue; a pretty good threesome plus one (centre) as I hit the golf course with Shane Warne, Greg Norman and Damian Oliver; the chunky NBA championship ring shadowed my two from the NBL. Bottom: Leroy Loggins (left) was an NBL opponent and a Boomers team-mate, but always a hero and legend, while Lanard Copeland (right) has a special place in my heart, to

HWT/Fiona Hamilton

HWT/Colleen Petch

Opposite page: my wife Melinda (bottom right) is responsible for a lot of good things, including (main pic, clockwise from top left) Courtney, Phoebe, Annie and Mason; (bottom left) Courtney shows her support, even if her spelling is a little off.

This page: the two faces of mate and business partner Nigel Purchase (top left and right). Middle: with fellow Olympian Rechelle Hawkes (left) just before I carried the flag and she read the athletes' oath at Sydney 2000; my mum (right) has been my biggest supporter. Bottom: three rough-heads at the Sydney opening ceremony me, Barry Barnes and Shane Heal.

HWT/Colleen Petch

(except maybe ourselves and our fans) thought we could. We didn't feel content with losing, but we did feel a sense of satisfaction with our overall season, given we'd never won a play-off series before. To get through to the grand final and lose in three games to the best team of the season was certainly no disgrace. But could we regroup and go one step further the next season?

Having gone so close to winning the NBL Championship in 1992, we knew we had a good team, so we made only one change to the roster, albeit a fairly significant one. The Tigers signed Mark Bradtke, who was destined to become the best and most dominant big man ever to play in the NBL. I'm not exactly sure how Hogey ended up with the Tigers, but it might have been the best thing that ever happened to our club in its NBL era. Hogey had played five seasons with the Adelaide 36ers before a falling-out at the end of 1992 saw him sign to play in Spain with a team in the southern city of Murcia. But his fans hadn't even had a chance to miss him when he was back in Australia by the start of 1993. His contract with Murcia was in two parts: pre-Christmas and post-Christmas. After playing to Christmas, Hogey was set to complete the deal, then had a change of heart. He threw on his backpack, went for a quick holiday around Europe and came home to Australia. As soon as Hogey stepped through Customs at the international arrival hall, NBL clubs were lining up to woo him. For a brief moment it looked like he might have gone to the cashed-up Perth Wildcats, but fate smiled upon the Tigers. For whatever reason – we assumed we had done a good recruiting job, but a reasonable influence might have been the fact that his future wife Nicole Provis lived in Melbourne – he signed with the Tigers.

Hogey came to us a little late in our pre-season preparation, but that didn't stop everyone assuming that the Tigers, as runners-up and having signed Hogey, were overwhelming favourites for the 1993 title. In some respects that was a fair judgment. But it was a long way from the truth once the season started and we were 1–5.

The pressure was mounting after we dug a hole for ourselves that our opponents gladly pushed us into. Slowly, things turned. We got our act together and recovered to a 16–10 win–loss record and third place on the ladder. At least we went into the play-offs with some momentum and confidence, which showed when we swept the Wollongong Hawks 2–0 in the first round and blanked the Magic in the semi-finals, winning 108–106 and 89–72, to set up the best-of-three grand final series against the Perth Wildcats.

The Wildcats were the standout team that season, going 21–5, but they still had to work hard during the play-offs, being forced to a third and deciding game in both series against the North Melbourne Giants and Brisbane Bullets. The Wildcats won the deciding game in each series at home, which was a big key for them. The 'Cats were undefeated at home that season. The Perth Entertainment Centre was a fortress.

The play-off format called for the Tigers to have our one and only home game as the series opener before going to Perth for games two and three, if needed. We had to win game one at home to have a chance of winning the title, so we were pumped when we took the floor in front of a sold-out Melbourne Park crowd, which for the first time was totally full of Tigers fans and not split for a derby. We won 117–113 (I had 41) in a spectacular and entertaining game. We also got a little lucky when the Wildcats' Scott Fisher missed a lay-up and the referees might have missed the nudge he received on the play. It was the old thing about needing some luck and we rode it as far as it would take us.

So we headed for Perth with a 1–0 series lead, needing to win one more game to land the championship. But we were never really in game two at the finish and lost by seven, 112–105. The series, the season, would go the distance. With growing doubts about whether we could do it, the Tigers needed to create history to win the title. There was a distinct feeling we had blown our chance and the Wildcats, with the home court advantage, had the momentum. The history we fought was that the Tigers, in ten NBL seasons, had never won a game in Perth. So now we faced one game for all the chips at a place we'd never won at. Clearly, the general expectation was that we wouldn't win.

Fortunately we didn't feel like the odds were insurmountable and it was almost like we had nothing to lose. We made a reasonable start and the Wildcats' dynamic point guard, Ricky Grace, was restricted by foul trouble, which was a big advantage for us. Andrew Vlahov, the Wildcats' blue-collar strongman, got away from us and had about thirty-five points, but Lanard Copeland came up big and the Tigers followed his lead. Frankly, we were up against it and the crowd gave us a sample of what it must have been like for the Christians with every Roman in the Colosseum barracking for those damn lions. There wasn't much love for us at the PEC that day, but, importantly, we weren't overawed. We were in the game at half-time and by the third quarter we owned a double-digit lead, hoping like hell we could hold it. By late in the fourth quarter, the worry beads were being polished with constant and frantic rubbing as the Wildcats made their unsurprising charge at us and the title.

Scott Fisher and Vlahov just wouldn't let the Wildcats fade away and they worked their butts off to whittle our lead to six. The Wildcats had us on the back foot, like the Christians trying to keep away from the lions just long enough for luck or fate to intervene. As it was, the lions Perth sent after us were so close we could smell their jungle breath. Lanard Copeland missed a free-throw and the Wildcats responded with a three-pointer to cut our lead in half. I'm not sure if 'panic' described our state of mind, but 'anxiety' might have understated it.

Then I got fouled and went to the free-throw line. In those days, when a team was in the bonus situation after the opposition had fouled too many times in a quarter, we would shoot a one-and-one from the free-throw line. Simply, if you made the first, you got a second shot. If you missed the first, it was play on. I missed the first free-throw and the Wildcats rebounded the ball, looking to cut the margin to one or tie the game with a three-pointer. Andrew Vlahov decided to go for the tie.

The clock was down inside ten seconds when Vlahov launched his shot from the top of the three-point arc. With the ball in the air, there was a very real sense that it was going in, the crowd was going to explode and we would be blown to smithereens. The hoop gods were with us. That ball did everything except go in the basket. I've often thought about that shot and wondered what emotions Vlahov must have felt on seeing that ball take a U-turn off the ring and fall into my hands with about five or six seconds left. I imagine that Vlahov would have replayed the shot in his mind for many years and thought 'If only ...' I sometimes still get the shakes thinking how devastating it would have been for the Tigers had Vlahov's shot gone in. Situations like that might have been easier to deal with if the shot had been an airball or had been blocked. To get so close is tormenting.

I secured the ball and waited for the Wildcats to foul and send me on another trip to the free-throw line. The Wildcats' tactic was desperate but logically sound. If I missed the first free-throw, which was entirely possible given our last two unsuccessful attempts, they could still tie the game and go to overtime. If I made one, the game was over. Perth called a time-out to set up a play if they got the rebound. All I could think about in the Tigers huddle was the upcoming free-throw. 'Just make one,' I kept saying to myself. 'Just make one.' When you've taken and made thousands of free-throws in games, at training and just shooting around as a kid, it shouldn't be a big deal. When you've got a championship on the line, nerves tend to complicate things a bit.

I was so nervous about missing the free-throw and Perth going down and making a three that I went into some kind of meltdown. I couldn't control my body and wondered how I was going to make the shot. All I had to do was go to the line, aim at the back of the ring and shoot. Nothing else. I just told myself to rely on the technique that had been good for thousands of free-throws and hope it would be good for at least one more. I just had to make the first shot. I made it. We were up four and, unless we committed a dumb foul while Perth made a three-pointer, we couldn't lose.

The sense of relief when that first free-throw went in was just enormous. But the drama was not finished. As I was about to release my second shot, somebody in the crowd threw a big ball of paper onto the court right in front of me. Distracted, I tried to pull back the shot, but it got out of my hand and missed. After the Wildcats rebounded the ball the referees stopped the game so they could clear the ball of paper off the floor. I thought I should have got another shot, but the refs gave the ball to Perth from the side, just to prolong the game and the minuscule possibility of something going wrong. I knew we couldn't lose, but was worried not everyone was aware of the situation. So I was just told everyone, 'Don't touch them. Just completely let them go.' The Wildcats made a basket on the buzzer, but it didn't matter. Game over. The Tigers were NBL champions.

At the final buzzer relief and jubilation immediately burst from every Tigers player, coach and supporter. It was exhilarating and it was exhausting. We had spent every drop of energy getting to this point, yet the adrenalin boost from winning made us forget about any pain or fatigue. Sharing this moment with my team-mates was important, but sharing it with my dad was paramount. That was when I put the headlock on him, as a way of hiding the tears of elation that were spilling from me. It was a Kodak moment, but I don't need any photographic reminders of that special embrace that hopefully showed my dad how much I love him and what he's done for me, the Tigers and basketball.

One of the few good things about playing that title game so far away from home was that we got to share the immediate after-game celebrations with the people who were really close to the team. There were a few board members with us, but in the locker room it was just the team, the coaches and support staff sharing moments of reflection and revelry before the media arrived on the scene to record our glory.

Most people expected us to be in the grand final in 1993. That said, we did not have a totally dominant season, but we had a very strong team. We had a great starting five with Lanard Copeland, Robert Sibley, Dave Simmons, Mark Bradtke and me, while Warrick Giddey, Stephen Whitehead and Ray Gordon came off the bench ahead of Andrew Walter and Nick Tenner. It was a good mix of people and players who created a balance, had a good understanding of their roles and combined for a great result.

We didn't stick around Perth after the game. We headed for the airport and a flight home to a reception I never thought I'd live to see. The game had been live on television, so the club organised for a big screen at a venue so as many family and fans as possible could watch together. When we touched down at Melbourne Airport at about 11 p.m., it was like they had all made a convoy to greet us. We walked off the plane with the trophy to be met by hordes of celebrating Tigers fans and for a few minutes in our lives we knew how the Beatles and Rolling Stones lived for much of theirs. There must have been about two thousand people there and the place was just going off. The booing in Perth had been drowned out by the cheering back in Melbourne.

chapter fourteen

A SHOT WITH
THE BULLETS

GOOD though Brett Brown is as a basketball coach, he might be even better as a salesman. As a coach, he won an NBL Championship with the North Melbourne Giants, he went to the Olympics as a Boomers assistant and he has worked in the NBA with the San Antonio Spurs. As a salesman, he was one of the best, topping sales in the greater Boston region for the AT&T telephone company in the United States before coming to Australia via a coaching stint with Auckland in New Zealand. But possibly his biggest and best sell job was convincing the Washington Bullets to sign me to a couple of NBA ten-day contracts.

During January 1994, Brett and I were working a school holiday basketball camp for kids at the Bankstown Stadium in Sydney. It was hot, it was the NBL off-season and I wondered if I really wanted to be there. Then I heard someone yelling: 'Drew! Drew!' Brett was heading towards me waving a sheet of paper in the air. It was an expression of interest in me playing in the NBA.

The approach came right out of the blue and, as luck would have it, only got to me because of Washington's connection with Brett. Brett was coaching the North Melbourne Giants and somebody from their office called to say there was a fax from the Bullets, asking about a couple of players they were interested in. One of those players was me.

The Bullets (now the Wizards) had been decimated by injuries, their season was long over in terms of contending for the play-offs and they decided to look at a few players on short-term deals. Brett whacked on his salesman's hat and went to work on the Bullets and their general manager John Nash, pitching me as though I was their only option. I shudder to think what he said. I sometimes wonder whether they thought they were getting a cross between Larry Bird, Michael Jordan and Magic Johnson ... which might have explained their sceptical looks when they eventually saw me. Either way, the Bullets took a punt on me, although they didn't exactly stake the ranch with the ten-day contract they offered me. For them it was a low-risk, low-investment venture and for me it was a chance to play in the NBA and pick up some handy cash. Neither party had anything to lose. Everyone was set, except our good friends at the Immigration Department.

I have battled some pretty tough defenders and double teams in my career, but I don't think any were as frustrating as the red tape involved with immigration laws. Before I could think about taking an NBA three-pointer, it was revealed the visa process would take longer than the ten-day contract and the injured guys would be back on the floor. The Bullets decided to forget it. For the time being. In a piece of worthy foresight, my visa was processed in case another opportunity came up. At least then I could pack a bag and go. Not that I had the suitcase sitting at the front door and a taxi to the airport on standby.

It was yet another setback for me in terms of getting a crack at the NBA and I was almost resigned to putting the bat in the rack. I had been the last man cut with the Seattle Supersonics before the 1989–90 season and then almost walked into a job with the Portland Trail Blazers. The Blazers had wanted me to go to veterans' training camp in 1990, but that went in the bin when I suffered the blood clot in my shoulder that September. But in early 1992, the Blazers renewed contact. I came home to the flashing light on the answering machine and was shocked to hear a message from Brad Greenberg, the Trail Blazers' director of player personnel. Portland was heading to the play-offs, but Greenberg's brief message indicated they had a hole that needed filling. I initially thought it was somebody pulling a prank, but I returned the call and sure enough, it was the real Brad Greenberg and his enquiry was genuine: Portland had an injury and they needed a perimeter shooter as emergency cover. It was simply a matter of wearing a uniform as a contingency and Greenberg was up front about it. The Blazers were ready to go if I was, but the folks at US immigration were not. Getting the necessary green card would take more time than Portland had, so the deal was knocked on the head, just like this latest approach from the Bullets. Three shots, three air-balls. I was ready to get on with the NBL.

While I got ready for the 1994 NBL season and the Melbourne Tigers' championship defence, the Washington Bullets were thinking of ways to keep their roster full. Players had dropped with injury all season. Rex Chapman had dislocated his ankle, Kenny Walker and Larry Stewart were on the injured reserve and the Bullets wanted Calbert Cheaney to join them if the NBA would allow an expanded injured reserve. Over the course of the season, the Bullets used twenty players and none appeared in all eighty-two games. So they were really banged up and desperate. They must have been because they called me for help. It wasn't a complicated conversation. The Bullets asked whether I was interested in going over for a ten-day contract. I agreed. It was a simple negotiation and I flew to Washington DC to play in the NBA. This time the only complication was the need to abdicate as King of Moomba before I left Australia. The organisers of Melbourne's March festival had appointed me as the Moomba monarch to lead the parade in full kit of gown and crown. Unfortunately for the Moomba folks, when it came to dressing up or dressing for the NBA, there was no contest.

I didn't go to Washington with any great expectations. I was fully aware it was an on-the-job tryout situation for me. If I did any good and didn't embarrass myself, there might have been the chance to return to the Bullets' next pre-season camp. Bullets general manager John Nash had communicated with my dad, so he knew what he was getting and pretty much guaranteed I would get a second ten-day contract when the first expired. Under NBA rules, teams have to either sign a player outright or release him after his second ten-day contract. I knew the Bullets weren't going to sign me for the rest of the season, but that was fine by me.

The only hitch on arrival in Washington was that I could not officially join the team. The Bullets had a player named Ron Anderson on a ten-day deal to help cover injuries and I could not sign my contract until Anderson's ten days expired. It was like the Bullets tried to hide me until then. I watched the first game on television in the locker room with John Nash, the GM, as he talked me through it. There was no reason given why we weren't behind the bench or in the stands and I didn't ask. That's the experience of being a 28-year-old rookie. I couldn't train with the team until I had signed, either. I was able to do some physical testing, so they could gauge what kind of Downunder Adonis they had. Throughout the Australian summer, I did some weights work and I was in good shape. I must also have been pumped up with adrenalin and pent-up nervous energy.

Lying on my back, I had to perform as many leg presses as I could, lifting half my body weight. I hadn't exactly shown I was Mr

Universe in other tests, but I attacked the leg presses with enthusiasm. Too much enthusiasm. When you talk about pushing the limits, I went beyond the stratosphere of mine. I pushed and pushed and pushed. By the time I finished, A. Gaze was to be written on the wall chart as the Bullets' record holder for maximum leg presses.

Pumped from my record-setting performance, I headed for the court and shot around by myself for a while. It was good that I enjoyed it because I could hardly walk, let alone shoot a basketball or lift a weight with my legs later that night. It was the worst muscle pain I have ever experienced. After I cooled down, my legs just killed me. I lay in bed that night unable to move, knowing I was in big trouble. If it wasn't some kind of paralysis of the legs, it was almost certainly the end of my contract with the Bullets because I wouldn't be able to get out of bed for training the next morning. I went to sleep, hoping it would ease. When I woke in the middle of the night to visit the toilet, I barely made it.

At least by the morning I could walk. Barely. It was walking in the fashion of a slow, stooped, eighty-year-old peasant woman loaded down with firewood in the mountains of Peru. As far as working out with the Bullets and coach Wes Unseld for the first time was concerned, I had no chance. So while one side of my mind dealt with the pain in my legs, the other side tried to come up with excuses why I couldn't work out. I didn't have one, except the truth. As the Bullets finished their team training, I was summoning the courage to tell Wes Unseld, one of the toughest players in the history of the NBA, that I couldn't practise because I had sore legs. I was sure Wes would have one word for me: wimp. Fortunately, and this is why I believe there must be some kind of god, Wes had another word: dentist. He had a problem with a tooth and needed to get it looked at. Wes apologised for cancelling the work-out, and I could have kissed and hugged him. Instead, I did my best to look disappointed. I waited for Wes to leave and I limped out behind him, happy the fickle finger of fate was on my side for once.

The finger of fate turned out to be the middle digit with a mind for revenge. While Wes Unseld's dentist's appointment let me off the hook, the pain in my legs had not totally subsided before my first NBA game against the Denver Nuggets a day later. As I got changed, I noticed the trainer attending some of the players, so I asked if he had anything that might help my legs. He gave me some liniment-type stuff to rub in and warned me to wash my hands when I'd finished. The first thing that happened when I rubbed this stuff onto my legs was that they went from being really sore to being on fire. This stuff, whatever it was, was stronger than Arnold Schwarzenegger. My legs glowed like embers and my face was starting to match – whether from the spreading heat or from embarrassment, I wasn't sure. Maybe both. Fortunately, I still had the presence of mind to wash my hands when I finished. Which I did right before I visited the toilet cubicle for some last-minute, tension-relieving, pre-game preparations just before Wes Unseld's team talk.

I took a seat with the rest of the Bullets and waited for Wes to provide last-minute instructions and go over the Nuggets. But before he could get warmed up, I was already burning up. In all the wrong areas. It wasn't my legs that were the problem; it was my bum. Even though I had washed my hands, some residue of the liniment had persisted and had obviously made its way to an inner cheek, if you get my drift. The delayed reaction occurred as I sat right in front of the coach. Hot though it was, I thought I would get through it. But while Wes Unseld talked Xs and Os, the burning sensation just got hotter and hotter and hotter. As the new guy, I tried to be cool in front of the team, but underneath that calm veneer I was a panicky kid whose bum was burning. I didn't want to stick my hand down my strides and soothe my backside in front of everyone, but I had a sauna sweat going. I had no hope of concentrating on the coach and as soon as he finished I pelted into the shower room to douse the flames. It wasn't the pre-game preparation I had in mind for my NBA debut and I still get nervous when somebody opens a tube of Dencorub.

Even on a struggling, banged-up, somewhat dysfunctional team that was 18–41 and going nowhere in a hurry, I didn't think I would get much opportunity. Given I had had little preparation with the team and didn't have an intimate knowledge of the offensive structure, which added to my nervousness, I was prepared to sit and wait for my chance. I didn't wait long. Wes Unseld called my name and I checked into the game with 3 minutes 58 seconds left in the first quarter. I finished with four points (two free-throws and a long two) and an assist and thought I did okay without sending shock waves through the NBA. Perhaps the most surprising thing was that the Bullets beat the Denver Nuggets, 100–95, in front a sell-out home crowd of 18,756.

I made a modest contribution against the Nuggets, but I didn't have a feel for the offensive structure at all, which didn't help. That was okay, especially since coach Wes Unseld praised my defence to the media afterwards. Either way, it became quite clear from that first game that some of the boys on this team, at that stage of the season, were out there for themselves. They were keen and eager to win, but if a situation presented a shooting option and a passing option, they would take the shooting option whether or not it was the right or good option. Adhering to the ideal of the saying 'there's no "I" in team' was not particularly strong for this group. Nor did the situation get much better during the seven games I played during my two ten-day contracts. Not that the environment encouraged the situation to get better. Over the twenty days I officially spent with the team, I reckon we had what I considered one proper training session. The rest of the time, we had walk-throughs and shoot-arounds. With all the injuries and roster changes, it was understandable that practice was disrupted and the constant losing took its toll on enthusiasm, morale and camaraderie.

Even though I never really got used to the Bullets' structure, I played enough that, in an extended situation with more opportunity, I felt I could play in the NBA. It was just that the Bullets players were in what you might call survival mode. I don't want to be disrespectful, but their style of play was like a highly talented game of pick-up ball. There was a distinct lack of sophistication about the offence; it was power and athleticism with little time for subtlety. It was a freelance game with quick-hit moves like isolation plays and a two-man game while the other three players on offence stood to one side and watched. That was not my strength, so I ran around and came off a few screens, hoping to be on the end of a pass for a shot. It wasn't what I was used to with the Tigers and, to be fair, I didn't expect the Bullets to change for me.

The NBA has evolved, both on and off the floor, as my time with the San Antonio Spurs in 1999 proved. The Bullets' training facilities were fine without being over the top, the US Air Arena, where we played home games, was old, we split our travel between commercial and chartered flights and the Bullets owner, Abe Pollin, had a reputation for keeping his hands in his pockets. These days, everything is first-class in the NBA. Expense rarely seems to be a barrier when it comes to training facilities, state-of-the-art venues and charter flights in luxurious private aircraft.

Overall, being with the Bullets was an excellent learning experience. People reckon they know the NBA because they watch television, read magazines and visit the Internet. That's not even getting close to what the NBA is really like. You cannot help but be impressed by the athletes playing the game in the NBA. The pace, strength and athleticism is way, way above that in the NBL and to see it up close and compete against it takes you to another level of appreciation. You might think the NBL is a good league with good players and athletes, and it is. But the NBA is another world.

Even how team-mates co-exist in the NBA is a lot different to the friendly mateship culture we have and cherish in Australia. Most of the guys on the Bullets were team-mates only in the sense that they wore the same uniform on game nights. In Australia we did things together. We ate as a team and hung out together, forming bonds and friendships. In the NBA it wasn't that easy: any out-sider was viewed as a threat to someone's job and the next phone call could be to say you'd been traded to another team. Most of these blokes made a lot of money and lived a good life, but they didn't seem that close and there didn't seem to be a lot of camaraderie among the team. The NBA glitz and glamour you see on television was far removed from the reality I experienced with the Bullets. It was a lot different in front of the telly 20,000 kilometres away in Melbourne to how it was at the coalface, seeing the revolving door of players coming and going, seeing the dog-eat-dog attitudes, the media pressure, players trying to live up to massive expectations and massive salaries and others who were just trying to survive in the system and stay in the NBA.

Don't get me wrong. There were some good players and some good blokes with the Bullets: Calbert Cheaney, Rex Chapman, Kevin Duckworth, Gheorghe Muresan, Pervis Ellison, Kenny Walker, Don McLean, and Doug Overton who played in Australia for the Wollongong Hawks before he went to the NBA. They were all pretty decent guys, who knew they had to adjust and follow the cut-throat, perhaps mercenary, nature and culture of the NBA rather than reveal their true nature as people. In some respects, these guys had the chance to make a lot of money to set up them-selves and their families for life. Since some of them came from poor and underprivileged backgrounds, they were going to be protective of their sudden wealth and fame and would not give it up without a fight. The way most protected the golden goose was through their stats, especially their scoring, even to the detriment of the team.

Even though I knew Doug Overton from when he played in the NBL as an import with Wollongong, there was a distance between us in Washington. He was polite and friendly, but he didn't really go out of his way to make me feel welcome, either. There was almost an element of competing with team-mates for survival, about trying to keep your job and doing whatever it takes. On the other hand, there was the night, maybe my last with the Bullets, when a group of us went out and we somehow took a wrong turn and ended up in a gentleman's establishment. okay. It was a strip joint. I was minding my own business when one of the less attractive females, shall we say, started paying me some over-the-odds attention. I tried to explain she had it wrong, that I hadn't paid for her performance. But she told me it was a gift and gestured towards a group of blokes. A few of the Bullets had chipped in for a going-away present. Which just went to show perhaps they did have a heart and a sense of team. Or maybe they were glad to see me leave.

Perhaps the best moment of those twenty days with the Bullets was when I answered a knock at the door of my hotel room the night before my first game. It was my mate Grant Cadee, who had flown to the US without telling me. He wanted to see me play in the NBA and figured he would surprise me. Even after only a few days in Washington, I was never so glad to see a friend. I wouldn't say I was disillusioned by my experience with the Bullets but when the second ten-day contract finished, I wasn't bitterly disappointed. I could have kept going had I needed to, but it was a grind, even for that short period.

One other aspect of my time with the Bullets was the situation involving coach Wes Unseld. Unseld was a quality person and a long-time favourite son of the Bullets, but during my time there, tension existed between him and general manager John Nash. The pair did not exactly agree on players and the future of the team – which, in the NBA, was usually the responsibility of the GM. I think Unseld felt that public comments by Nash did not help him coach players who might have felt they were on the way out. It also seemed Unseld had an unusually big workload for a head coach and there wasn't a lot of help for him, which would have added to the pressure. In fact, I'm sure the pressure had got to Unseld by the time I finished my stint with the Bullets. So much so that Unseld reckoned I was reluctant to shoot and he praised my defence. Which made him one of the few people to have ever said those things in the same sentence before or since.

Another shortcoming within the Bullets, and the NBA at the time, was the lack of knowledge or recognition of foreign players and respect for them. During the 1980s and early 90s, the number of foreign players in the NBA was minimal. Now they are common in a league that has become much more cosmopolitan and worldly-wise when it comes to marketing, media and recruiting. In the 1980s and 90s, foreigners were considered oddities and teams played safe with home-grown talent. These days it's different as the NBA starts to embrace the global game. Not before time, either.

Ultimately my time with the Bullets was a great experience. I was twenty-eight, closing fast on twenty-nine, and did not really think I would go back to the NBA. The Bullets invited me back for training camp, but the Tigers were in the semi-finals and I didn't want to bail out. People have had a hard time understanding my reluctance to jump at NBA offers, but for me, it's what matters most at the time. It's about making and sticking with a commitment and most of the time what mattered and what I was committed to was the Melbourne Tigers. I left the Bullets satisfied that, looking at it as objectively as I could, I could play at the NBA level. A lot of other players could, too – if they got the right mix of circumstances, role, team and being in the right place at the right time.

One example of being in the wrong place at the wrong time was when Melinda, who was pregnant with our first child Courtney, and I were on the way home to Australia from Washington. Melinda had joined me for the second of the ten-day contracts, recognising the special opportunity we both had. It stopped being special when we paused in LA for some shopping and a look around. We had time to kill between leaving the hotel and checking in at the airport on our last day. So we packed all our bags into a hire car and headed to Beverly Hills for lunch and shopping. Sounds good? Too good to be true. When we got back to the car, everything was gone. All our bags, Walkman, baby clothes, airline tickets, passports and my Bullets playing uniform. Gone. All of it. The thief was so good, he even took the lint from the mat in the boot. This was a big downer to end the experience. It was just a pity Brett Brown didn't sell insurance.

chapter fifteen

ALL GREEK TO ME

THE Greek language in its written form looks like somebody dropped a Scrabble box into a blender for five minutes then just poured the contents onto a page. It's impossible, unless you are Greek or a linguist, to decipher. But when you peer out the window of a fourth-floor hotel room and can clearly make out your photo on the newspaper poster at the street vendor's footpath stall, you can bet you also have something to do with the headline, whether you can read it or not. Even being unable to read a syllable of Greek, I knew exactly what the story was about. It's not hard to know when you have supposedly accused Greek basketball of being corrupt, organised, bent, on the take and open to bribery. That will usually get a headline or two whether you're in Greece or Greenland. As I peered out that window, calling over team-mate John Shasky to confirm that I wasn't hallucinating, I would have gladly swapped Greece for a season in Greenland if I'd known what was coming, especially the need to sleep with a kitchen knife for protection.

From when the controversy started to when it ended, I just wanted to get out of Greece. I was getting towards the end of the 1995 season with Apollon Patras and, in an interview with then *Herald Sun* basketball writer Chris Appleby, I made what I thought were innocuous remarks about some aspects of Greek basketball – specifically about the attitude of always looking, sometimes to ridiculous lengths, for a scapegoat in defeat. As I told Chris Appleby, every time we lost a game it was the same line from the fans: 'We don't have money, we cannot pay the refs, so we lose.' Then you'd get in a taxi and hear from the driver: 'We don't have money, we can't pay the refs.' I didn't know whether that was true or not, but at the time there was a cultural belief that bribing referees and officials, or at least doing them special favours, went on. I never saw one single sliver of evidence that it did, nor was there one game when I thought the refs were bent. There were games when I thought the refs were terrible and we got screwed, but I never saw any evidence of cheating, even though the theory was rampant and kept alive by the Greeks, which is what I explained to Chris Appleby for his story.

Some of those theories had developed into folkloric tales of how certain players had managed to gain Greek citizenship, like one of the young players on our team. The story was that the kid, who was born in Yugoslavia, gained his citizenship after the club got the town drunk to say that he was the boy's father, then got someone else to verify it and another person to issue the naturalisation papers. That was the story and you've got to place the emphasis on 'story'. There were so many stories that you started to wonder whether there was some truth to them. Otherwise the Greeks were better storytellers than the Brothers Grimm.

Certainly, the conspiracy theorists were never short of material during a Greek basketball season. Like the big televised Euroleague game between Olympiakos and a Russian team. For a while I couldn't believe what I saw. The Russians had only five players. A complete team had arrived in Athens the day before the game, but half of the team and the coach suffered food poisoning. So while the five fit players were getting their butts whipped by Olympiakos, the other five had their heads in toilet bowls at the hotel. Anyway, two players fouled out, leaving the Russians with three on the court and the game turning into a blowout for the Greeks in front of fifteen thousand fanatical supporters. Then, with about five minutes left, Olympiakos pulled two players to leave the game as a farcical, three-on-three, full-court contest. Next day the rumour mill cranked up to high with the notion that somebody had spiked the Russians' food. It might have been coincidence that they got sick, it might have been the airline food or it might have been a virus back home in Russia, but there was never a conspiracy theory left unspoken in Greece.

That was the mindset among the Greeks that I tried to relate to Chris Appleby. The culture meant there was always drama in Greek basketball because of the emotion and importance attached to it by the fans and the community. There was a lot of money at stake, particularly with large clubs like Olympiakos and Panathanaikos, who spend big with the intention of winning big. It's like that throughout Europe, though perhaps not as fanatically and dramatically as in Greece. Throughout Europe, football is king, followed by basketball. In Greece at that time, basketball was the number one game, with the emotion, passion and media scrutiny to match. It's similar to how most Victorians regard the AFL – only the Greeks tend to get a bit more hysterical about it. I found it to be even more so in far-flung Patras, which had no soccer team to share even a smidgen of the spotlight. Unfortunately, my explanation to Chris Appleby might have been lost in the translation. The story that appeared in the newspaper under his by-line said I accused the Greeks of being corrupt. Which might have caused a mere ripple of interest, except for Melbourne's large Greek community.

A few days later, as our game ended, a couple of Greek journalists ran up to me on the court, demanding, 'What is this you say in the

Australian newspaper that Greek basketball is corrupt?' We'd just finished the game, so I wasn't exactly ready for that question, but I told them I didn't believe I had said that. I couldn't speak Greek and they only spoke a little English, but I tried to explain as best I could. Obviously, from what transpired, I didn't do a very good job.

From that impromptu post-game news conference, things moved more quickly than Lanard Copeland on a fastbreak. When I got home that night, I called my mum and dad to ask what was going on in Melbourne with this story. While I was on the phone, I had an eye on the TV. Next minute, my head appeared over the newsreader's shoulder. I didn't know what was being said, but I knew it was about me and I knew it wasn't about how many points I'd scored that night. As I channel surfed, I stopped at another station with a news ticker moving across the bottom of the screen. The only word I understood on the ticker was 'Gaze'. Next day when I was on the front page of the Greek newspapers, I well and truly knew I was up to my neck in trouble. Which is a fair whack of trouble when you're 201 centimetres.

When I arrived at training, the players asked: 'What is this? What you say this for?' I explained my take on the culture and that was what I had told the journalist. I don't know if they bought my story, but it never seemed to be a major issue within the team. Maybe it was because there were already conspiracy theories evolving about how and why the story had been written. We were heading towards the play-offs, so there was speculation that it had been created by another team wanting to upset my relationship with Patras. There was talk that it was contrived by a team trying to sign me for the next season. Why worry about the truth when there was always a conspiracy theory to fall back on?

There were more questions from the media when we arrived at Athens airport to fly to Thessaloniki for our next game against Aris. About twenty journalists and TV crew fired questions before we took off and there were another twenty media guys with more of the

All Greek to Me

same when we landed. It was like cramming all my NBL media commitments from one season into a few hours. Fortunately, I was able to get a little peace and quiet in my hotel room, until I drew back the curtains next morning and saw that newspaper poster with my head on it. The way I felt, it might as well have been a WANTED poster. Worst of all, I got the feeling some Greeks had no problem whether I was captured dead or alive.

For the next two weeks, I was convinced elements were at work to make sure my trip back to Australia would be in a pine box. Much of it, if not all of it, was the product of an active, rattled mind that believed the corruption accusations were reason enough for somebody to keep me quiet. So for two weeks, I treated every noise, every out-of-the-ordinary situation, with dread, fear and over-the-top caution.

It all started when, out of the blue, the phone in my apartment was disconnected. I knew the account was paid up, but when I picked up the receiver, there was nothing. I thought, 'Is this a penalty by some disgruntled phone company employee/basketball fan for my comments? Is somebody coming and I can't call for help?' Whatever the reason, it was an uncomfortable feeling that got worse in the silence of the apartment. The heater in the apartment made clicking noises, which I had never noticed before. It had probably been doing this since I arrived, but now it surely meant something. Had somebody tampered with it while I was at training? Would it explode? My head was swirling and I decided to take out some insurance.

My apartment in Patras was quite big, with three bedrooms (plenty of room for intruders to hide while waiting to ambush me), so I dragged a mattress down from one of the bedrooms to the living room. My plan was to sleep on the living room floor and at least confront any intruders. Then I made sure the television was on twenty-four hours a day, so it seemed somebody was always home or there was more than one person in the apartment. That also helped take my mind off this whole ridiculous situation. Lastly, I went to the kitchen and got the biggest carving knife I could find and put it next to the bed. The only problem was figuring out how I would use the knife. If I waved it at whoever was supposed to come for me, maybe that would be enough to ward them off.

While I was prepared and armed inside Fortress Gaze, there was still one surprise waiting for me outside the apartment block. The club had given me a BMW 5-series to drive and I always made sure I locked it wherever I parked. One morning during this saga, I went downstairs to go to training and found the car unlocked. I couldn't guarantee that it was the only time I had forgotten to lock the car, but I didn't think that at the time. My first thought was that somebody had broken into the car and tampered with it, maybe cut the brake lines. Then I thought somebody may have connected a bomb that would explode when I turned the ignition key. Everybody's seen those movies and there I was, standing beside my car, not wanting to even open the door for fear of getting blown to smithereens. Nor was it a situation I could get help with. I couldn't exactly ring the club and say 'I think someone's put a bomb in my car.' They'd have thought I'd lost my mind. I thought I had. So I sucked up my gut, held my breath and gently opened the door. Nothing. Phew! Next step was to start it. If anybody was watching from the apartment windows, they were treated to a Monty Python skit. I had one leg in the car and one leg out, trying to lean away from the car as I prepared to turn the key. As if that was going to help in case of an explosion. I finally, tentatively, turned the key, the car started and I drove to training, making sure the brakes worked well before I reached every intersection.

Funny and ridiculous as it is now, I lived in genuine fear at the time. There was no question, with the benefit of hindsight, that it was a self-inflicted situation, with my mind playing games. But after hearing the tall tales of what teams will do to make sure they win games, make the play-offs and avoid relegation, it was no wonder. According to the stories, exaggerated or otherwise, people were capable of bribery, food poisoning and whatever else. So what was to stop them getting rid of the skinny Aussie with the loose tongue? At best, they might have just cut that tongue out. The funny thing was my team-mates' anger peaked at a small grumble and, aside from the massive media attention, that was it. There were never any threats of retribution or violence against me. The fans spat on you, abused you and threw stuff at you during games as a matter of course every week, so there was nothing different there. But my mind had a field day. Talk about conspiracy theories. I had become more Greek than the Greeks.

One thing about Greek basketball, and perhaps all of Greece, is that the sense of organisation can be as jumbled as their alphabet. Apollon Patras was a professional club and the players were paid decent money, but we never had things as simple as training uniforms and there was a distinct lack of knowledge and resources. Nor did we ever get paid on time. I did get all my money for the season, which is never a given in Europe, but I never got a payment on time. The club always had an excuse: they were waiting for television money, waiting for sponsors' money. They were all worthy excuses, but they used them all, and more than once.

At least I always knew when I was just about to get my money. All I had to do was listen for a motor scooter pulling up outside the apartment and a knock at the door a minute or so later. The first time I got paid in Greece, I didn't know what the hell was going on. There was a knock on the door and when I answered, I recognised a bloke from the club office. He couldn't speak English and I couldn't speak Greek, so the talk was minimal. But he got my attention when he slung off his backpack, unzipped it and dumped US$25,000 in cash onto my kitchen table. Then he just walked out, jumped on his Vespa and presumably went to make his next delivery.

There it sat on the table: US$25,000 in US$20 bills, like I had just made the biggest withdrawal from the world's biggest ATM. But what the hell was I going to do with so much cash? When I played in Italy, I would go to the bank and wire my payments back home.

In Greece there were apparently laws about transferring money internationally and it wasn't so easy to do. What I had to do was wait until somebody came to visit me and I'd send some cash home to Australia with them. In the meantime, I stashed the cash in various places around the apartment. Some would go under the toilet seat, some would go in the closet, some behind a kitchen cabinet. I made sure to spread it around in the hope that if I got robbed the burglars wouldn't find all the cash. It probably wasn't ideal, but you do what you have to do. The other aspect of these payments was tax. I asked about tax, the club gave me a form (written in Greek naturally), I signed it and it was sent off somewhere, I got it back with official-looking stamps and signatures, and whatever money I received was mine to keep. It all seemed haphazard and dicey, the way they went about it, but there's got to be an element of trust and I trusted they were doing the right thing.

The other thing that seemed a bit risky was the way the office guy rocked up on his Vespa with a backpack of cash. What would have happened if he was knocked off his scooter? What if he was robbed? What would happen to our pay then? It was all a bit of a gamble, which seemed in keeping with the way things were done. The Greeks have grown up with this and are conditioned to it, but when you're not used to it, it can be very amusing and sometimes frustrating.

One day, Patras's other import, John Shasky, refused to train because he had not been paid for so long. He sat out training and they gave him a little bit to get back on the court. If John hadn't gone on his mini-strike, he would have got nothing. We were always being told 'tomorrow, tomorrow', but tomorrow never seemed to arrive. The longest I ever waited to be paid was about five weeks. We were due our next payment and still hadn't got the previous one.

It is not uncommon for European teams to withhold money when a team is not winning. Somehow, the team officials believe it will make the players try harder. But as far as I can see, the negative impact on morale just has the opposite effect. They think not to getting paid is an incentive. It's not. It just adds to the general chaos. When you sign with a European team, the base deal involves accommodation, a car and a salary. But let's face it, nobody ever goes to play in Europe for free board and the chance to drive a car. We were there for the money, even if it was delivered on a Vespa.

I was signed by Apollon Patras midway through the 1994–95 season and played fourteen of the twenty-six regular-season games. Not that – surprise, surprise – it all went so smoothly from the start. I was supposed to replace Reggie Jordan as one of Apollon Patras's two imports, but when I arrived, Reggie was still there. Apparently, Reggie had to sign off on his deal to complete his release, but that hadn't been done, so Reggie had to play the next game. I had trained all week on the assumption I would play and Reggie was nowhere to be seen until he walked in on game day ready to play. I was out, he was in. Don't ask me how this all worked; it just did.

My first game for Apollon Patras was on the road at Thessaloniki against PAOK and we lost. It was a difficult situation for me because I was coming out of the NBL off-season and hadn't been doing much when I got the offer to go to Greece. I had about fifteen points, which was okay considering the circumstances, but making a good first impression at home was more important. I had something like twenty-eight points, we won and we went from there. Impressing the home fans mattered because although they were usually loyal and supportive, they could also be a bit feral. During one game, things got so bad, with coins and missiles being thrown onto the court, that we had to run and take cover under the Perspex shelter that protected the team benches while the club president got on the microphone to try to calm the crowd.

The season was definitely a mediocre one for Apollon Patras. We didn't get relegated, which was the club's first goal, and we made the play-offs, although in Greece, almost every team makes the play-offs. We lost to Aris 2–1 in the best-of-three first round play-off series and it was something of a shock when we pinched one game. There was certainly a sizeable gap between the haves and have-nots in Greek basketball, where Olympiakos, Panathanaikos, PAOK and AEK usually bang the big drums and the others tap their tambourines. There were a lot of good players in the league, which featured a slow-down, physical style of game, but I averaged about 30 points per game and savoured the experience on and off the basketball court. While there was never a shortage of dramas, it was a good overall experience in a beautiful and historic location.

Patras, with its population of about 200,000, is situated in the south-west of Greece about two hundred kilometres from Athens and is an important commercial centre and busy port, servicing the Ionian Islands and Italy in particular. The city, which dates back more than three thousand years and endured more than one invasion and occupation by Turkish forces, is divided between the Old section, with its landmark Venetian castle, and the New section, with its modern shops and port. During the reign of the Roman Emperor Nero, the patron saint of Scotland, St Andrew, visited Patras on a mission for Christianity. Unfortunately, St Andrew suffered a martyr's death by crucifixion.

It seemed the Apollon Patras fans knew their history. There were many times when they wanted to re-enact the crucifixion of St Andrew, using referees and opposition players for the sacrifice. In short, the fans were crazy. Our 4500-seat stadium was an ample playground for a male-dominated crowd whose raucous chants often featured gross profanity, suggesting an opposition player had an incestuous relationship with his mother, or did something against the law with a goat. They were hard-core fans and only needed the most obvious call to go against the home team to bay for the referees' blood. They had no hesitation launching coins and other missiles onto the court in protest and disgust, which didn't always cause the game to stop while the floor was cleared. Unless it got really bad, the refs would allow play to continue; otherwise they would highlight the pandemonium. Plus, the sooner the game was over, the sooner they could escape. Unless there was a barrage of drachma, the refs kept play going and kicked the coins to the side as they walked up and down the court.

Getting spat on was nothing unusual, either. There was one game against Daphne, which had my former Seton Hall team-mate Nick Katsikis on the roster. The gym only held about five hundred people with three or four rows of seating around the court. It was claustrophobic, especially when we went off at half-time leading. That was the signal for some of the crowd near the player tunnel to lean as close as they could and deposit spit bombs on us. The local police, who seemed to outnumber the fans, did nothing about this despicable behaviour from the local crowd.

When I first saw this crowd behaviour, it seemed idiotic, stupid, disgusting and against all standards of normal demeanour in sport. But in some quirky way, once I got to understand the culture, I respected the passion the people had for the game and their teams. Not that I condoned their behaviour; I just understood it better. My interpretation was they weren't doing it to hurt someone or to be destructive. It was part of the passion and so different to the NBL. In places like Townsville or Adelaide, which have the most vocal crowds in the NBL, the home team will be at the free-throw line and everyone will go quiet to help the shooter's concentration. In Greece, it's the opposite. People clap and get excited as if their energy will transfer to the player. It took me a while to get used to this when I was at the free-throw line, as it did the whole crowd thing in Greece. We have an expectation and belief Australian footy fans lead the way, in the world of sport, with their devotion, passion and commitment, but the Europeans are much more demonstrative with their team support. It was exciting to be part of it when things were going well. But when we struggled, the fans vented their frustrations and it was not nice to be on the receiving end.

In keeping with the crowd atmosphere, the Apollon Patras coach, Kostas Petropolis, was pretty fiery when the mood took him. He was a good coach and wore his heart on his sleeve. One night after we lost at home there was an almighty din coming from outside our locker room. It was Kostas banging on the door of the referees' room, crying and yelling out in Greek. Inside the locker room, the players vented their spleens, too, and some were in tears. It was enough for me to ask what was going on. Apparently, Kostas was demanding of the referees, and particularly one he had some history with, 'Why are you cheating us?' Even the players thought they'd been diddled by the refs. While there had been some dodgy calls, we couldn't blame the officials for our demise. The dubious calls were there in every game, so it wasn't like it was a surprise. Maybe the others saw something that made them feel they got shafted, but I reckon it was more to do with their emotions and the Greek habit of looking to pass the buck for any problems.

Our coach, Kostas, was also a smoker. Not that this placed him in the minority. Like for the Italians, I think it is a birthright of the Greek male to smoke as much as he likes, where he likes, when he likes. At every gym we played in there were massive 'No Smoking' signs. They might as well have been posters of the Marlboro Man with invitations to light up because that's what nearly everyone in the crowd did. We played in a pall of smoke every night. On one occasion, a policeman stood right under the 'No Smoking' sign. Naturally, he was smoking.

Some of the players smoked, although it was not permitted on the team bus that took us to most of our games. Not until the coach lit up, that is. This was the signal for the players to start puffing away, giving those of us who didn't smoke at least a taste of it. At the club, the players only lit up in the locker room after the game, but the coach rarely missed an opportunity. During a drinks break at training, he'd duck off to the side of the court and light up to get a fix before we resumed. One night, as we came down the stretch of the season, I looked over at the bench while we were playing and he had one burning. It must have been a stressful night at the office. Never mind that some of us were in danger of going from passive smokers to the real thing, that's just how it was. You had to get used to it.

The facilities in Greece were vastly inferior to those I had enjoyed in Italy, some of them making the old Albert Park Stadium look like a modern palace. The courts and rings were okay, but the locker rooms could be dreadful. There were often holes in the walls, the showers would be putrid and in some you couldn't swing a cat. At one place, there was one shower to cater for the whole team. In Australia we call it a hose. It was so primitive it wouldn't have passed any health regulations. This was a league spending millions of dollars on talent, yet barely a drachma to look after it.

The facilities and the smoking were not the only cultural differences in the locker rooms. It extended to the players and their post-game victory celebrations and, shall we say, the closeness among team-mates. In short, the boys from Apollon Patras liked to jump around in naked embraces after a win.

One night after winning a really important game, everyone was excited, emotions were high, a few blokes lit up, and the locker room was a great place to be. As I stripped off to head for the shower, I heard singing and chanting from the Greek guys already in the water. As I entered the shower room they all had their arms around each other, jumping up and down with their old fellas slapping around as free as birds. I've got to admit that it caught me off guard because it was unusual to see and I wasn't that comfortable sharing nudity.

The European blokes go for the kiss-on-each-cheek greeting, which is obviously part of the culture. But for blokes like me and American John Shasky, even that took some getting used to. So just imagine running into that shower scene. It was a bit of an awakening. Now picture the next scene, as the Greeks, perhaps sensing my unease at their, shall we say, familiarity with one another, played it up for all it was worth. There was never another team on which I played where blokes were so comfortable with each other that they grabbed each other by the stork!

On one occasion one of the players was naked on a seat in the locker room when another guy came along, sat next to him, leaned over and cupped his genitals in his hands. He looked at me and said, 'What is wrong Androos? What is wrong with this? This is good. This not problem. We are friends.' Obviously very good friends. Clearly they were just joking, but all jokes aside, I'm not touching another man's penis – and I reckon that goes for ninety-nine per cent of the other blokes I ever played basketball with. The more of a reaction the Greeks got from me and Shasky, the more they played it up. But I'm telling you, if anybody had tried that in the Melbourne Tigers' locker room, I would have been far less tolerant than I was of the Greeks.

I was, after all, just a visitor to their country, enjoying a great experience. I loved Greece, I loved my team-mates and the fans, I loved the basketball there. But for the life of me, whether it be their alphabet or naked blokes acting up in the locker room, there were a lot of things about Greece that I will never ever understand.

chapter sixteen

ALMOST BRONZED AUSSIES

THE game clock in basketball can be calibrated to tenths of a second. That's how far a game can be broken down: to one-tenth of a second. It's still possible for a game to be won or lost in that time. It's a finger snap, the blink of an eye. Given that, one whole minute is a relative eternity.

If there was any time from my career I would like back, it would be the last minute – or part thereof – of the last game the Boomers played at the 1996 Olympic Games in Atlanta. It was the closest the Boomers have been to winning an Olympic medal and we couldn't get the job done. With maybe less than a minute to go against Lithuania in the bronze medal game, the scores were tied. I would love the chance to have those seconds again, to maybe get it right, or at least be satisfied in my heart that I played it like I would have liked. In reality, I don't feel like I got it right. That's not to say we would have won the game if I had, but I would just have preferred to do it differently.

That loss down boils down to one play. It was a one-point game when Mark Bradtke made a pair of free-throws with 2:18 left. Lithuania came up empty on the next trip down the floor when an errant pass came to me as I dropped to the baseline to help out defensively. So we had the ball and a chance to take the lead. We worked through our offence, trying to find the open man for a shot, but Lithuania stepped up its defensive intensity and pushed us out of what we wanted. None of us could get a good look or a passage to the basket. The ball came to me near the top of the key. As the shot clock got to within two seconds of expiring, I put up a hurried shot that missed off the back of the rim with 1:32 left. Lithuania got the rebound and went down the other end, then Sarunas Marciulionis made two free-throws to make the lead three.

Shane Heal came back on the next possession and made an incredible fall-away jump shot from the corner to make it 72–73 with 1:03 to go. Almost thirty seconds later Arvydas Sabonis converted a bullish three-point play to put Lithuania four up before Scott Fisher made a put-back for 74–76. Then came the play that really broke the Boomers' backs. Marciulionis made one free-throw with seventeen seconds left to make the margin three, but missed the second. If we secured the rebound, we'd have plenty of time to get up the floor and get a good three-pointer away to tie the game and maybe send it to overtime. But the long rebound was tipped back to Marciulionis, who was fouled and sent to the line again with ten seconds to play. He missed the first but made the second for a four-point buffer. Shane Heal's three-pointer missed, Lithuania made two more free-throws with virtually no time left and we had lost, 80–74.

Within the space of little more than a minute, Lithuania took charge of the game and the bronze medal. It was a long ninety seconds that might have been so different had we used those twenty-two seconds of possession, which ended with my hurried shot, differently and better. If we had made a field goal on that crucial possession, maybe we would have won the game. Maybe Sabonis and his Lithuanian mates, not me and the Aussies, would be ruing a fourth-placed finish if I could have had that last minute back. Maybe.

Maybe my mind has played Chinese whispers all these years, but with the scores level and a big play to be made, I don't believe I was assertive enough. Given the nature of the game and the way I played in the tournament, I would have greater peace of mind if I had been assertive and tried to make something happen, even if it didn't quite come off. In the quarter-final against Croatia, I made the pass to Tony Ronaldson for the winning basket. I made something happen. Against Lithuania, I didn't when I needed to. I was not proactive enough to get something done. In a game that can be decided by tenths of seconds, less than one minute could have altered Olympic history.

The Atlanta Olympics were Barry Barnes's first as Boomers head coach and they were my first as Boomers captain. There were a few dramas and controversies to deal with along the journey to Atlanta, but selection wasn't one of them. The 1996 Olympic team almost picked itself, which was one reason we had such a good tournament. The roles and personalities were established within the team, everyone got along well, nobody tried to do things they were incapable of doing on the basketball court and anybody who didn't play much didn't complain. There truly was a team mentality about this group, a sense that we could achieve something if we all worked and sacrificed together. It's a rare thing, but we had that feeling.

The main selection talking point centred on Luc Longley, although it wasn't so much about selection as it was about his availability. Luc had just won an NBA Championship with the Chicago

Bulls, placing him alongside Michael Jordan as a member of one of the greatest basketball teams of all time. But Luc had to decide whether to play for the Boomers and shoot for an Olympic medal or have surgery and get ready for the next NBA season. Luc opted for surgery and to go to Atlanta as a supporter and TV commentator. That was his call and it created a couple of points of view. Actually, it might have gone close to polarising opinion. The public perception in Australia was that if the Boomers had Luc, a medal was almost a given. The players, being frank, knew that wasn't the case. Luc would have been a factor, but he hadn't played for Australia since the Barcelona Olympics and, I'd have to say, given some injury problems he had endured, I don't think playing for the Boomers was high on Luc's priorities at that stage of his career. Not compared to earning millions of US dollars and chasing NBA titles in the same team as Michael Jordan, anyway. When you put it in those terms, it was an understandable decision and I don't think there was any resentment or disquiet about it among the Boomers.

There was probably one selection dilemma involving Perth Wildcats team-mates Ricky Grace and Scott Fisher, who were both born in the United States and became Australian citizens during their NBL careers. But under FIBA rules, national teams are permitted only one naturalised citizen, meaning it was a choice between Grace (a guard) and Fisher (a forward) to go to Atlanta with the Boomers. For some time, it seemed Grace was the clear favourite, with talk he had been given a nod and a wink. Fisher was in the squad, but the selection strategy changed when Luc Longley decided not to play.

It certainly wasn't a straight case of Longley out, Fisher in. Fisher still had to prove he deserved his place in the Boomers twelve and, through a combination of performance and his big personality, he played his way into the team. It wasn't that Grace faltered or his game went off; it was that Fisher put forward such a compelling case of what he could bring to the table that he got the call. In fact, not only had Fisher jumped over Grace, he played himself ahead of blokes like Pat Reidy and Andrew Vlahov, proving beyond doubt that he deserved selection.

One of the first things you noticed about Scott Fisher was his persona: supremely confident, which some people could construe as arrogance. You knew he was around and you knew he would get the job done. But one thing you might wonder about Americans who naturalised was how deep was their desire to represent Australia and feeling of honour in doing so. For a bloke born in San Jose, California, like Fisher, how did it feel to be an Aussie and wear the green and gold? When I was a kid, I looked up to blokes like Rocky Crosswhite and Ken James, who were Americans playing for the Boomers as naturalised Aussies. I consider Fisher, whose background and personality enabled him to unashamedly display his nationalistic pride, as Australian as me, but it often seemed he was *more* proud and felt *more* obligated representing Australia than the Australians – and that felt good for all of us.

As it turned out, Fisher had a good Olympic tournament, but perhaps his finest performance was on the eve of the Games. At the major events, the Boomers had a tradition of rookie night, where the players, coaches and staff who were at their first Olympics or world championships had to entertain the rest of the team with a cabaret act. In Atlanta, Tony Ronaldson and assistant coach Brett Brown performed as the Music Men, assistant coach Alan Black and team manager Tom York were terrible, and Brett Maher and Pat Reidy teamed up to do an unusual rework of the song *Killing Me Softly*. Only Scott Fisher went solo on rookie night and his rendition of *Mac the Knife* was unforgettable. So when it came to playing or performing, Fisher had no problems fitting in with our team.

Another new face from leftfield was Tonny Jensen, whose selection perhaps demonstrated what it means to be in the right place at the right time. Tonny, who was playing for Brett Brown at the North Melbourne Giants at that stage, had been around the NBL for a few years without being a spectacular player. But his 1996 form for the Giants got him a look from the coaching staff and he did enough in the right games to become an Olympian. In a very short time he went from working in the abattoirs of Albury to playing basketball at the Olympic Games at Atlanta. Unfortunately, his demise was almost as sudden. By the time Sydney 2000 arrived, Jensen was struggling to stay in the league. He had suffered through a severe illness called Krohn's Disease, which can be life-threatening, came back to play a season with the Canberra Cannons in 2001 and was immediately gone from the NBL. But he will always be an Olympian and will always have been a member of the team that went so agonisingly close to winning a medal.

There was almost one late change to the team for Atlanta when Pat Reidy broke his hand during the warm-up series against Lithuania. It happened at the Glasshouse in Melbourne, which was the home stadium of the North Melbourne Giants, and there was little time for it to mend properly. Which was exactly what the coaching staff thought when they called me in after the game. Barry Barnes said he needed to start thinking of a replacement player in case Reidy couldn't go to Atlanta. A similar situation had happened in 1988 when Robert Sibley took a broken scaphoid bone to Seoul and could not play a minute at the Olympics. Instinctively, I told the coaches that come what may, they had to take Reidy to Atlanta. He had been picked, he was in the team and, with all due respect, we had plenty of players for his role, we could cover for him, so he would not be greatly missed on the court. We had an obligation to let Pat go to the Olympics and achieve a lifelong dream.

Pat went into hospital that night for surgery and his situation plagued me for every minute of the drive from the Glasshouse to home. We couldn't replace him on what was basically the eve of our departure for the Olympics. That night, after a little more contemplation, I called assistant coach Brett Brown and impressed on him the need to keep Reidy in the team. I told Brett that Pat might never get the chance to go to another Olympics. That was not the overriding factor, but while I felt good about going in to bat for Pat, it was about what was good for the team: to bring a new player into the Boomers at that late stage could have been unsettling. I played every card I had. I don't know if I had any influence, but Pat Reidy went to Atlanta and played and that was a victory in itself.

I also had an injury concern on the eve of departure for Atlanta. On the final weekend before the NBL season broke for the Olympics, the Melbourne Tigers had a road double against the North Melbourne Giants and the Canberra Cannons. I hurt my calf muscle in the Giants game and thought I was in some trouble, maybe out of the Olympics. We injected the calf with a painkiller to numb it for the Cannons game and I managed to get through. After a few days of treatment I was good to go, but had I known what was about to unfold in Salt Lake City, I would have undergone transplant surgery to make sure I was on the court.

The Boomers' only official game in America before heading to Atlanta was against the United States Olympic team in Salt Lake City. It was a warm-up game in the truest sense because we knew we wouldn't win and they knew they wouldn't lose. But it was a game that got both teams more than ready for the Olympics.

The Americans won the 1994 World Championship in Toronto, but the NBA players did not enhance their reputations in doing so. In the eyes of the international basketball community, they conducted themselves poorly in Toronto with their on-court antics and trash talking. It was poor for their image and basketball's image and, thankfully, USA Basketball made sure it had a line-up at Atlanta that was more in tune with the expectations and etiquette of international basketball. The US team for Atlanta included future Hall of Famers Charles Barkley, Scottie Pippen, Reggie Miller, Hakeem Olajuwon, Karl Malone, John Stockton, David Robinson and Shaquille O'Neal. It was because of these guys that our game in Salt

Lake City attracted a sell-out crowd and a live national telecast. It was a situation most teams would have found intimidating. The Boomers didn't.

Our mindset going into the game, even though it was an exhibition, was that we would not take backward steps. We felt we belonged on the court with these guys and we deserved their respect. It was important that, while we were rank underdogs, we did not just roll over like puppies and have our bellies scratched. We wanted to know how good we were going into the Olympics and we wanted to see how far we could push the Americans. So we had a crack and Shane Heal served it to the Yanks by the bucketful. After a slow start, we worked our way into the game and then Shane caught fire, hitting shots from all over the floor. Being the kind of guy he is, Shane's levels of bravado and confidence rose with every shot he made. Shane in that mood was a man not to be messed with, as a man of a similar nature, Charles Barkley, found out.

After taking a jump shot, Shane was landing when Charles made a late lunge trying to put him off his shot. On his way through, Charles clipped Shane's legs and sent him to the ground. Not surprisingly, Shane took offence at this because, in a universal understanding of basketball rules and etiquette, when a guy leaves the floor, he's entitled to come back down safely. So, unhappy with that treatment, Shane reacted like he would whether it was Charles Barkley, Michael Jordan, some scrubber in F grade or a mate in a pick-up game at Lilydale. He gave Charles a spray. I think he suggested Charles's mouth had some connection with the male appendage, but he expressed it in slightly cruder terms.

That was enough to get Charles's attention. He did a double-take and tracked back to see what the problem was with the little fella. When Charles arrived on the scene, Shane delivered a few more choice words and a shoulder to the chest as the exclamation mark on the expression of displeasure. Shane did not cop crap from anyone and he made sure Charles and the rest of the Americans knew it, with a confrontation that threatened to get out of hand before the referees intervened and calmed things.

The encounter between Shane and Charles certainly got the crowd buzzing and it showed we were not prepared to bow and scrape to the Americans and we were not overawed. The US team was probably expecting to be treated more royally, and that's when the trash talking started between Andrew Vlahov and Karl Malone, yapping like a couple of fox terriers on the subject of respect and how it should be doled out. They were only warming up when a time-out was called and they crossed paths on the way to the team huddles. By now Shane Heal had joined Vlahov in the verbal stoush with Malone, who was joined by Barkley, and I could see where things were going. As captain I had to fly the flag, get in there, settle things down and get my boys out of the fray. I wish I hadn't felt so brave for once in my life.

I arrived on the scene with everyone grabbing hold of everyone else and out of the corner of my eye I saw Shane had his fist cocked ready to throw one. Keep in mind that Malone was 206 centimetres and 116 kilograms against Shane's 186 centimetres and 79 kilograms and you can see Shane was fighting way out of his division. But I also remembered what he told me about the laws of street fighting: if you're going into a fight you know you can't win, always throw the first punch so at least you've landed one. That appeared to be his mindset with Malone. So like the referee in a boxing match, I got between them and placed one hand on Shane and one on Malone. Immediately, a sense of dread surged through my body as I realised I too was fighting outside my division. When Malone looked at me I knew I was in the wrong place. Without another second passing, I whacked Shane on the arse and said, 'C'mon, it's a time-out, let's get to the huddle.' We got out of there as quick as we could. Well, I did, anyway.

When we got to the Boomers huddle, Vlahov was still fired up and so was coach Barry Barnes, who could be an emotional character.

Barnesy's message was fairly simple: 'Fuck 'em. Don't take any backward steps. Be sensible, but no backward steps.' Fortunately, things had cooled down by the post-game media conference featuring Shane and Charles because both guys operated under the theory that although you played hard, what happened on the floor stayed on the floor. Charles was cool afterwards and he and Shane became instant buddies, with respect for each other as competitors. Even though we lost, 118–77, Shane earned respect and notoriety for his twenty-eight points and his confrontation with Charles, which was splashed all over the TV and newspapers and, soon after this excellent performance and the Olympics, he signed with the Minnesota Timberwolves of the NBA.

What that game and incident did for the Boomers as a team was significant. Even though we lost the game by forty-one points, it set the tone for the Olympic campaign, showing a demeanour and attitude in keeping with where we thought we stood. We wouldn't be pushed around, we wouldn't be disrespected, we would play hard and we would be shooting for a medal.

The Boomers were drawn to play South Korea on the first day of the tournament, which was the first day of the Olympics. That provided a conundrum for coach Barry Barnes, who was worried about the team marching at the opening ceremony, then backing up to play the next day. He discussed it with me and said he hadn't made up his mind about the team marching, but he felt inclined not to because of the physical strain it could place on the team. Olympics opening ceremonies aren't just about marching a lap of the track and watching the flame being lit. There's hours of standing, sitting and waiting before getting the call to the arena. It's a long day that turns into a late night and it can be very draining, especially in hot weather. What Barnesy said made perfect sense, but with some of the first-time Olympians urging me to persuade Barnesy to let us march, I told him the Boomers should take part in the opening ceremony.

Our performance was crucial, but a lot of blokes on the team had not been to an Olympics. Having been to three before Atlanta, I knew the opening ceremony was a big part of the whole Olympic experience. With no disrespect towards South Korea, we knew we could win that game whether we marched or not. If we couldn't beat South Korea without any sleep we weren't going to go far in the tournament, anyway. But being involved in the opening ceremony could be as important for team morale as a win on the court. The benefits of marching, with the euphoria and excitement, far outweighed the negatives. I didn't think it mattered who we played, we had to march. As long as everyone took care of themselves, we would be okay. So we all marched, saw Muhammad Ali light the Olympic flame and soaked up the experience and the inspiration that it was. Just before the ceremony closed, we gathered as a team and headed for the exits to make sure we were on one of the first buses back to the village. We were probably tucked up in our bunks before some of the athletes got out of the stadium. We were ready to play.

Not that we were living in luxury accommodation in the Olympic village, which was really a dorm building on the campus of Georgia Tech university. It was pretty primitive accommodation in sweltering conditions with bunk beds in tiny rooms. Shane Heal and I shared a room, so we had no trouble agreeing to disassemble the bunks, get rid of them and sleep on our mattresses on the floor. It was cooler and gave us more space and greater comfort.

At least the security was better than the sleeping arrangements. In Atlanta, the security was high-tech. In Barcelona, Phil Smyth and Leroy Loggins had swapped their accreditation passes, complete with photo identification, to see if security would pick up on it. The Spanish security guards didn't bat an eyelid as they checked the passes, which was slightly surprising considering Phil is white and Leroy is black. At Atlanta, they would have had trouble pulling the same stunt because they checked your ID by swiping your finger print at every checkpoint.

The major security scare in Atlanta was when a pipe bomb exploded near the end of the Games. Some of our guys were there the night the bomb went off, but we were pretty much back together and accounted for by the time we heard the shocking news. It had the potential to be disastrous for some of our group. Fortunately, all was well. [Andrew – were others injured?]

We opened the tournament against South Korea like we owed Barry Barnes a favour for letting us march at the opening ceremony. We won, 111–88, as Shane Heal hit twenty-three points and dished eleven assists and I had twenty-six. It was the perfect start, but we ran into a brick wall in our second game, losing to Yugoslavia, 91–68. This time Shane and I only managed sixteen between us. In all honesty, we were supposed to lose this game and as Yugoslavia progressed through the tournament undefeated until the gold medal game, you could understand why. So our mindset and confidence was unruffled as we prepared to play Brazil in a game that, in the great Olympic traditions of pivotal contests, we needed to win.

I might be accused of slight exaggeration here, but it turned out to be one of the finest games in Olympic basketball history as the Boomers eventually got over Brazil, 109–101 in double-overtime. To play overtime was not all that common. Playing two extra five-minute periods at the Olympics was rare and we had Shane Heal, Andrew Vlahov and Scott Fisher to thank for not needing a third. Vlahov and Fisher did an outstanding defensive job on Brazil's scoring machine Oscar Schmidt, keeping him to just five points after half-time, while Shane had thirteen of his thirty-five points in the second OT period.

The Boomers trailed by fifteen in the first half and by as much as twelve in the second before three straight three-pointers from Shane Heal tied the game with about ten minutes left. Oscar, who was one of my heroes, a five-time Olympian and an all-time great scorer who would have been an impact player in the NBA had the Americans been more open to foreign players during his prime, had a chance to win it near the end for Brazil and I missed with a prayer from halfway as time expired. Then Brazil tied the first overtime with a tip-in at the buzzer after we had led by five with two minutes left. Shane made a four-point play on the first possession of the second OT, then fired another triple, then made a couple of free-throws and, finally, it was game over.

Going into the Brazil game, we knew it was going to be big. We had identified Brazil and Puerto Rico as the must-win games if we were to avoid the United States in the knock-out quarter-finals. With the Olympic crossover system for the quarter-finals, the top four teams from group A played the top four teams from group B in a 1 v 4, 2 v 3 scenario, with the losers dropping out. So, theoretically, the higher we finished the better our chances. Simply, we didn't want to finish fourth because we knew the US would be top of its group. When we beat Puerto Rico 101–96, we were thinking we could finish as high as second in our group if we beat Greece.

The win over Puerto Rico meant we wouldn't finish lower than third, so we had avoided the Americans in the quarters. Then we thought about whether it was better to finish second or third. The question became: which team would we rather face in the quarter-finals – Lithuania or Croatia? The general feeling was that we would probably prefer to play Lithuania. We knew a lot about the Lithuanians, we beat them in a pre-Olympic series, albeit without giant centre Arvydas Sabonis, and we felt comfortable about our chances of beating them again. We never for one minute contemplated throwing the game against Greece, but you could bet your life that the Greeks thought through the same scenarios. In fact, after we beat Greece, 103–62, there was a lot of talk that the Greeks might have tanked it to get their preferred quarter-final match-up. After looking at our situation, we were always going to come back to the same conclusion: we play to win every game. Not everyone said the same thing about Greece after we towelled them up.

Even though we would have preferred to play Lithuania in the quarter-final, our opponent was Croatia, a country with a fine basketball tradition and a team we'd never beaten. Not that the Boomers had often played Croatia, formerly part of Yugoslavia. But the fact was that we'd never beaten the Croatians and their 1996 line-up had talent like NBA players Tony Kukoc and Dino Radja, so it was never going to be easy. Which is part of what makes quarter-final day at the Olympics so special. It is make-or-break for eight teams in a knockout situation where previous results count for nothing. In some respects, it seems almost unfair that a team with a 5–0 or 4–1 record, which the Boomers had, could be eliminated from the tournament with a loss in the quarters. Part of the beauty also is that a team that scraped into fourth place with a 2–3 record has a chance to stay alive for a medal. Either way, your tournament comes down to one game.

As it panned out, the game against Croatia came down to one play on the second-last possession of the match. There was nothing in the contest the whole way and, as time ticked down, scores were level and we had the ball. It went through my mind, as Shane Heal brought the ball up the floor, that this was the type of scenario where I wanted the ball, and wanted to be the one to decide the game and our Olympic campaign. It sounds conceited, but that was how I felt. Sometimes there is uncertainty in how you feel about wanting the ball, but I was feeling positive and I wanted the ball. I wanted the shot to win the game and I knew I would get the chance.

We called a play known as First Option. I was on the left wing and took a pass from Shane Heal, who then cut, using Mark Bradtke in the high post as a screen to lose his defender. The return pass to Shane wasn't on, so Bradtke set a screen for me to drive right and into the key. The defenders switched on the screen, which left me guarded by Stojko Vrankovic, who was 221 centimetres and slow enough for even me to get by off the dribble. I started to drive and the defenders moved into help positions to stop me getting to the basket. I pulled back to the top of the key to try to isolate Vrankovic and drove down the right side, forcing Tony Ronaldson's man to leave him to help Vrankovic defend me. I flicked the ball to Ronaldson on the right wing and, in a classic catch-and-shoot effort, the Bear made the three-pointer and was fouled as the defender desperately tried to get back and block the shot.

Ronaldson was on his back in front of the Croatian bench and we were going nuts. We ran over and had Ronaldson in a group bear hug, knowing that if he made his free-throw with 34.1 seconds left, we would be four points up and Croatia would need a near-miracle to beat us. Ronaldson made the free-throw, Croatia made a basket and Shane Heal made a few free-throws to seal it, 73–71, as Croatia fouled to stop the clock in desperation. Finally, time ran out and we were back to a place we'd only been once before: the medal round at the Olympic Games. The Boomers were ecstatic, to say the least. After the game to decide whether you play for pride or medals, we were playing for medals.

As history shows, we were consigned to playing for bronze medals, which was no surprise given that our semi-final opponent was the all-conquering, all-NBA United States line-up. Which not only presented a massive challenge but also threw Shane Heal and Charles Barkley back into the spotlight after their confrontation a couple of weeks earlier in Salt Lake City. So there was some extra interest in this return showdown between the Yanks and the Aussies. The truth of the matter was, when it came to Shane and Charles, there was no animosity between them and they were fine. When Shane played for the Timberwolves in the NBA, he actually got Charles to sign some photos of the incident in Salt Lake City and had them framed.

The Salt Lake City game hardened the American resolve and there was no way known they would be shown up in the semi-finals of an Olympic tournament in their own country by the upstart Australians. This was the business end of the tournament and they didn't want any slip-ups. At the same time, we weren't going to roll over and, like in Salt Lake City, we promised to take no backward steps. We got out of the blocks and had an early lead only to fall behind by a few baskets just before half-time. I was a little sad to hear the half-time buzzer because I had twenty-one points and was going along okay. Yet while we were only ten points down, we might as well have been forty or fifty behind because the pervading feeling among the team was that we didn't have a snowflake's chance in hell of winning. We still had our respect and credibility to play for, as did the Americans. Reggie Miller told me so.

After my big first half, the Americans cranked up their defence and their yapping, especially Reggie. As I went to the free-throw line for some rare second-half points, Reggie got in my ear. 'That's the only way you'll score now. We've put a cork up your arse. You better enjoy these free-throws, man, 'cause we've put a cork up your arse.' Kinky as it sounds, it wasn't very sexy at the time. Nor did Reggie get any slack from Shane Heal, who couldn't back off, regardless of the game situation. Reggie wore goggles and one time I inadvertently flicked the goggles and they dislodged. I apologised to Reggie so he knew I didn't mean it, but he was looking at me in a weird way. I repeated the apology. Twice was too much for Shane. 'Fuck that,' he said. 'You said you were sorry once. If he doesn't want to take your apology he can stick it up his arse.'

I was trying to maintain the delicate US–Australian basketball relations and Hammer gave me a spray for it. That's maybe the thing I respected most about Shane. No matter the situation, he competed hard and the game was never over until the final buzzer, regardless of what the scoreboard said. Shane refused to lose face to the Americans and I think the whole team achieved a similar result. We were beaten, 101–73, but certainly not disgraced and, most importantly, we were still in the hunt for a medal.

Our good form justified our belief that we were a red-hot chance against Lithuania in the bronze medal game. Lithuania had played well, and only lost to Yugoslavia by eight in the semi-final, but the big difference between us and them was one giant man, Arvydas Sabonis. He was such a massive bloke with massive talent to match. He hurt an Achilles tendon at an early stage of his career, which was spent mostly in Spain before going to the NBA, and there was a common belief that, had he not suffered that injury, Sabonis could have been the best player in the world. I saw Sabonis before he got hurt and he was a freak. He was 220 centimetres tall and weighed 135 kilograms, so he was a physical presence, but he also had great touch and mobility. He had the full package and, even on one leg, he single-handedly won the gold medal at the Seoul Olympics for the USSR. This day in Atlanta, he virtually single-handedly beat us with thirty points, thirteen rebounds, three assists and five blocked shots.

The game went back and forth until that final, fateful minute and my shot that clanged off the back of the rim. The Boomers scored again after that shot, but there are moments you just know decide basketball games. That was one. If we made that field goal and took the lead, I firmly believe we would have had the momentum to win the game. It was like another moment when we were three up and if we stopped Lithuania on its next possession and then we scored to be five or six up, it would have made it hard for them to win. Anyway, Sabonis got the ball on the perimeter, spotted up and made a three to tie the game. It was his third three-pointer of the game and underlined just how good he was, just how much difference he made to the team we had beaten in the pre-Olympic series. It highlighted the difference between Lithuania winning the bronze medal 80–74 and the Boomers getting nothing more than a consoling pat on the back.

For most guys the disappointment of losing the bronze medal game set in even before the final buzzer. With about two seconds left Lithuania had free-throws and we knew we couldn't win. By the time we reached the change rooms, the disappointment was overwhelming and the emotion overflowing. The disappointment was over the loss of the game and the lost chance for a bronze medal and some history for men's basketball in Australia. The emotion and tears were for other reasons beyond winning and losing.

This group had spent a lot of time together in the Olympic campaign and some of us had been together in the Boomers for ten years or more. For some, like veteran Ray Borner, the end of the Olympics meant the end of the road with the national team. There was a sense we had shared an incredible journey that was over, even though we had not quite reached the desired destination of Olympic glory. The hurt, of course, was magnified because we had got so close to the destination, only to stop short. The initial feeling was of personal disappointment, but looking our team-mates in the eye, that was when the true feelings and emotions started to get raw.

In some senses, the emotion experienced in the aftermath of a loss like Atlanta was like suffering a death in the family. That is not meant to sound trite, because the depth of loss or time of grief is nowhere near so severe after losing a basketball game as after the death of a loved one. But for a short while, at least, there was no hurt to match it. It was a hurt shared by every player, whether they had played forty minutes or none, and every member of the coaching and support staff. The feeling was totally shared, which just proved again what a tight bond this team had formed. Barry Barnes spoke to us briefly, but I can't remember a word he said. It was just too emotional a time and I don't know a person in that locker room who didn't cry. We were as one to the bitter end.

After the initial outpouring of emotion, my process of recovery and rationalisation worked fairly quickly. You can always wonder what might have been, but it wasn't long before I was relatively content. I'm not saying I was satisfied with finishing fourth, but I had peace of mind and a sense of satisfaction from finishing fourth, which is an accomplishment. Look at it in the big picture of how many people play basketball around the world and there I was on a team of twelve great blokes who were good enough to finish fourth at an Olympic Games. Yes, we wanted to do better; yes, people felt we should have won the bronze medal game, but this was a team and a performance I was, and always will be, extremely proud of.

The public's post-Olympic reaction was a little disappointing. While we had done everything we could, there was an undercurrent of disappointment and a feeling in the community that we had failed by not winning a medal. That was wrong. Some may argue that I'm just consoling myself, but I know the difference between trying to con myself into justifying a loss and being justifiably proud of the Boomers' efforts in Atlanta. People jumped onto the theory that if Luc Longley had played we would have beaten Lithuania and won a medal, but I'm not buying that. Luc's presence would have changed the team dynamics, and the effect of that could not be guaranteed. Sure, we might have tamed Sabonis with Luc's help, but who's to say we would have beaten Brazil in the double-overtime game or got past Puerto Rico or Croatia? There was no guarantee that we would have done better over the course of the whole tournament if Luc had played. Given my time over, I would take Luc every time because he was a good player and a great bloke. But we went to Atlanta with the people we had, we achieved the best result the Boomers have had at any Olympics and I'm proud to say I was a part of it.

Our Atlanta campaign was as good as it could possibly have been without winning a medal. When you walk away from games or tournaments, the worst feeling you can have is to have to admit 'We're much better than the way we played.' The pressure and anxiety sometimes gets the better of you. In Atlanta we walked away satisfied that we had done the best we could and content in the knowledge that we were beaten fair and square. We did our best, we did whatever we could. We walked away disappointed, but with a clear conscience. Sometimes you have to acknowledge that the other team was the better team. You can visit the what-ifs as many times as you like without getting any satisfaction. I gained perspective from that saying of my dad's: the only times winning is important are in surgery and in war. It wasn't about life and death and we had done the best we could. We did our absolute very best in Atlanta, we got the best out of the team and I can live with that.

The only thing I find hard to live with is the last minute of the bronze medal game. One minute is the blink of an eye in a lifetime. But it's an eternity when you can't get it back.

chapter seventeen

GLORY WITHOUT A GUARANTEE

Winning one championship does not automatically guarantee that a second will follow. The history of the NBL had borne that out, with only three teams going back to back as champions in the first nineteen seasons. For the Melbourne Tigers, we had to endure history's lessons the hard way to realise that our championship in 1993 did not provide any special privileges. Certainly not on the basketball court, anyway, where we learned to appreciate the old saying that winning never comes easy. That was perhaps never more true than in 1996 when we went within one shot of winning the championship.

The Tigers went 21–5 in the regular season and in reality should have been 22–4 because we tripped up against the Newcastle Falcons to open a road double on the last weekend of the season. We closed the regular season against the Brisbane Bullets in Brisbane and, almost unbelievably, went back there to start the play-offs a few days later. Just as unbelievable was that we lost that first play-off game in a best-of-three series by twenty-one points and were on the verge of elimination, showing that our 21–5 season was worth nothing in the finals. Fortunately, we recovered to beat the Bullets in games two and three at home to make the semi-finals and a similar scenario against the Canberra Cannons. After rolling along during the regular season, we were under all sorts of pressure in the play-offs. Like the Brisbane series, after dropping game one, we won both home games against the Cannons to set up a best-of-three grand final series against our old rival, the South East Melbourne Magic.

Unlike in 1993, the Tigers were under pressure to win the title in 1996, simply because of our excellent regular-season record. In 1993, given what we did during the regular season, we weren't really expected to win it all. This time, we were. That we played the Magic just added to the whole scenario. There was plenty on the line in this series and we had more to lose than most. That notion became even more acute when we opened the grand final series at Melbourne Park by winning 100–89, meaning we needed only one more win for a second NBL championship. It never came. Six nights later, the Magic pipped us 88–84 in game two to level the series, then we were obliterated, 107–70, in a Sunday matinee massacre, losing the third and final game of the series in the most embarrassing fashion imaginable.

The hardest part of that loss was probably the fact that we were so close to winning game two and the championship. The Magic was two ahead, with about twenty seconds to go, when Lanard Copeland launched a three-point shot from the top of the arc. The ball hit the ring, did a lap, took a peek into the basket and spun out. The Magic got the rebound, made a couple of free-throws, won the game and went on to win the title. That's how close we were to winning. I'm convinced that if Copes had made that shot, we would have got a stop on the Magic's possession and we would have won the title. After the finger of fate flicked Andrew Vlahov's shot off the rim in 1993, now it poked us right in the eye.

It was a demoralising loss that left us wondering what might have been. But while we wallowed in wonderment and, to a certain extent, self-pity, the Magic was pumped and looking ahead to game three. If there was a harbinger for game three it came the day between games when Ray Gordon copped an elbow and broke his nose at practice. Whether it was mental or physical or a combination of both, we were down the next day and got poleaxed. It wasn't even a contest. It was a complete and total flogging and by far one of the biggest and most embarrassing losses we ever had.

The seasons since winning the 1993 NBL Championship were not great for the Tigers in terms of play-off achievement. In 1994, we finished on top of the ladder with a 19–7 record, eased through the first round of the play-offs and then bombed in the semi-finals against the Adelaide 36ers. The Sixers got us in game one by thirteen and we led game two until Rob Rose made a couple of miraculous shots to put them into the grand final against eventual champs the North Melbourne Giants. No disrespect to the Giants, who were coached by my friend and former Tigers assistant coach Brett Brown, but had we made the championship series, I feel we would have won it. Could have, would have, should have. Bottom line was we didn't.

As we prepared for the 1995 season, we believed we had a good shot at winning the title. Then we received a blow nobody saw coming: Mark Bradtke left – temporarily at least – to spend time on the pro tennis tour with his wife Nicole (née Provis). The news was broken to me, Lanard Copeland and Dave Simmons after a round of golf with Mark at Yarra Bend one afternoon. As Hogey dropped his bombshell, I'm sure the three of us all thought the same thing: 'What the hell!' As we rationalised Mark's decision to follow the tennis circuit, we looked at the positive, which was a chance for a young Chris Anstey to play and get more NBL experience. Within a couple of years, Anstey would be an NBA first-round draft pick with a multi-million dollar contract. We could clearly see his potential, but he added to our problems by wanting to leave the Tigers. Of all teams, Anstey wanted to play for the Magic.

After Hogey decided to go with Nicole on tour, we talked him into playing with the Tigers whenever he was in Australia. It was a good compromise as we believed it would ease the pressure on Anstey from time to time during the season and keep Hogey's hand and mind in shape for when he did return to the NBL full-time. But Anstey's departure for the Magic threw us for a loop and left us without a full-time big man in the middle. We had signed Blair Smith from the Brisbane Bullets, thinking he would develop and be a backup. But with Hogey and Anstey both gone, Blair became our starting centre.

Blair was never a superstar in the NBL, but he was good for us, fitted in well and worked hard. It was a bit like that for the team during 1995 as we ground out a 14–12 record to finish in the eighth and last play-off spot before losing to the Perth Wildcats in the first round. The Wildcats had home-court advantage, but because of venue availability problems, this series was arranged on a home–away–home schedule rather than the normal away–home–home. We upset things a bit when we beat the Wildcats in Perth to open the series, so we only needed to win one of the next two, but we couldn't get it done. We lost game two at home, then got eliminated with a four-point game-three loss back in Perth. Interestingly, Blair Smith had his best game of the season in game three and the Wildcats went on to win the title.

Maybe things just weren't meant to be in 1995. But when Mark Bradtke came back full-time in 1996, we stepped up several notches with an excellent regular season and went close to winning the title in game two of the grand final before losing so embarrassingly in the third and deciding game. The response to that 1996 grand final loss was that we had to make changes. Specifically, we felt that the Tigers needed something fresh in one of the import spots. Lanard Copeland had been a remarkable success since signing in 1992, which meant Dave Simmons, a fan favourite who had been with the Tigers for eight seasons, was gone. It was a tough decision and it caused some angst, which was understandable given that Simm had been a pivotal player for so long. But it was a decision the club had to make. Ultimately, it proved to be totally vindicated.

In letting go Dave Simmons, who was a genuinely hard-working power forward, the Tigers needed a player who could give us something extra to add to our arsenal. We needed a power forward to do what Dave had done, but with the ability to score consistently from outside. The man we signed was Jarvis Lang, who came highly credentialed and with excellent athletic ability, which was a bonus for marketing because we felt that, with the running game we could get into, he would draw people. At college at the University of North Carolina-Charlotte, Lang had a reputation as a shooter, a rebounder with the ability to put the ball on the floor and get to the basket, often above it. But there was a catch: Lang had knee problems. Even so, we thought we needed to roll the dice and we brought Lang out on a trial situation. The doctors took a look at him and they said that, while they might be some issues with his knees, he should be okay.

If we thought the health of Jarvis Lang's knees was our main worry, we soon got a fairly rude wake-up call. After splitting the opening weekend on the road to the Brisbane Bullets and Townsville Suns (this was before they became the Crocs) to be 1–1, we went into a serious tailspin, slumping to a 2–7 win–loss record that had eyebrows raised, jaws dropped and heads scratched. This was not how it was meant to be for a team that went within a shot of winning the title the year before.

During that poor start, there were two situations that indicated the 1997 season was not going to be normal. One was that, of our two wins in the first nine games, one was against the South East

Melbourne Magic, which showed we weren't as bad as our record indicated. The other was the game we won against the Adelaide 36ers but lost on a technicality when Mark Bradtke was ruled ineligible because he didn't have a clearance after his season in the NBA with the Philadelphia 76ers.

We knew Hogey, after playing with Philly between NBL seasons, would miss the first three NBL games, so being 1–2 with the big bloke returning to the Tigers line-up was no need for concern. Hogey returned on the weekend of a double against the Adelaide 36ers and South East Melbourne Magic and he just took the Sixers apart with thirty-one points and eighteen rebounds as we won 94–89. It was exactly what we wanted, but the amazing high became a crushing low when Hogey called me on the afternoon of the Magic game to say he couldn't play that night because of a red-tape snafu. Not only that, there was a chance we would be docked the Adelaide win from the night before because, while we thought all the paper-work on his clearance was done and stamped, the NBA had not notified USA Basketball, causing a broken link in the chain.

The bottom line was that Hogey couldn't play against the Magic and we forfeited the Adelaide game. Somehow, though, we managed to beat the Magic. It was slim pickings when it came to wins for the Tigers, who lost an appeal to have the technical loss to Adelaide overturned. Nothing seemed to go right and by the time we were 2–7 and then 3–9, we were grossly under the pump. So much so that some people felt we would not recover to make the play-offs, while then-*Herald Sun* basketball writer Chris Appleby went out on a brittle limb and called for my dad Lindsay to step down as coach. Just to add to the mix, Jarvis Lang's knee played up. Actually, the knee was stuffed. Lang couldn't train and he had played only eight games, so we had to address the issue. Lang had minor surgery to have the knee checked out and the doctor wasn't sure he would be able to play. Lang missed a couple of games due to the surgery, so we decided to cut our losses and make a change.

We had talked to people about imports we could sign and out of the blue Brett Brown, my friend and North Melbourne Giants coach, rang. He was in Sydney and had bumped into an American by the name of Marcus Timmons, who had played in the Philippines after spending the 1996 NBL season with the Illawarra (now Wollongong) Hawks and was looking for a job. Showing the strength of the basketball fraternity and the ability to momentarily set aside rivalries, Brett suggested we take a look at Timmons. We checked him out with Hawks coach Brendan Joyce. Joyce didn't exactly have good things to say about Marcus's attitude, which caused us to have doubts, but the bottom line was that we needed somebody to replace Jarvis Lang and we needed them quickly. The other factor was that Marcus was the type of player we had been looking for when we signed Jarvis. So we asked him to come down for a trial and after a couple of training sessions we knew he was the bloke to help us.

Signing Marcus Timmons might have been the significant turning point of our season. Marcus gave us defence, rebounding and size and he could hit a perimeter spot. He was the perfect fit for us. Soon enough we went from 3–9 to 6–11 and that eleventh loss, at the hands of the North Melbourne Giants on 7 July, was the last defeat we suffered in the regular season. In the most amazing turnaround, we won the next thirteen straight games to close the regular season with a 19–11 mark in second place on the ladder. From a team that couldn't win a raffle if we held the only ticket, we had become a team that couldn't lose, as we showed during the streak by coming from eighteen down in the fourth quarter to beat the Magic.

Finishing second on the ladder guaranteed us a semi-final spot, which allowed us to take the winning streak to fifteen games by sweeping the North Melbourne Giants. That gave us another grand final showdown with the South East Melbourne Magic and a chance to tie and then break the NBL's record for successive wins, which stood at sixteen and was owned by the Sydney Supersonics. Frankly, while everyone talked about the streak and the chance to claim the record, the most important thing was winning the championship. From an impossible position at the start of the season, the Tigers were two wins from achieving the highly improbable.

Playing in a grand final provided enough motivation and edge on its own. That we played the South East Melbourne Magic, our arch enemy, simply increased that motivation and determination by a factor of about ten. The Tigers–Magic rivalry had plenty of genuine feeling, especially among the players. One reason for the keenness of the rivalry was that Magic coach Brian Goorjian always pushed an angle, always tried to tweak some knobs and push some buttons. The Magic played hard, they didn't take backward steps and they portrayed a bad-boy image by wearing black uniforms and taking on the nickname of the Men in Black from the movie of the same name. The theme worked a treat and they were probably the most disliked team in the NBL. Goorjian didn't shy away from the notion and there has been no greater manipulator of the media. I have no problem with Brian and I respect and admire his genius at working the media, trying to gain an edge. Good on him.

One example of how Goorjian worked the media and put thoughts into people's minds was in the lead-up to the 1996 grand final series between the Tigers and Magic. We had played the semi-final decider against the Canberra Cannons on a Sunday and next day we had a recovery session with a swim and a walk. Instead of just walking, some of us played nine holes of golf at the Sandringham course, which backs onto where the Magic trained. So Lanard Copeland, Dave Simmons and I played golf and a television news crew filmed us. It gave Goorjian an instant propaganda angle from which to build the culture and image of the Magic with the claim that they work harder than anyone else, blah, blah, blah. So we were on the news playing golf and the next night it was Goorjian's turn in front of the cameras, pumping up his players as the hardest working team in the league, working on their game and fitness while the Tigers were relaxing and playing golf. We thought Goorjian had lost his mind, but later we came to appreciate that he used this forum to motivate his players and develop the culture of his team as well as to gain whatever extra edge he could. If he thought it would help his team win, he would do it and you've got to respect him for that. The Magic did win the title that year. But twelve months later, we were ready.

Rod Laver Arena at Melbourne Park was filled with fifteen thousand fans for game one of the best-of-three grand final series and we gave the Magic a pasting, just like they had done with us in game three a year before. We won by thirty-seven points, 111–74, so there was a sense of revenge about it. It wasn't our prime motivation at the start of the game to win by so much, but when we knew we were around that number, we felt we should try to grind them into the floor. We also wanted to set the tone for the rest of the series, whether it lasted one more game or two more games. We wanted to send a message.

Our win in game one equalled the NBL record of sixteen straight wins and we were unbackable favourites for the title. The Magic was clearly under the pump. But if there is one thing to be wary of, it is a Brian Goorjian-coached team with its back to the wall. As a basketball coach, Goorjian is a street fighter and he'll do whatever it takes to win, so we knew something would happen before or during game two to try to get the Magic back in the series. What happened was that Goorjian pulled a major switch in his line-up. He removed NBA-bound Chris Anstey and import guard Brian Tolbert from the starting five and put in teenager Frank Drmic and veteran big man John Dorge. Given the timing, most coaches wouldn't have contemplated such a change, but Goorjian did and his move was vindicated with an 84–78 win to square the series at 1–1. It was a physical game, they shut us down defensively, our winning streak was over and, with a perceived shift in momentum, we were one game away from being seen as chokers.

The second game was played on the Wednesday night, so we had Thursday and Friday to recover and get ready for the third and deciding game on the Saturday night. Nor were we without our problems and concerns. I had rolled an ankle that went shades of black and blue, while there was a distinct tension among the group, from not really knowing which way this series and season would end. We need not have worried.

If we made a statement with our win in game one of the grand final series, the Tigers made two pretty big statements in game three. In fact, Warrick Giddey, the ultimate unselfish role player who epitomised the ideal of doing whatever it took to get the job done, made both of these statements without saying a word and the Magic got the message loud and clear: we weren't to be messed with. The first significant moment came early when athletic Magic forward Sam Mackinnon went for a dunk and Wozza went up to block the shot and broke Mackinnon's nose. Some felt it was accidental, some felt it was deliberate, but I suppose it depended what colour you were wearing. The Magic was still on its Men in Black trip and looked like being ready to fight fire with fire and not be intimidated. Then Wozza set a screen for me at the centre line as I brought the ball up the floor. I was closely guarded by Mike Kelly, the best defender in the NBL, and I ran him right into Wozza. Kelly didn't see Wozza and got flattened – legally, I might add – and it wobbled his legs and might have taken a bit of an edge off the Magic.

The big basketball play of the game came just before three-quarter time from none other than Lanard Copeland, the bloke who looked like he couldn't play at his first training session but was on the verge of a second NBL title with the Tigers. We blew open the game for a twenty-point lead during the second period before the Magic rallied in the third, cutting the half-time margin from fourteen to eleven. As anyone will tell you, if a charging team gets the margin into single figures, it creates doubt among the leading team and generates confidence and belief in the team making the move.

So we really needed a couple of baskets to hold off the Magic. Copes delivered, making two jump shots and taking the ball to the basket on a drive to pump the gap back to seventeen points. The Magic responded with four straight points to reduce it to thirteen, then Copes stepped up again and landed another jump shot right at the buzzer to end the third period. Any thoughts of the Magic seizing the initiative and the momentum were gone. The Tigers led by fifteen and there was no way known we would let this one escape, finally winning 93–83. Fittingly, Copes was named MVP for the grand final series and we were all wearing our championship rings.

It was certainly a season to remember, especially since it had started like a season to forget. We were 3–9 and climbed out of that hole, we fought adversity and criticism, we became only the second NBL team to win sixteen straight games and we won the championship. All that gave the occasion a bit more significance, as did the fact that we beat the Magic, our arch rival. If anything, the rivalry went up another notch after that grand final for two reasons: we claimed the Magic's title and Warrick Giddey had given back some of the physicality the Magic was more accustomed to dishing out. Mark Bradtke had thrown petrol on the bonfire earlier in the season by telling the media that the Magic was soft and was not really living up to the bad-boy image. It added to the theatre and rivalry between the two teams who reached the ultimate point of the NBL season. There was no doubt that playing the Magic in three of the four grand finals the Tigers were in added to the games and meant something to the fans. With the intensity and atmosphere, the contests were often spectacular and the games amazing. That was diluted when the Magic merged with the North Melbourne Giants to become the Victoria Titans in 1998. While the Titans were considered by some to be the Magic in a different wrapper, it changed the rivalry and things was never the same again.

Having said that, we would take a championship no matter who it was against. We were just happier than a monkey with a boat-load of bananas to have won another one. Our win in 1997 was different to that in 1993, not only because of how the season panned out but because we won the title at home and got to share the complete experience with the fans. Having been there before, the second time is never the same as the first. Don't get me wrong, they're all enjoyable. But they're different, and you never know when you're going to get the chance to win another one. There are just no guarantees.

chapter eighteen

GAINING THE NBA SPURS

THE quarter-finals at the world championships usually make for one of the best days of basketball on the planet. Normally, I would have preferred to be playing, but the Boomers failed to get out of the group stages at Athens in 1998. It was a disappointing tournament for the Boomers and my mood on quarter-final day probably reflected that. I just wanted to sit quietly by myself and watch the four games.

So, of course, just as I was settling in, I noticed this bloke heading in my direction. I shrunk into my seat a little, hoping he might catch on to the body language. But he kept coming. I thought he might have been an autograph hunter who remembered me playing with Apollon Patras, or maybe he knew my dad and wanted to say g'day and pass on his best to the old man. It turned out he was neither. My new mate introduced himself in English that carried a strong Polish-sounding accent, but I can't say I caught his name. I kept one eye on the game and the other (and an ear) on him as he started up a bit of small talk.

'Andrew,' he said, 'do you have any interest in finishing your career in the NBA?'

There were two possibilities. Either he was an agent trying to rummage up some business or it was a set-up by my room-mate Shane Heal. As far as I knew, Hammer wasn't in the building, so I kept listening and maintained a polite level of interest. I told my new mate I'd never shut the door on the NBA, but it was unlikely, given the late stage of my career, that I'd be heading back to the big league. Besides, the NBA was in the middle of a serious labour dispute and there were doubts that the 1998–99 season would even go ahead. But this bloke would neither take a hint nor be deterred.

'Andrew, you know the situation with the lockout and that teams are not allowed to talk to anyone, but I'm a scout for the San Antonio Spurs,' he said as he pointed to the seats on the opposite side of the court in the Olympic Sports Hall, where Spurs coach Gregg Popovich was sitting. 'Gregg Popovich is here and would like to meet you, but he is not allowed, so I'm here to sound you out. Coach Popovich has a tremendous respect for you and your career and what you've done and he feels with the team he's got he needs more perimeter scoring. Would you consider playing for the Spurs?'

Despite what this bloke was saying, I was still on the lookout for a wind-up and, in the back of my mind, I wondered if this bloke was legit or whether he'd just lost his marbles all together. But the working side of my brain warned me not to be hasty, so I threw a harmless grenade back his way.

'I'd consider anything and if the opportunity came up that would be great,' I said, following the company line and pausing before adding the kicker. 'Mate, do you know how old I am?'

'Yes, thirty-three,' he said without missing a beat or consulting a media guide. 'We understand all that, but Coach Popovich is just looking for someone to hit a perimeter shot.'

With that, he gave me his card, which carried the distinctive NBA and Spurs logos and his name. It all looked and sounded legitimate but, having had NBA interest that fizzled to nothing before, I didn't really think too much more of it. Not until the Boomers shoot-around the next morning as we got ready to play Brazil in the play-off for ninth and tenth. Coach Barry Barnes sidled up and mentioned that somebody from the Spurs had spoken to him about me and indicated they were quite keen about trying to sign me. My new mate had covered some ground.

When I got back to Australia from Athens, I mentioned the conversation with the Polish bloke to Grant Cadee, a mate and agent, and Brett Brown. Grant, who had several good NBA contacts, followed it up with the Spurs director of scouting and assistant general manager, RC Buford. When they got off the phone, RC went and checked it out with Gregg Popovich. Sure enough, the interest was real. What I couldn't really explain was how a grey-haired 33-year-old Australian was a chance to play in Texas after a conversation with a Pole in Greece. When they say getting an NBA job is about being in the right place at the right time, this had to be it. Maybe.

The Spurs' interest in me probably started a year or so before the world championships in Athens. Larry Fehrenbacher, a former coach of the US Air Force basketball team, was a friend of Gregg Popovich and my dad. The lines of communication had remained open between the three of them and I think that was how Pop became aware of me. It was a bit like that with other NBA interest I'd had. Somebody knew somebody who knew somebody else and my name got mentioned on the way through. Initially, I didn't regard the Spurs' interest to be much more than that. At thirty-three, I just never thought it was realistic. But the more we examined the situation and the more we put some of the pieces together, the more the Spurs' interest seemed more than passing.

RC Buford saw the Boomers finish second at the Goodwill Games in New York on the way to Athens, so that was a tick. The Boomers did well at the Goodwill Games, which were played at storied Madison Square Garden. We beat Argentina, Lithuania and Puerto Rico, but lost to the United States in the final, 93–85. We actually took the Americans, who were a team of college kids, to overtime after I missed a shot from the perimeter at the end of regulation with the scores 79–79. I ended up with twenty-five points against the Yanks and averaged 22.4 for the five games of the tournament, so I did reasonably well. But the worlds in Athens were another story as the Boomers slumped to ninth and I managed 16.9 ppg. It wasn't the form I thought would have the NBA wanting my name on a contract.

Grant and Brett maintained contact with RC Buford and he actually visited Melbourne for a week to help with the adidas ABC basketball camp that I was part of. RC, who had been an assistant coach at Kansas University when it won the 1988 NCAA Championship, provided an NBA presence and some serious basketball knowledge. It also gave me, Grant and Brett a chance to pick his brain on several fronts, not least of all the Spurs' interest in me.

I remained ambivalent about the whole NBA thing. It was a long shot, particularly with the labour dispute between NBA players and owners. The season, which was delayed by the dispute over a new collective bargaining agreement, was in increasing jeopardy of not being played the longer the impasse continued. But it was still early days in the dispute when we spoke to RC in Melbourne and he actually confirmed that the Spurs wanted me for the season. As soon as the lockout ended, if it did end, I would be offered an NBA contract. There was nothing in writing, because NBA rules prevented teams from talking to players during the lockout, but RC gave his word and there was no reason to doubt it. I was going to the NBA. That's if there was a season. Definite though RC was about me signing for the Spurs, he was just as definite in his reading of the labour situation that there would be no season.

There was a season in Australia and the NBL went ahead as normal from October. So, while keeping mum on the NBA deal, I went into action for the Melbourne Tigers. We started the season 10–0 and were on a tear as I wondered whether I would finish the season with the Tigers or the Spurs. The more the Tigers won and the more the NBA situation remained unresolved, the more appealing and the more realistic was the prospect of staying with the Tigers.

While I continued playing with the Tigers, I received information from inside the Spurs – from a pretty a good source. Brett Brown, who lost his job as a coach of the North Melbourne Giants when they merged with the South East Melbourne Magic, picked up work with the Spurs. When the Giants went south, Brett talked to the Spurs and the Boston Celtics, where he had contacts, and offered his services for free. He was prepared to do an internship to gain experience as a coach and an insight into the NBA way. San Antonio bit on the offer and Brett's initiative was rewarded. We regularly exchanged email and by December it looked like the NBA season was dead. Then, almost out of nowhere, by January, it looked like the season would go ahead. The NBA and the players association had a two-week window to get a deal done. Until then, there could still be no official talk to players.

With the NBA season becoming a strong possibility, I was like a duck on a pond. I was serene and relaxed on the surface, but I was working furiously below the surface. To be ready to go to San Antonio as soon as the NBA flicked the green light, I needed a visa. Given my experience with US visas, I knew I couldn't just show up and get a stamp. Fortunately, I had some help from the US consul general in Melbourne, Tex Harris. Tex just happened to be a big basketball fan. Even better, he was a Melbourne Tigers fan. The complication I had securing a visa was that I needed an NBA contract as proof of work. Because of the lockout, I didn't have a contract. A verbal agreement didn't count with the US immigration authorities. Without the relevant visa, I couldn't get an NBA contract. I believe it's called

Catch 22. I needed to be in San Antonio for the opening of an abbreviated training camp, so I said to Tex: 'I have a deal, but I don't have a deal. Can you help?' Tex understood the situation perfectly and expedited the process. I got the visa stamp in my passport. The other obstacle we had to overcome was getting to San Antonio. Only a few people knew what was going on, so it was like an underground operation trying to get organised. Because I hadn't signed a contract with the Spurs and, going strictly by the rules, hadn't spoken to team officials, they could not fly me in. I had to buy my own ticket and be in town ready for camp when it opened. If anyone bought the story that I was doing that on spec, I have some prime real estate in the Arctic Circle that they might be interested in buying.

There was speculation in the Australian media that I was going to the NBA and I held the line that it was a possibility, nothing more. But I went on a road trip with the Tigers to Townsville and Brisbane during January knowing that the two games we played would be my last in the NBL before going to the NBA. We lost a tight one to the Townsville Crocodiles on the Friday night and we beat the Brisbane Bullets in overtime the next night. I had forty-five points against the Bullets and got an early night. I had to catch the first flight out of Brisbane on Sunday morning for a media conference in Melbourne. Publicly, at least, it was finally on. Almost five years after the briefest taste, I was going back to the NBA with the San Antonio Spurs.

When I arrived in San Antonio, the NBA season, to all intents and purposes, was ready to go just as soon as the loose ends were tidied on the collective bargaining agreement. Then the pre-season could get underway officially, knowing we would have a two-week training camp, a few pre-season exhibition games and a fifty-game regular season. The lockout wiped thirty-two games off the normal 82-game season. Even though teams could not practise with coaches present until the agreement was signed, just about all the players on the Spurs pre-season roster were in town by the time I arrived.

There wasn't much time for cuts to be made and places won, so it wasn't a big group for the camp. At least I didn't have to worry about making the team. I was already assured of a roster spot and signed my NBA contract. Given my previous service at training camps and the two ten-day contracts with the Washington Bullets, I was granted a pay status higher than a rookie. So I wasn't on the lowest NBA salary level, but I wasn't too far above it, either.

When I got to San Antonio, the team was in place, at least on paper or in the heads of Gregg Popovich and RC Buford. With core veterans Tim Duncan, David Robinson, Sean Elliott, Avery Johnson and Antonio Daniels in place, complemented by re-signing free agents Jaren Jackson and Malik Rose, the Spurs signed more old guys: Steve Kerr, Mario Elie, Jerome Kersey and me, raising the average age of the team to almost thirty-one. There were also four guys in for tryouts: guards Chris Garner and Brandon Williams, forward Gerard King and centre Brett Robisch. Those veteran free agent signings probably diminished my chances of playing a regular role for the Spurs. But I never went to the Spurs believing I would play decent minutes, anyway. The possibility of playing ten or fifteen minutes a game was never mentioned by the Spurs. Depending on who the Spurs signed it might have been a chance, but it was never discussed. I knew without even talking to Gregg Popovich that I was there for insurance purposes only. If somebody went down injured, I might step up. Certainly, my contract was guaranteed, but my playing time was not.

Almost from my first day in San Antonio, we were in practice situations – initially with informal scrimmages, then in more structured and supervised sessions with the coaching staff. Until the coaching staff got involved, the scrimmages at the University of the Incarnate Word were basically glorified, highly-talented pick-up ball sessions. Pretty much all the players were there, with Avery Johnson running the show in lieu of the coaches. Avery called the shots, decided who would play and on which teams. I knew Avery from my tryout with Seattle in 1989 and I knew David Robinson from the 1986 World Championships and 1988 and 1996 Olympics, so I was relieved and pleased when Robinson walked right up and welcomed me the first day of practice. Going into an uncertain situation, David's welcome was reassuring because these guys could ice you right from the start if they wanted to.

I held my own in the scrimmages and I don't think I looked out of place but I realised very quickly the amazing level of athleticism, strength, speed and skill these guys brought to the table. Not just the superstars, either. I was matched up against Chuck Person, who had been with the Spurs the previous season but was about to be sent to the Chicago Bulls in exchange for shooting guard Steve Kerr in a sign-and-trade deal. Some people assumed Steve's signing snuffed out my chances of playing, but I don't believe that was necessarily true. I actually thought Steve's signing was a great move. This was a guy with three NBA Championship rings and a ton of experience. He also became one of my best mates on the team as the season evolved.

During training camp, we did fairly strenuous weights sessions. It was as I pumped a little iron during my second day on the job that everyone on the team learned about my prowess in the gym. There I was, having long considered a weight room as something at the front of the doctor's surgery, flexing my puny guns alongside blokes like David Robinson, who I'm sure was actually chiselled from marble and granite. Robinson was known as the Admiral because of his service in the US Navy before playing in the NBA and not even Michelangelo could have sculpted or depicted him in finer form than he actually was.

Not wanting to be put off by these Adonis types, I was prepared to have a crack. I wanted to impress. The problem was that I wasn't sure about converting metric weights to imperial. Going from kilograms to pounds, it turned out, was not my strong suit. One of the strength and conditioning coaches, who had actually been on the

World's Strongest Man TV show, asked me how much I wanted on the bar for the incline bench. I figured ten reps with about eighty-five kilograms would be fine. But between us, we had no idea what that was in pounds. So they whacked some weights on the bar and I got ready to lift. I swear, I managed to just get the bar over the cradle hooks that kept it in place while resting. While I immediately sensed I was in a bit of strife with the weight, I didn't give in. I had to make an attempt. Boom! The whole thing was on top of me and I felt like I was fighting for my life. I was trying to get the bar off like it was a tarantula about to bite. The only thing was this was an extremely heavy tarantula. As I flailed beneath the weight, I yelled out, 'I haven't got it!' As if nobody there knew that.

Now I'm sure this was a very funny scene if you were watching, as testified by the number of team-mates doubled over with laughter. So much for making a good impression. I wanted to tell them we'd miscalculated the weight, but I don't think they would have bought it, even if they had stopped laughing long enough to hear the explanation. They did eventually ask if I was all right. Trying to shield my acute embarrassment, I quickly gathered my coolness and shrugged it off as nothing. Yeah, right. While I acted like nothing happened, they would have thought, after seeing that and the scrimmages, 'He's old, he's not particularly quick and, clearly, he's not that strong.'

Fortunately, my inability to raise weights above my head, or my chest for that matter, did not disqualify me from social activities. Steve Kerr, Will Perdue and Malik Rose often invited me to hang out with them, go to dinner or a movie. Maybe they just felt sorry for the slow, grey-haired, old weakling from Australia. If they did, I certainly tested their patience.

One day Will and Malik invited me to a movie and gave me directions to the cinema, telling me to go this way and that and, crucially as it turned out, to make sure I turned right at the access road. After driving for about thirty minutes, I was still no closer to the cinema. I had no mobile phone to call them, so I stopped and asked people for help with the directions, but I still couldn't figure out where I was going. It was like the Leyland Brothers meets Gilligan's Island. I eventually pulled over at a public phone and called Will on his mobile. I explained I had followed their directions several times, but I could not for the life of me find Access Road. It was then that Will patiently explained I should have veered right onto *an* access road. I was looking for Access Road. Hey, it was an honest mistake. If they had said I had to turn right onto a service road, I would have been fine. Call it an international miscommunication. But by now the boys had to be thinking, 'He's old, he's slow, he's not strong and he's not very bright, either.' The saving grace for me during these embarrassing situations might have been that I was Australian. You know, 'It's okay, he's from Australia.' A bit like Basil Fawlty would explain Manuel the Spanish waiter with 'It's quite all right, he's from Barcelona.'

With the Aussie connection, the Spurs marketing people thought they had a perfect role for me, helping with the season-opening Tux and Tennies Ball. The Tux and Tennies Ball was a tradition in San Antonio where everyone dressed in their best formal attire (tux) and wore tennis shoes (tennies). It was a big deal and the folks in the marketing department asked if I'd film a video clip to open the function. They wanted me to impersonate Steve Irwin, the Crocodile Hunter, for the cameras. Which was fine with me. It was just that I had absolutely no idea who Steve Irwin was. Big as he was on American TV, I had never laid eyes on the bloke who is now just as big an icon at home. So now the Spurs must have thought I was some kind of impostor. I was from Australia and I didn't even know the Crocodile Hunter. They couldn't believe it. Who is this guy?

Anyway, they explained the Crocodile Hunter and his hyped-up enthusiasm for baiting and wrestling crocs and asked me to be just like that. The only difference was, dressed in khaki shirt and shorts

and topped with a bush hat, I had to fight through the jungle track-
ing the Spurs' Coyote mascot. Obviously they'd seen my thespian
work on the Channel Ten sports reports back home. So I examined
the script and gave it the all-clear. Actually, I was quite happy to do
anything the Spurs wanted, except take out the garbage, at that
stage. So as I parted the dense undergrowth, I whispered to the camera that, miles from civilisation and medical help, I was hunting one
of the world's shrewdest, most dangerous, feared animals. With that,
I dived onto the Coyote, bound him up with rope and posed
triumphantly in best Crocodile Hunter fashion.

I could only hope my performance went over well at the Tux and
Tennies Ball but the evening gave me an instant introduction to the
San Antonio community and the wider Spurs organisation. I think
it also showed the players, coaches and whoever else that I was not
on an ego trip. I was happy to mix and fit in and do whatever was
best for the team. Given I had already shown that I was old, grey,
slow, weak and not very bright, I had surely proven that I was worth
keeping around, if only for comic relief.

The serious business of getting ready for the season continued,
but the more I looked at the guys in training camp, the more I wondered about my place in the scheme of things. I knew I wouldn't play
much, but when I looked at the guys in camp and the eventual fourteen players who were contracted (twelve active, two on the injured
reserve), something just didn't seem right. Every time I considered
the make-up of the Spurs roster, it just kept hitting me between the
eyes that we were overloaded with guards and were skinnier than a
stray cat when it came to genuine big men.

I had a strong sense of déjà vu as the situation seemed very similar to the one I had experienced during my tryout with the Seattle
SuperSonics ten years earlier. No matter which way I mentally listed
the players, no matter how I rationalised the roster and the rotations, we had more guards than the Pentagon. It just didn't make
sense. I looked at the players signed, I looked at myself and I figured

if you were going to carry insurance, which I was, surely it would be with a big man, even if only for scrimmage purposes and as injury coverage. Not that I shared this theory with the coaching staff.

Maybe I thought too much, or still felt like the new boy, but I was a bit gun-shy early at practice and in scrimmages. Frankly, I knew the Spurs had signed me, but I just wasn't sure how long I would last. I never felt deflated because I never went there with an expectation of much anyway. But, while it was great and I really wanted to be part of it, did I fit in? That was the question swirling around in my head.

The harsh reality was that my role would be very limited, maybe even more limited than I conservatively envisaged. I always knew that, but there were other factors at play as I reflected on what I had given up to be there. For one thing, the Melbourne Tigers were a red-hot chance to win the NBL title. But I stepped back, looked at the Spurs' situation and weighed it up for what it was. When I made the decision to go to San Antonio, I said it was about having an experience. The other factor was that this superstar team was considered a championship chance. Whatever my role was, it would be nice to be part of that.

The pre-season exhibition series started with a road game against the Houston Rockets and was my introduction to NBA travel, the modern way. During my brief stint with the Washington Bullets in 1994, we mainly flew on commercial airlines, mixing with the public, hanging around in departure lounges. Not with the Spurs of 1999. We flew charter, in our own aircraft, making regular business class travel feel like you were crammed into a Fiat Uno driving over one hundred kilometres of speed humps.

A few of us still lived in a hotel when the exhibition season started, so Malik Rose drove us to the airport. Malik knew where to go and it wasn't to the check-in counter or a curb-side drop-off. No sir. Malik drove us right onto the tarmac and under the wing of the aircraft. We jumped out, an attendant grabbed our bags from the boot, Malik drove to a park about a hundred metres away and we walked up the steps to the aircraft. It was impressive, to say the least. At the back was a section for travelling media, the coaches were in the middle and the players were at the front. We were early and needed to know the seating rules, so Malik pointed out who sat where and which seats were available for the new guys. You certainly didn't covet, let alone sit in, a seat that belonged to one of the veterans. Mind you, these seats that people had laid claim to were no ordinary airline seats. They were massive leather chairs with more leg space than my lounge room. It was like you could get anything you wanted on board, too. I honestly thought that if I asked, a Japanese geisha would have come by for a foot massage. It was that good. Mind you, while I was initially overawed by our jet, some of the guys who had been on other NBA teams rated other teams' charters better. Whatever.

There was no doubt that charter flights were and are a luxury perk of playing in the NBA. Some might say it's an extravagance. But given the NBA schedule and the need to travel vast distances in a short time, it makes sense to go straight from the arena after a game to the airport and fly to the next city or home, giving the players extra rest and preparation time. When the NBA owners invest so many millions of dollars in paying players, there's no point hurting that investment by skimping in areas like travel. With the charter aircraft, the Spurs flew to every corner of the US but never once went through an airport terminal. In fact, it became so natural to bypass the airline terminals that when I came home after the season, it felt a little weird lining-up at the check-in desk.

Flying on charters was only one part of the largesse associated with the NBA. A bigger part was the amount of money paid to players. The salary cap for the 1999 season was US$30 million per team, although there were avenues to legally spend more. The Spurs' cap that season was US$40 million, but with the shortened season it was calculated on a pro rata basis at US$24.5 million. Sometimes you could lose sight of the amount of money dished around. I was on close to the minimum of about US$350,000 (about US$220,000 pro rata), but I was counting dimes compared to blokes like David Robinson (US$14.8 million), Sean Elliott (US$5.3 million) and Tim Duncan (US$3.4 million). Let it be said that Duncan's latest contract is worth about US$122 million over seven years. Nice work if you can get it.

It was big money and the players reflected that with their jewellery, clothes and houses. The big earners had the best of whatever they wanted, but one thing about this group with the Spurs was that they did not flaunt their wealth. Several players, especially David Robinson, were very generous with their donations to charity. In fact, David donated many millions to promote education in San Antonio and even funded the building of a school. So it was no surprise to any of us who have spent time with the Admiral that the NBA named its award for community service award after David Robinson.

David is a genuinely humble man and it was humbling to be invited to his house in San Antonio. My wife Melinda and I visited for dinner one night and we knew it would be something special when we approached and saw the house was on Admiral Way. We were not let down once we stepped inside and were given a grand tour. It was a mansion, though in no way over the top. It was two-storey, with tennis court and pool, as you would expect. The big comparison for me was the Admiral's master bedroom, which, combined with the walk-in dressing room and en suite, was bigger than the two-bedroom apartment Melinda and I shared with our daughters Courtney and Phoebe in San Antonio. You just could not help but be impressed by the house and by David himself. He was all class, a terrific human being.

The other telltale sign of money among the players was their cars. Some guys might have had three or four cars and there was a sprinkling of Mercedes-Benzes, Porsches, Land Rovers and whatever else in the players' parking lot. Again, I let the team down. I drove a rented Pontiac, which didn't really fit the NBA image. But I wasn't on my own. Steve Kerr, despite a contract that earned him almost US$2 million per season, drove to work every day in his six-year-old Honda. Steve was a bit of a battler in the NBA pay stakes during his career and loved his Honda. He copped some flak about his wheels from time to time, but it fitted his image. When I returned to San Antonio a year later, I was pleased to see Steve had traded in the Honda. I was not surprised he had got himself a family-oriented Volvo. It was a modest and humble car for a modest and humble man.

As the lockout had delayed the start of the season by about three months, the NBA and the teams were eager to make sure they got the fans, some of whom were highly critical of the labour dispute involving blokes who earned millions of dollars, back on side pretty quickly. The Spurs had always been a community-minded organisa-tion and held an open practice at the Alamodome before the first exhibition game. More than five thousand fans turned up to watch us go through a few drills and a very low-key scrimmage. At the end of the session, some of the fans got autographs from the players. But, because of the massive demand, especially of the superstars, the fans went into a lottery to be eligible for an autograph. Not only was it a lottery to get an autograph; the draw also determined which player's autograph the fans would get, lining up at designated tables to do so. So imagine the letdown for the many young San Antonio fans who hoped to get the signature of Tim Duncan or David Robinson and drew the short straw of Andrew Gaze instead. They only had to look a couple of tables down the line and curse at how close they were to getting the big prize as they shuffled away with the consolation.

It turned out that the exhibition season didn't give those fans who saved their Andrew Gaze autographs much hope of a spike in the price of their newest piece of memorabilia. Although, as it happened, the exhibition season might have been the most I played with the Spurs. Our first exhibition game was against the Houston Rockets at Houston's Compaq Centre. We had sixteen players on the roster for the pre-season games, which meant minutes were thin, even for the big names. I subbed into the game in the third quarter, played about eight minutes and hit a three-pointer. Steve Kerr had the ball in transition from defence to offence, a defender ran to him, he passed to me in the corner, I squared up and let it fly. Bang! The best way to describe my first game in a Spurs uniform was that I didn't stuff up.

At the end of the exhibition season, the Spurs retained Brandon Williams and Gerard King as contracted players on the injured reserve. Every team carried extra players so that, rather than calling up guys from outside the NBA in case of injury or a roster change, guys were ready and familiar to the team and its offensive and defensive plays. In a fifty-game sprint, which was what the shortened season was, having guys on tap would be crucial. For me, it would mean something else.

Once the regular season started, I was not in the playing rotation at all. I could safely say my tag was twelfth man and I saw as much action as the bloke carrying the drinks for the Australian cricket team. I was strictly a junk-time player, getting bits and pieces here and there at the end of games that were decided on the scoreboard. There is a very good reason why junk time is called junk time: the basketball played is junk. Rubbish. Garbage. Not wanted by anybody. It's usually every man for himself, desperately trying to make some kind of impression in one or two minutes. Watching this stuff, I sometimes wondered how guys made it to the NBA. It could be that bad. The thing was, though, if that's all you got, you had to take it, be grateful and do the best you could.

My first NBA points for the Spurs came in a 99–81 win over the Seattle SuperSonics when I knocked down a three-pointer. Being the consummate team player, I even had an assist to Jaren Jackson.

A handful of games later, we blew out the LA Clippers, 114–85, at home. That 39-point margin meant I was a pretty safe bet to get into the game. It was even better when I hit back-to-back three-pointers.

The pressure was on, though, when the Denver Nuggets called at the Alamodome on 13 March. There were 32,982 people in the arena that night but only a few I was worried about impressing. Fortunately, my team-mates put a big margin into the Nuggets en route to a 92–61 victory for our seventh straight win, so I was able to get in for late-game action and score three points. They were valuable minutes and valuable points, although maybe not too memorable. In fact, they might have been precious because I don't think reporter Liz Hayes and her crew from *Sixty Minutes* would have been too happy taking home video of me sitting on the bench all night.

The *Sixty Minutes* crew was in the United States doing a piece on me and fellow Aussie Luc Longley, who was with the Phoenix Suns. The only difference was that I would play random minutes and earned near the minimum wage, while Luc averaged twenty-four minutes per game for 8.7 ppg and 5.6 rebounds and had just signed a new deal worth US$36 million. Not bad cabbage, but being 218 centimetres will help. Not that *Sixty Minutes* treated us any differently. They laid on a black stretch limo for the Gazes to ride around San Antonio on a nice Sunday afternoon so they could film me doing something. The way the season was going, even the TV cameramen were getting more shots than me.

One of the advantages, if you could call it that, of sitting on the bench all night, was that I got a good idea of what the crowd thought. Usually, if an American sports fan thinks something, he or she will articulate it some way sooner or later. As the Spurs struggled through the first dozen games, their fans said what they thought and a lot of it wasn't very pleasant. From my spot on the bench at home games, I heard plenty from the seats behind. The fans were harsh and did not miss. After a 6–8 start to the season, coach Gregg

Popovich was in the gun and some of the fans were all too willing to pull the trigger.

During this bad trot we played the Utah Jazz at home and got killed. They pulled our pants down to our ankles and Pop got ejected after blowing up at the referees. Down about twenty after three quarters, the only good thing was that junk time started earlier than usual and I managed to get some extended minutes. But it was a position none of us wanted to be in. After that game, I spoke to Brett Brown about the situation and even the coaches had been talking about how dire the whole thing was. In American sport, if the head coach gets fired, the whole coaching staff might follow him out the door, so a lot of people were concerned about the team not getting it right on the floor. The pressure, along with the speculation in the media about Pop's future, was mounting.

Gregg Popovich took over as Spurs coach in controversial circumstances during the 1996 season. He was general manager and Bob Hill was the coach, but coaching without David Robinson, who was out injured. The Spurs were 3–15, so Pop fired Hill and took over the dual role of coach/GM, which he still held when I arrived. The Spurs barely recovered and finished the season 20–62, the worst record in franchise history. There was a payoff: the Spurs won the draft lottery and landed Tim Duncan with the first pick. That certainly helped Pop rejuvenate the team, but if he couldn't coach he would have been found out, with or without Duncan and Robinson.

There was no doubt Pop had done his coaching apprenticeship. After playing at the Air Force Academy, where he was captain in his senior year and had a tryout for the 1972 US Olympic team, Pop completed his five-year military service commitment and spent a lot of it touring Europe as a member of the US Armed Forces basketball team. You could understand why Pop, having played in the old Eastern Bloc countries, did not have an aversion to adding veterans and foreigners to his teams. He became an assistant coach at Air Force, then moved to a little Division III school, Pomona-Pitzer

University in California, and served eight seasons as head coach. From there, he went to the Spurs as an assistant under head coach Larry Brown, then moved back west as an assistant coach with the Golden State Warriors under Don Nelson before returning to the Spurs as GM in 1994. So it wasn't like Pop was just off the street when it came to coaching. He'd done his time.

Coming from a military background, Pop was naturally a disciplinarian. But not rigidly so. He was also flexible. He understood the superstar mentality of the NBA, but he was not beyond giving either Robinson or Duncan a verbal spray if he thought it was needed. If you read stories about Pop, inevitably it will either be said, implied or deduced that he is a player's coach and a coach's coach and normally cool under pressure or in a crisis. There has always been talk, but never publicly from the man himself, that he worked as a US spy or a covert military operator in Russia. The only such talk I heard within the Spurs was during the rocky start to the season. The grapevine had it that Pop told his assistants he wasn't under pressure. Pressure, Pop told them according to the tale, was working solo under the nose of the Russians during a Siberian winter. Simply, Pop is a good guy. He is also smart and humble, always off to the side of any celebration when he should rightly be the centre of attention. Although there was one time, after we escaped with a win over the Phoenix Suns on a Sean Elliott three-pointer at the buzzer, when we saw a different side of Pop. It wasn't really a side we wanted to see, either. We were already in the locker room when Pop burst in, stripped off all his clothes and lay stark naked on the floor pumping his fists. Then he got up and got dressed. It was a good win, but not that good.

Perhaps the best thing about Pop was that he never forgot about you. That all came home to me during my time with the Spurs, especially when I was on the active roster and rarely playing. Even though Pop was under pressure, he still had time for me. He always remained positive and he never stopped encouraging me. At practice or if I was shooting around by myself, if Pop passed by, he never failed to tell me, 'Stick with it, you never know what's going to happen or if a chance might break.' He never made any false promises and he never offered insincere hope. He was a genuine bloke and, frankly, he was the only reason the Spurs signed me. So I certainly didn't want to see him sacked. As it was, the Spurs beat the Houston Rockets to start a run and we went 31–5 the rest of the regular season. It saved Pop's job and it saved the Spurs' season. So Pop didn't get the elbow, but little did I know I was about to.

chapter nineteen

HAVE YOU GOT A MINUTE?

HAVE you got a minute? Usually, it's a rhetorical question. But when the boss says it, it's not so much rhetorical as it is foreboding. As San Antonio Spurs coach Gregg Popovich said these five words, he motioned for me to cross the hotel foyer. He didn't have to say another word. I knew what was coming.

Ever since training camp, I'd felt the balance of the Spurs' active roster wasn't right, that while I was there for insurance among the guards and small forwards, I was insurance that the Spurs didn't really need. They had more parachutes than the air force in those positions. But, as I have said, we were supermodel thin in the big-man positions and, since our game was based around two of the NBA's best in David Robinson and Tim Duncan, it would have been disastrous if one of them or their backup went down. As it panned out, back-up centre Will Perdue spent thirteen games on the injured reserve, but when David's back tightened and he sat out a couple of games the alarm bells rang loudly for the coaching staff.

When it came to sizing up the insurance business, I was like the Man From The Prudential. I had it down pat. Not that it was hard to see. Malik Rose was a 200-centimetre forward playing as an undersized centre and Jerome Kersey, who was of a similar build, did his best work from the perimeter. The obvious move was to bring in 205 centimetre Gerard King from the injured reserve and make him our fourth-tallest player behind the seven-foot trio of Robinson, Duncan and Perdue. Even if he didn't play, which was likely, at least he was there and ready to go in a game situation, if only for a minute here and there to rest one of the bigs and maybe waste some fouls down the stretch.

Surely, I thought, there would be a time when I'd go on the injured reserve. Maybe it was my pessimism taking over, but for a while it seemed like nobody else thought the same. Maybe they did but were too polite to discuss it in my presence. Anyway, for about two weeks, I constantly asked Brett Brown, who was involved with every coaches' meeting, about my situation and whether Gerard King would take my place on the roster. Every day, Brett placated me and reassured me the situation had not even been raised in the coaches' meeting. He was honest and up front, so I just kept training when the schedule allowed and wondered what was up. About a week later, the wheels started turning somewhere other than in my brain. Brett mentioned to me that the subject of a roster change had been raised by the coaches. Naturally, he needed to tell me this in confidence. As a coach, he didn't have to tell me. As a mate, he did.

Even though I mentally tried to prepare for being removed from the active roster, when it became a realistic possibility my thoughts started drifting. It was a confusing time. I wasn't sure when it would happen or how long it would be for. One thing that did enter my consciousness was that the NBL season was heading towards the play-offs and the Tigers were a chance to win the championship. Frankly, I thought if I got placed on the injured reserve, maybe I would have been better off back in Australia. 'I love it and I'm happy to do it and I'm enjoying the experience,' I told Brett Brown one night. 'But the NBL finals are coming and, if this happens, do you reckon I should say thanks, but I'd prefer to go?' Brett, although sympathetic to my situation, was straight and to the point: 'You should try and stick it out.'

In my head and maybe my heart, if I wasn't playing for the Spurs, I would have preferred to be at home playing for the Tigers. While I was on the active roster, at least there was always a chance I would play. If I was on the injured reserve, I knew I had no chance. At thirty-three, I didn't really know how much time was left in my basketball career and I wanted to make the most of it, whether it be in the NBA or the NBL. I was torn, so I called my dad. As always, he was the perfect sounding board, let me get things off my chest then said what he always said: 'It's your decision. Do whatever you feel is appropriate and I'll support you.'

For about a week after Brett alerted me to the coaches' inclinations I waited for the move to be made. It happens all the time in the NBA. Players move on and off the active and injured lists, trades are made, players are signed and there's not any real fuss made of it, unless it involves a superstar. The news usually ends up in the fine print of the newspapers, amid the agate, under the heading 'Transactions'. I'd read those things hundreds, maybe thousands, of times and not given it a thought. Now that it involved me, I dreaded the newspaper five-point like some people dreaded the death notices and obituaries.

It was early April with thirty-three games of the fifty-game schedule gone. The season was right back on track for the Spurs as we prepared to play the Rockets in Houston. The day before the game we trained in the morning and were due to fly to Houston that afternoon. After training, Gregg Popovich called me aside. I braced myself. 'Andrew,' Pop started, 'we're in a situation where we're thinking about activating Gerard. If that happens, it would mean you'd have to go on injured reserve.' Rather than just send me on my way, Pop explained what it all meant and why he was considering the move. It was as I thought. With David Robinson's suspect back, Gerard was the logical guy to have in uniform in case of emergency. Basically they were changing the size of their insurance policy from my 201 centimetres and 95 kilograms to Gerard King's 206 centimetres and 113 kilograms. It made perfect and logical sense.

'You remain part of the team,' Pop said, trying to soften the blow. 'You train with the team and the expectation is the same as if you were on the active roster. The only thing is you don't suit up at game time. If someone else gets hurt, you're straight back in, but this is how it is and I just wanted to let you know this is how we're thinking and to make you aware of it and let you have time to think about your situation.'

I drove home before going to the airport for the short flight to Houston with my head swirling. I spoke to Melinda about the situation, discussed the options and weighed them up as best I could. There were only two choices: stay or go home. What prevailed was the thought that burned in my brain all along: my sense of obligation to the Spurs and Gregg Popovich. They gave me this opportunity, I entered it with my eyes wide open, I knew the situation I was getting involved in. I'm sure if I had told them I was cutting my losses and returning to Australia for the rest of the NBL season they would have understood and wished me luck. But I felt a sense of obligation to stick it out and see it through to the end.

'Andrew, have you got a minute?' Finally, the words I had dreaded and expected. We had been to our game-day shoot-around at the Compaq Centre in Houston and had just got off the bus back at the hotel, when Pop called me aside in the lobby. He didn't muck around. 'We're going to go ahead and make the change,' Pop said. 'We're going to do it for tonight.'

'Fair enough,' I said. 'I understand. No problem.'

Pop's parting words were: 'The trainer will be in touch and explain the process.' Later that day, the telephone rang in my hotel room. It was the Spurs' head trainer, Will Sevening. He asked: 'What injury do you want?'

'Well,' I said, trying to figure what part of my healthy body would make a good excuse, 'my ankle's been playing up a bit.'

It was comical and frustrating. I was fit and healthy, but had to go through the charade of being injured. There was no test to even make sure the injury was genuine, which made a mockery of the whole thing. The NBA should just allow teams to carry fourteen guys with two listed as reserves so they can make changes whenever needed. Why the need for make-believe? But while I dealt with my phantom injury, the disappointment was all too real. My disappointment arose on two fronts. One, I was further removed from my goal and desire to play a full season in the NBA. Whereas I had a small chance of playing, going on the IR meant I had zero. Two, I kept thinking about what was happening with the Tigers, who eventually lost a close two-game semi-final series against the Victoria Titans.

It was a time of self-doubt and second-guessing: had I made the right decision to join the Spurs in the first place? Should I have pulled the pin and gone home? Had I let down people in Australia because I was in San Antonio and not playing? Had I given up a chance to win another NBL championship? I really had no answers to my own questions and they all highlighted my disappointment and dejection. Whichever way the Spurs or I wanted to paint the situation, being placed on the injured reserve when I wasn't injured was a kick in the guts. Much as I understood it and expected it, it was a kick in the guts that still hurt.

During a normal eighty-two game NBA season, teams would be expected to cop injuries. But during the lockout-shortened campaign, the Spurs went through relatively unscathed. Will Perdue's thirteen games on the IR was the most by any of the players in the rotation. Tim Duncan, Avery Johnson and Sean Elliott played in all fifty games, while David Robinson, Mario Elie, Jaren Jackson, Antonio Daniels, Malik Rose, Steve Kerr and Jerome Kersey missed a combined twenty-four games, and not all of them were through injury. It was indeed rare to go through a season with such good health. The Spurs' good health might have been my bad luck.

After a while, I realised moving to the injured reserve really only changed my status officially. It didn't alter my standing among the guys on the team. They didn't treat me any differently. I still sat on the bench, except that instead of a Spurs warm-up suit, I was in a business suit. Which did present a problem that first night of my IR duty in Houston. Because I had expected to be on the roster for that game, I travelled in casual gear and didn't have my suit with me. It was a jeans and windcheater trip, but when you sat on the bench in civvies, *more* was expected from the NBA fashion police. As I watched the game, Jerome Kersey leaned over and said in a half-serious tone: 'Man, do you know where you're at? This is the NBA. Don't come dressed like that again.' He was kind of joking, but he also made sure the NBA dress code, with Hugo Boss as God, was upheld. I made sure I wore my Sunday best the rest of the season.

Had I not been involved with such a great group of guys, being placed on the IR might have been a lot harder to accept. The Spurs provided a night-and-day comparison to my experience with the Washington Bullets in terms of people and the organisation. Whereas the Bullets were fragmented and played for themselves in facilities that needed work, the Spurs were a team that was united, headed for the ultimate achievement, surrounded by facilities and support staff that were the duck's nuts. The Spurs were a class organisation in every facet.

Probably the guy I was closest to during my season with the Spurs was Steve Kerr. We had a little bit in common: thirtysomething white boys born a few months apart who couldn't jump. Fortunately our perimeter shots carried us through our various careers. Steve's early NBA career was mainly as a journeyman, starting with the Phoenix Suns, then making stops with the Cleveland Cavaliers, Orlando Magic and the Chicago Bulls before landing with the Spurs as one of many veterans on the roster.

Steve's story was fascinating, and not just for being a member of the Chicago Bulls team that won three straight NBA Championships from 1995/96 to 1997/98, completing Michael Jordan's haul of six titles. Steve had been born in Beirut, Lebanon, and lived in France, Egypt and Tunisia, but grew up in the LA suburb of Pacific Palisades before going to college at the University of Arizona, where he was a fully fledged cult hero. A lights-out perimeter shooter, Steve blew out his knee and missed what would have been his senior year at college. But that was a mere hiccup compared to the greatest tragedy he endured: losing his father to an assassin's bullet.

Dr Malcolm Kerr, an expert on Middle East affairs, was president of the American University in Beirut. In January 1984, just as Steve was settling into his freshman season at Arizona, Dr Kerr was gunned down by Islamic militants as he stepped out of an elevator in Beirut. Typical of his inner toughness, Steve played two nights later. Just like the night he played through the game with the crowd from rival Arizona State chanting 'PLO, PLO . . .'

Even as he prepared to fly out of Beirut to begin college life at Arizona, the airport was bombed. Steve and his mother got away safely to the United States embassy, then were driven for eight hours through Syria to Jordan to fly home to the US. The man who drove Steve and his mother was later killed by sniper fire. I don't know what qualities Steve Kerr possessed before his father's murder, but the Steve Kerr I knew was a steely competitor who gave credence to all theories on deceptive appearance. The greatest, funniest, friendliest bloke off the court, Steve Kerr was one tough son of a bitch on it. He had to be, otherwise he wouldn't have survived a minute in the NBA.

Steve and I used to hang back after practice and play what we called the President's Cup, in deference to the team's golf event played between the United States and the rest of the world minus Europe. We would play one-on-one or shooting games and it all counted. Standing a mere 191 centimetres and weighing a scrawny 81 kilograms, Steve never took a backward step. Not to anyone. If we scrimmaged at practice, chances were Steve would be going hardest. He knew his strengths and limitations and, let me tell you, determination and will to work and win were not listed under limitations. If somebody tried to pull something sneaky at practice, they hoped Steve did not catch on. He wouldn't cop it. Not if you were twelfth man for the Spurs (Andrew Gaze) and not if you were the greatest to ever play the game (Michael Jordan). Which might explain why Kerr got into a fight with Jordan one day at Bulls practice. There was tension between the two after Jordan launched his NBA comeback from his first retirement and fling with baseball. Playing against each other in a scrimmage, the defensive engagements got more and more aggressive until, finally, they snapped. Jordan shoved Steve hard, Steve started swinging and so did Jordan. Steve finished the bout with a black eye and Jordan's eternal respect.

That was one thing Steve Kerr earned during his NBA career: respect. He earned a lot more respect than cash and he has five championship rings (two with the Spurs and three with the Bulls) to prove it. If he didn't have Jordan's respect and trust, Steve would never have received the pass from Jordan for the shot that won the Bulls the NBA title against the Utah Jazz in 1997. It was game six of the series. As time wound down on the contest, Bulls coach Phil Jackson drew up a play inside the huddle. Everyone in the stadium knew the ball was going to Jordan. Jordan, expecting a double-team from the defence, knew the next pass would be to Steve. Jordan told Steve to be ready. Steve told Jordan to give him the ball and he'd make the shot. He was as good as his word.

When you meet Steve Kerr after hearing stories of that title-clinching shot and other deeds, you would be tempted to say, 'Hang on, mate. Are you *the* Steve Kerr?' He's not an imposing presence, he's got that boyish look he'll still have when he's seventy and he'll be as humble and funny and friendly as he always has been. Which is pretty good considering there is not a country in the world in which Steve Kerr would not be recognised. He is famous worldwide for having played with Michael Jordan and the Chicago Bulls but, with his personality and the way he carries and conducts himself, he might as well be Sammy from the sawmill down the road.

Steve and Will Perdue were together on the second Bulls Three-peat team, so there were some great storytelling sessions focused on Michael Jordan and the Bulls. They would talk and I would just sit, listen and lap it up. They felt privileged to be part of the great Bulls era and were quite respectful of and complimentary towards Jordan. He helped make their careers and when general manager Jerry Krause broke up the team, it was with lucrative sign-and-trade deals that rewarded the players with contracts the Bulls might not have been able to engineer had the team stayed together. Either way, we were mighty glad to have Steve Kerr on our team, especially heading into the play-offs.

The play-off teams had to name twelve players for the post-season rosters, which, once lodged with the NBA, could not be changed for any reason whatsoever. Once that was done, so was I. It was an interesting situation for me and the other guy on injured reserve, Brandon Williams. We wanted the Spurs to do well and win the whole thing, but we wanted it to happen quickly so we could end our frustration and get off what sometimes seemed like a mouse's treadmill, doing lots of work but going nowhere. That said, the play-offs refreshed everyone and infused the team with excitement as we entered the business end of the season.

There was a small drama in the first round against the Minnesota Timberwolves. With the first two games in the best-of-five series at home at the Alamodome, the Spurs won game one, but dropped the second, handing home-court advantage to the T-Wolves. That was a shock for everyone and a wake-up call. In a best-of-five series, one slip can be crucial, but the Spurs caught it in time, won both games on the road and advanced.

Next up was the Western Conference semi-finals and a best-of-seven series against the LA Lakers, who were still developing into the powerhouse that they became in following seasons. With big man Shaquille O'Neal in the line-up, they could not be underestimated. But with Tim Duncan and David Robinson doing their thing, we won the series in four straight games. It was a sweep but not an avalanche, with the margins six, three, twelve and eleven. In some respects I thought we got out of jail a bit against the Lakers, but nobody stopped to offer apologies. We were running like escapees towards the next round of the play-offs.

In the Western Conference finals, we were up against the Portland Trail Blazers. In a similar scenario to the Lakers series, we swept the Blazers in four games but got away with a couple of close wins to open the stand. There were two defining moments in this series: Sean Elliott tip-toeing along the sideline to win game two with a three-pointer that became known as the Memorial Day Miracle, and the Spurs' defence that held the Blazers to just sixty-three points in game three. Sean's triple, with just 9.9 seconds left after we had trailed by as much as eighteen, was enormous in the context of the series and the season and might have given the players a hint of destiny. The defence might have sent a message to show just how tough it would be to topple the Spurs in a best-of-seven play-off series.

After topping the Blazers, the only teams who could stop us winning the NBA Championship were the New York Knicks or Indiana Pacers. While the Spurs rested at home and got ready for the NBA Finals, the Knicks and Pacers slugged out a six-game series in the Eastern Conference finals. That gave us a ten-day break between the last game of the Trail Blazers series and the first game of the Finals. Since the longest break we had during the regular season was three days, it seemed like we were on long-service leave. Eventually, it was time to face the Knicks over the best of seven games for the NBA Championship.

It was almost same-old, same-old for the Spurs against the Knicks. We took the first three games (two at home, one at Madison Square Garden) 89–77, 80–67, 89–81 to at least be thinking about what size championship rings we would be fitted with. After game four, those thoughts came to a stop like New York traffic at peak hour. They were replaced by conspiracy theories. Listen to talkback callers on the numerous sports radio stations in the US and conspiracy theories are as much a part of the NBA Finals as David Stern presenting the Larry O'Brien Trophy to the winning team. The most popular conspiracy theory from the fans is that the NBA must have big-market teams in the finals to make the most of TV ratings and advertising revenue. Therefore, they argue, the officials work against the small-market teams in the play-offs. As the Spurs played game four against the Knicks, you could almost hear the conspiracy theorists dialling the talkback numbers. Let me say right now, I don't necessarily buy into these conspiracy theories, but if the fans out there had one that went along the lines of the NBA not wanting the Knicks to be swept in this series, I'd have to say the way the game was called did nothing to discourage that.

The Spurs lost 96–89 and, suddenly from coasting at 3–0 with one eye on cruising the San Antonio River in a victory parade, we were snapped back to attention with the reality that we would be in New York a little longer than anticipated. We didn't have a cockiness about us, but there was certainly a confidence about our chances of becoming NBA champions. We kept a lid on things, but there was a feeling of inevitability about the whole thing. It was decided before game four that we would fly straight out of New York that night if we won. When we lost, there was no panic. The confidence remained, we stuffed any thoughts of celebration and travel arrangements into our duffle bags and focused purely on finishing the series, the season and the journey in game five.

As time ticked down with game five still in the balance, most people were sure that, when it came to the crunch for the Spurs, the ball would go to Tim Duncan. Duncan and the Knicks' Latrell Sprewell owned this game as they duelled up and down the MSG floor. At one stage, for about six minutes at the end of the third quarter and the start of the fourth, they had twenty-eight of the twenty-nine points scored by the Knicks and Spurs. Sprewell had fourteen straight for the Knicks and Duncan was responsible for fourteen of the Spurs' fifteen. But for all their heroics, neither had pulled his team clear. That would be left to the most improbable figure and unlikely hero: Avery Johnson.

That Avery Johnson was with the Spurs, let alone on the floor with the championship up for grabs like a long, elusive rebound, was testament to his enormous persistence and massive heart. AJ was undersized for the NBA at 180 centimetres and 81 kilograms. He did not possess great offensive skills. He had played for five teams, including one previous stint with the Spurs that ended when he was released on the day he was a member of David Robinson's wedding party. He was once cut by the Denver Nuggets on Christmas Eve. There was a strong belief throughout his whole career that he didn't belong in the NBA. AJ made sure he did.

The two greatest attributes Avery Johnson took to any team were his basketball brain and his leadership. As sharp as a whip, AJ had the nickname Little General because of the way he organised his troops on the floor. He was smart, he knew the game and, boy, you'd better do as he said. While we had David Robinson on the team, with his massive public image and on-floor and off-court presence, there was never any doubt among the players that Avery was the leader. Certainly, AJ had no problem letting people know that was the case, whether it be in a vocal sense or in leading by example. If the situation called for it to be grabbed and shaken, Avery did it. David, as the team's figurehead, could be somewhat submissive in certain situations. When action had to be taken, AJ took charge and led his Dirty Dozen on whatever mission was needed in the war to win the title.

It was obvious from the first day of pre-season training camp, when the coaches were still off-limits due to the NBA lockout, that AJ was in charge, running the court, telling people who was on and off. It was as natural as breathing for Avery, so it would not have surprised many of his team-mates when he was appointed head coach of the Dallas Mavericks in early 2005. There was one game early in the season when Tim Duncan said something and Avery snapped back with a comment that he was leading the team and he was in charge. My first thought was that Avery was treading on thin ice if Tim didn't buy into this deal. There was no doubt Tim was the Spurs' franchise player and Avery could easily find himself traded and on the next plane out if Tim didn't like the situation. But to Tim's credit, and everybody else's, Avery's role was accepted and embraced and it was never an issue. His authority was never questioned. There was only one word to describe his team-mates' feeling towards him: admiration.

To see Avery operate in this environment might have seemed strange. But he was a bloke who had been kicked around the league, had dealt with rejection by coming back stronger, had had his confidence tested so many times it was ridiculous, had worked to get every gram of potential out of his body. So to be so close to an NBA Championship, AJ would not let this slide. He set the standards and made sure others lived up to them. As a leader, Avery was respected. As a bloke, he was well-liked. He was actually quite a funny bloke who spoke with a strong Cajun accent and fired his words so quickly I sometimes had to ask him to repeat stuff a few times. Like when he was talking about a situation that wasn't good.

'We're to' up,' Avery would say. 'We're to' up, man.' The first time I heard him say that, I couldn't figure out what the hell he was talking about. Usually Steve Kerr was my interpreter in such situations, but he wasn't handy. I was just so confused and figured 'to' up' meant 'toes up', as in: we've turned our toes up, we're dead. Which I finally conveyed to one of my team-mates. After he finally stopped laughing, I was told Avery's 'to' up' was actually 'torn up'. We're torn up. Hey, I thought I was close. In the same postcode anyway.

Avery was very religious, as was David Robinson. They were devout Christians and happy to share the Word of God. The most noticeable thing about Avery and David, given that they lived and worked in an environment where hard-core swearing was part of the everyday conversation, was that you never once heard either of them swear, curse or use profanity. I only have to drop a biscuit crumb to drop an F-bomb, but these guys were amazing. That was their level of religious commitment, that was their amazingly high standards and you had to respect them for that. But that's not to say their language was wishy-washy. Before every game, we came together for a prayer just before going onto the floor. Avery would solemnly lead the prayer and always close it in the same way: 'Amen. Now let's go and bust 'em in the mouth.'

Which was what I thought would happen to Sean Elliott as the players came into the locker room at half-time of game five against the Knicks. The contest was tight and there was a slight sense of the game and the series slipping away. Sean came in and said, in a general way, that we needed to look after the ball better and not commit so many turnovers. It was something that is said a million times a year in games around the world. Avery didn't take it that way. He took it personally. He exploded. In an instant, Avery was in Sean's face, taking exception to what he felt was, being the point guard in charge of carrying and distributing the ball, pointed criticism.

For a moment, I thought they might erupt into a physical confrontation. Sean stayed cool and tried to explain, but Avery was so caught up in the moment that he was one little ragin' Cajun. The coaches stepped in and separated them and cooled it off, but when the team went back out for the second half, I did not see Avery or Sean offer the other a hand of friendship or a conciliatory pat on the backside. That situation demonstrated how Avery was a fighter and did not take anything lying down. He was sensitive about his domain and he took criticism to heart. The only reason he was in the NBA was because every time he was criticised, he responded in way that had people shaking their heads and handing him his dues. With game five of the NBA Championship series on the line, Avery gave them the greatest response of his career.

After Tim Duncan and Latrell Sprewell had cooled a little, David Robinson scored a couple of buckets and Marcus Camby replied for the Knicks. Sprewell hit another bucket for a 75–72 New York lead, only for veteran Mario Elie to take a pass from Duncan and knock in a game-tying three-pointer. Then Sprewell made a pair of free-throws and Duncan went one of two from the line. New York led 77–76 with two minutes and thirty-three seconds left. That's a lifetime in basketball. It was time for Avery Johnson to make the shot of a lifetime. AJ got free along the baseline. He took a pass, sized the shot and from eighteen feet made a flawless jumper for a 78–77 lead with forty-seven seconds left. Nobody scored again as Sprewell's shot at the buzzer fell short. The Spurs were NBA champions.

The usual post-game scenes ensued after we clinched the NBA title. Hugging, high-fiving, spraying champagne and mugging for the cameras with smiles bigger than the entrance to Luna Park. Even though I did not play, did not even dress, I still had a sense of euphoria and achievement about the whole thing. It was impossible not to get caught up in the celebration of the Spurs' first NBA title. Being the rather excitable type, I didn't find it difficult to do.

What made the championship victory even more memorable and enjoyable was that I shared it first-hand with a couple of my best mates. Melinda, who was pregnant with our third child Annie, went home to Melbourne with Courtney and Phoebe not long after I went on the injured reserve. For the last few games of the championship series, their places were taken by my mates Wayne Peterson and Grant Cadee. In hindsight, sharing this occasion with them might have been the highlight of the whole season. It wasn't about them basking in my glory, which was minimal. It was that they experienced an NBA Championship celebration from the inside, which very few people in the world get to do. As the celebrations uncorked, Grant was actually in Phoenix, where my Melbourne Tigers team-mate Mark Bradtke had a tryout with the Suns and met us back in San Antonio. Wayne was in New York and made the absolute most of every moment. Every one of his New York minutes was packed with about eighty seconds of action when it came to the post-game locker-room celebration. In fact, he might have got into it more than I did.

Once the initial team-only celebration came down from its high, I slipped out to do a TV interview. As I left the locker room I saw Wayne, or Rattler as we all know him, at the door and told him to hang there until I came back and I'd try to get him in. So I did my TV interview and came back to where I'd told Wayne to meet me. No Rattler. I looked around for a few minutes, then thought, 'Stuff it, I'm not hanging around out here while the party's inside.' One of the first things I saw when I got back into the locker room was a familiar face wearing a Spurs championship T-shirt and cap, hugging Gregg Popovich and David Robinson and posing for pictures with them and the NBA trophy. It was Rattler. He had outwitted security that would shame even the United Nations building, which happened to be not far from Madison Square Garden.

Wayne and I, while opposites in a lot of ways, have been friends since high school. While I was relatively meek and mild at school, Wayne had a little bit of a wild streak and made regular visits to the principal's office for breaches of discipline that were probably more to do with his exuberance than anything sinister. His personality certainly lends itself to being loud and he has not been known to back down from confrontation or a difference of opinion. Growing up in the tough suburb of Port Melbourne as the only boy in a family of six children, he had an independent and competitive streak, which he carried onto the Albert Park basketball courts with the Port Colts. Knowing each other from school, we sometimes hung around at the stadium together, played one-on-one and got up to some mischief here and there.

There is no question Rattler was one of my biggest supporters. He's a very loyal person who values friendships highly, so once he's your friend, he's your friend for life, whether you like it or not. For him to bob up in New York for the championship series should not have been surprising. He wanted to be there to support me, perhaps thinking I might have done it hard as a non-playing member of the team. When it comes to his friends, a quick trip to New York and San Antonio is nothing for Rattler.

After the locker-room celebration, it was a very low-key and informal affair for the rest of the night. We had a team dinner at the hotel, then guys just went their own ways. I went to a club with Malik Rose, Rattler and a couple of others. It was a quiet night in most respects. It was late, we were drained from the emotion of winning the title and we knew the real celebrations awaited us in San Antonio.

The Spurs organisation prided itself on being a big part of the San Antonio community and the people of the city responded in kind. Just like when we touched down in San Antonio after the flight from New York. There might have been about fifteen thousand people at the airport to meet us and the team was presented on a stage before moving onto our next stop. One of the first to speak was David Robinson, who spent his entire career with the Spurs. The Admiral told the cheering crowd it was great to get a championship ring after so many years. Another veteran, Jerome Kersey, said the same and Avery Johnson said something similar. Then Steve Kerr took his turn at the microphone and mentioned how great it was that it only took him twelve months to finally get his fourth NBA Championship ring.

After the airport, there were no official functions until the river parade and presentation ceremony at the Alamodome the next day. The lack of togetherness immediately after winning the title surprised me. In Australia we wouldn't let each other out of sight for several days at least. A group of us made up for it, though. That first night back in San Antonio, Rattler, Grant Cadee, Steve Kerr, Will Perdue, Spurs director of media services Tom James and I had the best celebration you could imagine. In fact, you would have needed a pretty good imagination to have pictured this scene a few months earlier. But there I was with my mates from Melbourne, and a few mates from San Antonio, celebrating an NBA Championship. I even had a drink that night – that was how big it was. Everywhere we went, applause, cheers and congratulations washed over us like returning heroes. In reality, I had done nothing, or a minimal amount, to contribute to winning the title and I felt like a bit of an impostor. But the reaction from everyone was sincere and overwhelming. They didn't even mind my out-of-sync, disjointed dancing.

They also didn't mind an Aussie taking over. At one club, the house DJ welcomed us and the crowd responded. But that wasn't good enough for Rattler, who is the courtside announcer for the Melbourne Tigers home games and was the PA man for the 2000 Olympic Games men's final in Sydney. Wayne disappeared and the next we heard of him was when we did hear him. He had again used his powers of persuasion, commandeered the DJ's microphone and introduced us like it was game night: 'Ladies and gentlemen, please welcome, from your NBA Champion San Antonio Spurs, number 4 Steeevee Keeerrrrrr . . .' The crowd went nuts and it really added to the memorable occasion it already was. Once we left the clubs behind, we retired to Steve's place for a quiet drink and a debrief. This time Steve disappeared. Next minute, a door opened and Steve made his entrance, wearing his Spurs playing uniform and doing defensive slides across the kitchen floor. It was that kind of night. Of the four NBA titles he had won to that point, Steve reckoned it was the best celebration he'd had. Naturally, Grant and Wayne took credit for that. Aussie spirit, they reckoned. For me, the great reward is the contest. But even I had to concede that the celebration was pretty good.

The biggest part of the championship celebration was the parade and gathering at the Alamodome. San Antonio's river and canal system is the centrepiece of the River Walk through downtown. The parade had us cruising down the River Walk on tourist barges and boats as about 400,000 people lined the route. It was amazing as Rattler and Grant joined me for the cruise. At the end of the cruise, we paused for a drink and then headed for the buses to go to the Alamodome. As we walked to the buses, the NBA Trophy somehow ended up with Grant Cadee, who could not resist brandishing it above his head and drawing a massive cheer from the crowd.

The size of the crowd lining the parade route that day was testimony to the connection the people of San Antonio had with the Spurs. The Spurs were the only major pro sports franchise in a city of about 1.1 million people and the locals supported them royally. In the build-up to the NBA Championship series, the support and hype generated in San Antonio made Melbourne during AFL Grand Final week look like Ballarat during the Begonia Festival. It was extreme, unqualified and total support. People called out as we walked down the street and there were toots of recognition from drivers. And on game nights the Spurs fans made out-of-towners understand the definition of home-court advantage. The noise and passion they generated was incredible.

Which was just how it was as we arrived at the Alamodome and walked onto a stage in front of about sixty thousand people. It was an amazing atmosphere. Avery Johnson introduced the players, who each said a few words, Gregg Popovich said his bit, there were some video highlights on the big screen and, almost with the click of your fingers, it was over. We had a team meeting the next day, cleaned out our lockers and were gone. Some of us went to different cities, some of us to different countries never to play as a team again. But in terms of NBA history and the history of the San Antonio Spurs, we would always be together.

There was one small piece of business to tidy up before we all left San Antonio: the play-off bonus. I was unaware that we were in for a windfall until I heard a few of the players talking about it. 'Making paper' was the expression they had. 'Making paper.'

I wasn't sure how the system worked and, since I was not on the active play-off roster, didn't know if I was eligible for a share. But Steve Kerr and Will Perdue told me the players decided how the play-off money was carved up and everyone got a certain percentage. It turned out the play-off shares were not an issue. Avery did the talking in front of the group when it came to the bonuses. There was no discussion. The money was split evenly among the fourteen players. End of story. To me, that vindicated my decision to stick it out with the Spurs. It showed I was accepted and respected. The play-off bonus was a substantial amount of money as far as I was concerned, but it wasn't the cash that impressed me. It was my team-mates' attitude towards me. At that moment, I could not have been a more wealthy man, even without a dollar in my pocket.

Money was and still is a big factor in the NBA. Role players are instant millionaires these days. The money is ridiculous. But more power to the players if they can get it. Some of the money they don't even have to work for. When I signed with the Spurs, I was asked to join the NBA Players Association. The US$10,000 annual fee caused me to gulp, until the benefits such as royalties from merchandising were explained. I received a cheque for about US$30,000 at the end of the season as my share of royalties. There might not have been one Andrew Gaze playing top or card sold, but my Players Association membership entitled me to the same share of the profits as David Robinson, Charles Barkley and Kobe Bryant. I was happy to get it, but it made me shake my head in amazement sometimes.

Even the material spoils of victory were ostentatious. Like the NBA Championship ring. It is one chunky piece of jewellery. It's not the kind of thing I would wear around, if only because I'd be scared stiff about losing it. I'm not sure how much it's worth, but I'd have to guess quite a lot. Melinda, like all the wives and partners, received a pendant modelled on the players' rings, which was a nice touch.

The final piece in the Spurs championship ensemble arrived as a mystery package in the mail one day. There was a card in the letter box to say I had to go to the post office to collect it and pay stamp duty on it. I had no idea what it was. Nor did the woman at the post office. There were no identifying marks or names on the box, so I couldn't even guess. The woman said I had to pay eight hundred dollars to get the package, but as I politely pointed out, I wasn't paying the money without knowing what it was. She eventually opened the package and let me have a look. It was a watch from David Robinson, who bought one for all the players as a thank-you gift for a memorable season, for finally helping make his dream come true. It was inscribed on the back: 'NBA Champion 1999'. I was happy to spend the eight hundred dollars. The only problem is I'm too scared to wear the watch in case something happens to it.

When it comes to money, if somebody had said it would cost me $100,000 to experience the 1999 NBA season with the San Antonio Spurs, I would have paid it in a heartbeat. No questions asked. It was an extraordinary journey. Even though I only played in nineteen games for a total of fifty-eight minutes for the whole season, there was no hollow feeling. It was a totally fulfilling experience – the unique opportunity to see the NBA from the inside, of being part of the team that won the championship. It was an extraordinary reward for any sacrifices I made. As a basketball player, I got to see the absolute very best players every day at either practice or in games, and I was able to work on my game and keep learning. As a friend, I provided a unique experience for my mates Wayne Peterson and Grant Cadee, enabling them to join a title celebration and carry the NBA trophy. For them to be there was good for me, too. Hopefully, my being with the Spurs was somehow good for Australian basketball.

Sometimes it's hard to explain just what it was like that season with the Spurs. But trust me, it's a wonderful memory. Have I got a minute? If you want to talk about the Spurs, I can talk for as long as you want.

chapter twenty

ALL IN THE FAMILY

WE were just getting through the main course at the 1998 NBL awards dinner when, with my mother Margaret on one side of me and my wife Melinda on the other, one of them, considering my chances of winning the MVP, said: 'I hope you don't win it again.' As you can see, I didn't lack for support from the main women in my life. Unfortunately, I had to disappoint them, leaving their side to go and collect my seventh NBL MVP award. No doubt they were relieved that I made the return journey to and from the podium without embarrassing them.

Talk about being kept in check. Neither of them, whether it was my mum from my childhood days, or my wife during my adult life, ever let my ego get the better of me. Certainly, as Melinda would no doubt readily attest, I have no reason to fuel my ego when it comes to being romantic or the ideal, help-around-the-house husband. I try, but as Melinda would also tell you, I can be very trying.

Having said that, and I admit to the odd deficiency as a romantic and odd-jobs man, it should go on the record that Melinda chased me to get this lifetime partnership off the ground. Okay, chased might be a little exaggerated. But the way I remember it was she did at least make the first move. Melinda is the sister of my best mate Nigel Purchase, who grew up with me playing for the Tigers. Melinda often came to games and I often went to their house, but I never considered her anything more than my mate's sister. It was only once I twigged she had an interest in me as something other than Nigel's mate that I looked at her in a different light.

Never let it be said I'm slow on the uptake, but I think Melinda initiated our first date. We were both young (she was fifteen and I was a naive and immature eighteen) and I wasn't one of those blokes who was out and about on the social scene with the chicks flocking to me. Not that I could ever understand why not. Anyway, our relationship blossomed. I suppose if there is fate, this must have been it because it kind of just happened and progressed from nothing to the point where I can't even remember what it was like not to be with Melinda. We didn't get married until I was twenty-seven so we had a courtship that certainly went longer than a normal try-before-you-buy deal. Now that I think of it, Melinda could have no grounds for complaint. She knew what she was getting. Which was a fairly unsophisticated, unromantic basketball player.

I have no compunction admitting I was born without a romantic bone in my body. I am living proof that romanticism cannot be transplanted, grown or developed. I'm terrible when it comes to romance. There's never flowers or chocolates or whatever, but that doesn't mean there's a fault or flaw in our relationship. I'm sure Melinda would like a little bit more romance, but I think she realises you are who you are and it would almost be corny or fake if I started buying flowers. She'd wonder what I'd been up to.

So it was no surprise that my marriage proposal lacked violins in the background and rose petals scattered at my true love's feet.

Seeing as how we bought an engagement ring in Hong Kong three years before we were married and before we were even engaged (it was a good deal), we always knew we would get married. It was just a matter of when. For want of a better description, my marriage proposal to Melinda sort of just happened in the bathroom one day. It was, actually, almost conversational in keeping with my relaxed and suave manner when dealing with the opposite sex.

I had bought a house in Rusden Street, Elsternwick, and was moving in, but the message clearly conveyed to me was that unless I had plans for our future, Melinda would not be joining me in my house of residence on a full-time basis. It was indicated that it might be considered inappropriate for her to join me unless we were in a more formal relationship. So that was the ultimate, motivating factor in finally getting around to my proposal. I suppose I just needed a prod to do what I always knew I would do. Maybe it's a big deal for some people how they proposed marriage, but that doesn't guarantee success in marriage. Just because you're not romantic doesn't mean you don't have the total love and commitment I have for my wife.

Melinda was with me for almost my entire senior basketball career, so I give her great credit and thanks for sticking with me. I give her even more credit and thanks for sitting through so many basketball games, many of them shockers. It was good we got together at such a young age because Melinda quickly became aware of the commitment and requirements of competing at the highest level. She saw how demanding it was, dealing with travel and separation – and learning, if not always liking, that all this was a necessity of the business. We both learned to deal with the highs and lows of winning and losing and how that affected on us off the court. Melinda was also smart enough to know not to get into a post mortem of a game when it was best to ignore it. I think my mood was usually the give-away.

Not that she didn't voice her opinion about things when she felt strongly about them, such as our wedding. We were married at the end of the 1992 season, but there were a couple of things I had to take care of first. One was a post-season tour to the United States with the Tigers; the other was knee surgery. In that order. The problem was that the wedding was only about a week after the scheduled surgery, which was an arthroscope and shouldn't have caused much bother. Simply, Melinda felt I should skip the tour and have the surgery earlier so I could at least walk freely at the wedding. Perhaps because I'm a man, I couldn't see what the big deal was. I had the surgery, limped for a few days, but was pretty right for the big day. We were married at Melinda's parents' home and had the reception in a marquee on the tennis court. It poured rain all day, except for the hour when the ceremony was performed. Fortunately, I couldn't be blamed for the weather.

While Melinda might often struggle in with the groceries and ask me why the bedroom blinds are still down at noon on a sunny day, or wonder why the reminder to fix the toilet seat has been on the little chalk board for two years, I can honestly say she has been unstintingly supportive of my basketball career. When it was just the two of us, it was easier to make decisions and be flexible in what we did. But issues such as playing overseas and committing to one or two more seasons with the Tigers had more impact when we started our family. There was more pressure on me and I had to be more conscious of how my decisions and career path affected Melinda and our children.

When I played in Italy for Udine, we weren't yet married and Melinda wasn't that keen to go. We'd just moved into a house and we were going to uproot, live in a foreign country, then re-settle back in Melbourne in a few months. I had no problem with it, but I could understand why Melinda was hesitant, worried about the uncertainty of what lay ahead. The giveaway might have been when she burst into tears as I accepted the deal with Udine. It was the same when we went to Greece. Again, we'd just moved into another house and we had our first child Courtney, so it wasn't an easy thing for Melinda to do. But she also knew those situations were good for me as a basketballer and good for us as a family in terms of financial security. There were always significant overseas opportunities for me to consider and if I hadn't had the family I might have been more likely to accept them. But sometimes you have to sacrifice for your family and I have no complaints about that.

Away from basketball, Melinda has always looked after everything to do with our family and its existence, which made for a demanding job. It still does, actually. I won't admit she wears the pants, but she does play the major role in getting the job done at home. Because I could be away for long periods, Melinda made a lot of significant decisions about the kids and their education, made sure the bills were paid and the house and family functioned smoothly. To be honest, I couldn't tell you how a lot of things happened around our house. They just did and do and I probably should just get on the end of the line with the kids to collect my pocket money and brown-bag lunch every day. I should also remember to say thanks more often.

While I might not be too actively involved in the operation of the household and some of the decision-making, that doesn't mean I take any less than full responsibility in my role as a parent. The practical side might sometimes be lacking, but I can set an example and have an influence on the standards set for our four children. Sometimes, just being there is an important aspect of a parent–child relationship and, while I was often on the road or at a function or dealing with business, I was also at home a lot with the kids. Some fathers might be away from home between 6 a.m. and 6 p.m. and see their kids sparingly. With my training schedule, I was more often than not at home when the kids arrived from school.

I am acutely aware of my parental responsibilities, especially in an era that is so different to when my sister and I grew up in a largely innocent environment. Not that my moral standing and parenting skills led to my nomination as 2004 Victorian Father of the Year, which was an award based on profile rather than performance. I'm not naive enough to believe I was the best dad in Victoria that year. Not when there are so many other fathers who deal with a lot more family problems, such as physically and intellectually disabled kids, and do a brilliant, devoted and unrecognised job. That's real parenting, when your son or daughter is in a wheelchair and needs around-the-clock attention. It was more about having a public profile and a family that landed me that title to promote being a good father. If I can do that and be as good a dad as I can for my kids, I'll be reasonably happy.

Melinda and I believe we have given our kids a healthy environment to grow and develop in and, as they get older, they will learn, as I did, that the Gaze name can bring the good and the bad. They have been exposed to my relative fame in Melbourne and Australia since they were born, so it's not unusual for them to see kids wanting an autograph or a photo with me. What they need to know is how to behave in regard to having a famous name. The kids at school know who their dad is, but that's not to say my kids should be boastful about having a dad who is well-known and in the public eye. Who I am, in terms of fame or whatever, should be irrelevant to my kids and I think they have done a good job of handling that so far.

There is the possibility that my kids will cop flak like I did while growing up because of the Gaze name. Already we've had one pivotal moment when Courtney started playing basketball with the Melbourne Tigers under-ten girls. The kids picked their playing tops randomly from a bag and, as luck would have it, Courtney plucked out my number, number 10, which she was thrilled with. When they moved into under-twelves, their uniforms had their names on the back, too. Mindful of the extra scrutiny and possible abuse Courtney might receive from being identifiable, Melinda asked her if she wanted to keep her name off the top, but I felt she should keep it on, which she did. While I don't agree with juniors having their names on their tops, there was no use running away from the situation and I said it might have been worse for her to be the only kid without a name on her playing top. Courtney might not have understood why it was even an issue, and hopefully she never goes through what I did, getting booed and abused as a kid. But you are who you are. Be proud of it and deal with it.

I just hope our kids respond to being a Gaze, especially in a basketball environment, in a way that's not detrimental or a handicap to them. They will have a lot of opportunities because of their name and they've got to respect that and try to take advantage of the opportunities without any negative effect. I don't want them to be turned off the sport because they have to deal with extra pressure. I want them to love basketball and play because they love the sport. I don't want them to feel like they have to play. I also don't want them to play but forego the chance of good things because they carry greater and unfair expectations due to who their father and grandfather are.

I have a real desire for all four of our children to be involved in sport, not just basketball. There are so many benefits being involved in sport, but I don't have a burning desire for them to be elite sportspeople. I'd love them to develop a passion for a sport that gives them a chance to become elite, but if they don't it's not the end of the world. I feel like I can contribute to their sport as a father, supporting them and guiding them, but if you ever see me even remotely close to being an ugly parent, feel free to tap me on the shoulder and slap my face. I'm not one to criticise parents, but to see the behaviour of the parents of nine year olds at a basketball game can be interesting, to say the least.

Seeing my children born was the greatest experience imaginable. I'm sure all fathers say that, but it's true. It was big, it was exciting and it was a relief when the doctor gave them a quick once-over and handed them to Melinda. When Courtney was born, I faced an overwhelming sense of responsibility and new challenges each day. I'd never even thought about changing a nappy until Courtney was born. Then I had to think of ways of avoiding the job. Eventually I caught on and, by the time our fourth child Mason was born, I had a decent handle on the nappy thing.

Our four children – Courtney, Phoebe, Annie and Mason – are four distinctly different people with distinctly different personalities. If anything, there are some similarities between Courtney and Annie, but Phoebe and Mason are on their own. As parents, you learn not to give one more than the other, but you do treat them differently because of their personalities. You also do things differently because of the experience gained from each previous child. I like to think our children are all treated equally, as Melinda and I believe they should be, but they'll tell us quickly enough if they think we're favouring one or another.

At least in a few years I'll have a big, strong son to help me fight the wars with the women of the Gaze household. As the youngest, Mason still has some growing to do, but when he is old enough to defend his old man, I hope he realises what I went through for him. It was, just setting modesty aside, more than some men could handle.

After Courtney and Phoebe, I was a bit ambivalent about having more kids. Then we had Annie, which was fine, but Melinda really wanted to have a boy. If we'd had a boy earlier, we might not have had the four kids, but Melinda came from a family of four and she was extremely keen to have four. If she was going to have a fourth, Melinda wanted it to be a boy (not that she would have loved a girl any less) so she looked into optimising the chances.

I'm sceptical about all this stuff, but Melinda consulted a naturopath, who had a theory about how to increase the chances of giving birth to a boy. A lot of it was diet related and Melinda was on a high-potassium diet, eating bananas like an orang-utan, and eliminating dairy products. I had to have plenty of caffeine, so that meant lots of Coke as I don't drink coffee. Melinda had regular blood tests and it was almost like we were trying to produce a rare species of plant that only bloomed when Haley's Comet appears.

The other aspect of the program that involved me was a little more embarrassing. I had to make sure my testicles didn't get overheated. In fact, there was a preference to keep them cool, which meant cold showers straight after training and more than one session of applying ice. I did apply myself to the task, but the icing didn't go down real well. If you've ever seen the episode of *Seinfeld* that relates to shrinkage, you'll know what I mean. Sceptical though I am about determining the sex of your baby, we got the job done. It wasn't romantic, but who said anything about romance? Not me.

chapter twenty-one

CAN YOU KEEP A SECRET?

ONE routine event after arriving at the Olympic Games village was to attend a media conference. Media conferences weren't usually exciting, but they were something that had to be done, especially with the 2000 Games at home in Sydney and the massive local media interest. A week out from the Games opening, the Boomers flew into Sydney from Melbourne on the Sunday morning after playing the United States on Saturday night. On Monday, Boomers coach Barry Barnes, Mark Bradtke and I were summoned to the Australian Olympic Committee media conference, which was a regulation affair. We answered a few questions about our preparation, gave the thumbs up to the athletes' village, paid credit and respect to our opponents, said it would be nice to win a medal but as long as we did our best that's what really mattered. Harmless stuff.

There was one question not related to basketball. A reporter wanted to know what I felt about my chances of carrying the Australian flag at the opening ceremony. It wasn't a surprising question. There had been a lot of speculation about who would be the flag bearer and who would light the Olympic cauldron. Even though my name was mentioned as a potential flag carrier, I honestly never thought about it. I never really thought it would happen or that I was a realistic chance. It was the sole decision of AOC boss John Coates to name the flag carrier, but I was just thrilled people thought enough of me to mention me as a candidate. That was my answer to the reporter's question and I didn't think I would hear anything more of it.

When the mass media conference closed, we obliged a few reporters who wanted quick one-on-one interviews. That done, Mark Bradtke and I headed back to the village. We had only taken a few steps when John Coates, who hosted the media conference, broke off from a conversation and called us over. He thanked us for attending the media conference and especially for being so positive about the athletes' village. After a fair amount of controversy in the lead-up, the AOC was happy for any good feedback. We were engaging in small talk when John changed direction and tone.

'By the way, Andrew,' John started, 'it will be my decision who the team captain and flag bearer is and I just wanted to let you know that I would like you to carry the flag in the opening ceremony.'

I heard what he was saying, but there was something about the actual words that left me uncertain. I couldn't fully comprehend the situation and I needed clear-cut clarification.

'So,' I started tentatively, 'you want me to carry the flag?'

John Coates confirmed his decision. I would carry the Australian flag in front of the Australian team at the opening ceremony of an Australian Olympics. I was in shock and only just heard the rest of the details about the official announcement to be made by Prime Minister John Howard the next day. He asked if my mum and dad and Melinda and the kids were going to the opening ceremony and said tickets would be arranged. Melinda and my oldest daughter Courtney were already going, but mum and dad had planned to drive to Sydney, stop somewhere on the way and watch the opening ceremony on television. Their plans just changed.

There was one other thing, John Coates said. We were not to tell anybody. Not a soul. Only about six people knew I would carry the flag and that included the three of us standing there. In making his decision, John Coates obviously did not know how bad I was at keeping secrets. Hogey and I were so excited that within twenty seconds of leaving John Coates, we were on our mobile phones, calling our wives. I called Melinda, but I couldn't get the words out. I was too emotional. She must have feared something was wrong, but I finally got the message across and she called my mum and dad to tell them. I don't think I would have been able to. Hogey's emotional reaction was a thrill for me because it showed how much it meant to a close friend and it also showed it was okay for me to do the same. But the bottom line was, after those two immediate calls, Hogey and I had to keep the lid on and make sure it didn't get out in the twenty-four hours before the official announcement. We had this exciting news to share with everyone and we couldn't. It was like winning Tattslotto and having only $5 in your pocket for a celebration.

Hogey and I pulled ourselves together on the walk back to the village to decide a course of action. I wanted to tell everyone connected with the Boomers, so we decided to wait until the next day and let them know before the official announcement by the Prime Minister. It was the ideal compromise. The hard part was spending every moment among my team-mates, trying to suppress this amazing surge of joy, pride and excitement buzzing through me. When we got back to the village, I felt guilty about not telling the guys, especially my room-mate Shane Heal. We'd been through a lot together and he was keener than me that I should carry the flag, but

I couldn't let him know. It was a killer. It was almost like cheating on my wife, but I'd made the promise to keep quiet and I would do so. At least until the next day. Well, that was the plan, anyway.

A few hours after I was asked to carry the flag, the Boomers played our final warm-up game against Lithuania at Wollongong. That one-hour bus ride south of Sydney was tough, thinking about the game, trying not to think about carrying the flag. I hadn't been able to think straight all day, with this feeling of betrayal gnawing away at me. With about three or four minutes to go in the game, which we won 88–80, it all got too much. Hogey and I were at the opposite end of the court while some free-throws were taken and I said to him, 'At end of the game, I'm telling them. I've got to tell them.'

After the game, we headed to the locker room, where everyone was excited about the win to top off a pretty good pre-Olympic campaign. Coach Barry Barnes went through his usual post-game run down and as he finished I asked everyone not directly connected with the team to leave the locker room. With only the players, coaches and support staff there, Barnesy, knowing I was a candidate to carry the flag, started to mention how important the next day could be for the team with the announcement of the flag bearer. Before he could finish, I interrupted him and got out of my seat.

'Guys,' I began, 'today after the press conference with John Coates, he told me that I was going to be ...'

That was a far as I got before I broke down. But everyone realised what I was trying to say and they broke into a spontaneous celebration, cheering and yelling, surrounding and hugging me. It was like we'd won a gold medal. When I think of that moment, it was the reaction from my team-mates that made it even more special. That they were so excited just made it feel so complete. It made me happy that the team was happy and I hoped they would feel part of it, too. It was total euphoria. I was in locker rooms after winning an NBA Championship and when the Tigers won NBL championships but, while this was something different, it was the best moment you could ever hope for.

After the cheering died down, there was one more thing I needed to tell them. 'Boys,' I said, 'you can't tell anyone. Not a soul.'

Twenty-four hours is twenty-four hours. Except when it's the twenty-four hours during which I'm sitting on the powder keg that is the announcement of who would carry the flag at the opening ceremony of the Sydney Olympics. Then twenty-four hours seems like twenty-four days. At least my family and team-mates knew and that was the main thing. Still, what might seem to be a routine announcement was not guaranteed to be a smooth announcement. As my dad, knowing I could make a dill of myself without even trying, said to veteran sportswriter Ron Reed at the announcement, 'The next fifteen minutes could be interesting.'

Having settled down since telling the Boomers the news the previous night, I got toey again as I got dressed in the official Australian Olympic team uniform. As we left our huts in the village and the Australian athletes started to mass, I got a real sense of importance and occasion. It was the sense of being involved in something so very special that you needed to open your nostrils as wide as you could, take the biggest inhalation possible and hope that breath of memory sustained itself for the rest of your life.

So it was a case of on with the show as we arrived at the concourse area of the SuperDome, knowing that some suspected, others still did not have a clue and some may have twigged had they recognised my mum and dad and wife Melinda at the function. There were pre-announcement formalities with the introduction of all the previous flag bearers, which helped build the tension and excitement. Then Prime Minister Howard finally made the announcement. In another show of team pride and unity, and perhaps to make out they didn't already know, the Boomers swamped me again with their congratulations.

At this stage my old man's observation of an interesting fifteen minutes rang true. After all, it's not every day you grab the Prime Minister in a bear hug and try not to cry on his shoulder. As I headed to the stage, I was nervous and emotional and thought I might lose it altogether. So as I mounted the top step to be met by the PM's congratulations and handshake, I gave him a hug, put my head down and tried to compose myself. I don't know if Mr Howard thought I was a staunch Liberal voter, but I was buying myself time to get my stuff together for what I expected would be an emotional speech.

I can't really remember what I said with the Australian flag proudly tucked under my arm, but I remember what I wanted to say. While being at my fifth Olympics was the prime reason I was chosen to carry the flag, I sincerely believe my family history, with my dad attending every Olympics from 1956 to 1984, was a significant factor in John Coates's decision. I tried and wanted to say that, but I'm not sure whether I did or whether I made sense. What I do know is that when I looked out into the sea of people and saw my mum and dad and how proud they were, it was quite an emotional moment. So by now, John Coates must have been wondering why he had asked this sniffling, babbling fool to carry his country's flag at the opening ceremony.

With the formalities done, I posed for photographs with John Howard away from the presentation area. Given my emotional state, mixed in with the euphoria swirling around the place, I still didn't have my head on straight and wasn't sure exactly what I was supposed to chat to the PM about. But I'll say one thing for the PM: he was as cool as you like. He congratulated me again, said I made a great speech (so I must have made some sense) and made some small talk, asking where I lived. I told him Elsternwick, a suburb in Melbourne, to which he asked, 'Have you ever considered politics?' Again showing all my poise and composure, I blurted out, 'No. The problem with politics is too many people don't like you.' As soon as I said it, I realised who I'd said it to. Fortunately, the PM had a chuckle and seemed to understand where I was coming from.

There was more to this honour than hanging out with the Prime Minister. There were more formalities and media interviews to take care of, not to mention preparing for the Boomers' opening game of the Olympics against Canada. Perhaps the best part of being named the Australian flag bearer was what it meant to the people closest to me. That much was rammed home when I switched on my mobile phone and it was chock-a-block with messages from friends. You couldn't get another message onto the system, it was so full, and the fact other people were so happy made me happy. One bloke who didn't leave a message was one of my best friends, Wayne Peterson, who was in Sydney to work as one of the court announcers for the basketball tournament. After getting into the locker room without a pass to celebrate the San Antonio Spurs' NBA title in New York, wouldn't you know it that, even though he had no invitation, no credentials to get him past security and through the door, Wayne was at the SuperDome to see me officially named as the flag bearer. I don't know how he did it, and I'm not sure I want to know, but he was there and that was almost as big a surprise as being asked to carry the flag.

When it was announced in 1993 Sydney would host the 2000 Olympic Games, I knew straightaway I wanted to be there. I would be thirty-five, getting to the end of my international basketball career, maybe on the fringe of selection, but I had to be there. If I was only going to be twelfth man for the Boomers, I would take it. A home Olympics was something I was sure I wanted to be part of. Mind you, this was before I played at Atlanta in 1996, so I might have taken 2000 a bit for granted. Previously, I set my long-term goals from Olympics to Olympics, but when IOC president Juan Antonio Samaranch pronounced Sydney as the host for 2000, it was a done deal in my mind. I made a commitment to myself that I would do whatever it took to get there.

Atlanta loomed as my fourth and final Olympics. At least I was partially prepared for that. Until *the* announcement. Then all bets were off and the motivation to be in Sydney was massive. After all, how many athletes have competed at an Olympics in their own country? In the whole scheme of things, not many. Having experienced and appreciated the Olympics in three countries, to do that at home would be special. Cities and countries always responded to having the Games on home soil, with the host nation usually producing its strongest performance and best results. For what the Boomers wanted to achieve in gaining an Olympic medal, that had to be a plus. My mind was made up. I was going, even if it was in a reduced role. Little did I know then just how much of a role I would have at Sydney 2000.

The first of the routine chores at the Olympics was the accreditation process and checking into the athletes' village. Even at a home Olympics, the excitement factor was dulled by waiting in line for four hours to be processed with an athlete's pass that was to be protected with your life. Lose it and you'd certainly wish you hadn't. If you didn't have a pass, you didn't go anywhere, especially in today's high-security era.

That done, we moved into the village not far from the main Homebush Olympic precinct. The accommodation was like a holiday village, with portable cabins, and there was certainly a buzz around the place. But the buzz was replaced by moans and groans when the oversized basketballers inspected their quarters. Actually, there were no real complaints, but if we had been on tour, this standard and style of accommodation would have provoked uproar. Because it was the Olympics, it was accepted, even though it was a bit pokey and provincial. You could say the rooms were so tiny that when you put the key in the door, you risked breaking the window on the opposite side of the room. There was enough room for two beds, a shower and a toilet. I roomed with Shane Heal and we had to go outside to open our suitcases. Small and cramped though our accommodation was, it was a relief to finally get to Sydney. Not only had the Olympics been a long time arriving, the previous week had been incredibly tense and controversial on a couple of fronts for the Boomers.

After a seven-game tour of Italy and France, we were home for a while, then headed for Hong Kong to play the FIBA Diamond Ball tournament against a field that included Yugoslavia, Italy, Angola, Canada and China. Shane Heal went down with a calf injury, but we managed to beat European champion Italy and, in the final, world champion Yugoslavia. They were major victories for the Boomers in terms of prestige and financial reward. Or at least they should have been. The prestige was undoubted. The financial reward was not as forthcoming as the team thought it should have been.

As had been an issue in the past, most notably at the 1998 Goodwill Games and World Championships, I was dealing with Basketball Australia during the Hong Kong tournament about changes to our workplace agreement. More to the point, I was in discussions about being paid the money we believed we were entitled to as Boomers players. It wasn't the first time and it won't be the last, but the players were sick of continually coming up short because of BA's usual claim that it didn't have enough money.

There was some talk of going on strike, but we were never going to jeopardise our Olympic campaign. Instead, there was a suggestion within the group that if we wanted to make an emphatic point, we should boycott the pre-Olympic game against the United States at Melbourne Park. One of the issues pertaining to that game was that, even though it was played in Melbourne, USA Basketball owned the rights to the game and collected the big bikkies, probably a million dollars with the TV contract factored in. We got nothing except the opportunity to play. Basically, we felt it was a bad deal and nobody was impressed by the allocation of two tickets per player that was eventually extended to four with a couple of extras in the nosebleed section.

As it was, during the 1998 Goodwill Games, when we finished second, if the players got a share of the prize money from the Diamond Ball tournament it would alleviate the problem we and BA had with the financial shortfall affecting both parties. I was in constant contact with BA president John Maddock about trying to resolve the situation, but my negotiating skills again failed to deliver what the players asked for. Not that I didn't try my best.

It got to a stage where John might have been considered unreasonable in his refusal to accept the compromise I put to him. I went back to the team and, to avoid any more conflict that the players or BA might regret, I presented a scenario I knew was highly unlikely to come to fruition but would appease the troops for the time being. Basically, I bent the truth a little bit because I could see the whole thing ending in tears and acrimony. The only way to avoid that was to buy some time, even though John didn't want me to do that either.

The dispute over the money reached the stage where I told John that I would inform the team the matter would be addressed and ratified at the next BA board meeting, which would be after the Olympics. That would set the matter aside for the players to concentrate on the Games, and it would allow BA to come up with another proposal. It was the way to go, in my opinion. John didn't want me to tell the players that, but I did it anyway because we were heading towards a no-win situation.

I had (and have) total respect and admiration for John Maddock, a veteran Melbourne Tigers team-mate from my early days, and the job he has done for basketball in Victoria and Australia. I understood that he was acting under the direction of the BA board but things were made hard for me in this situation. I had one hundred per cent respect and sympathy for BA's economic situation, but it was as though BA had zero understanding of the team and the impact this situation could have on the team. It wasn't like it was a one-off situation. BA had a collective bargaining agreement with the players, but it seemed that more often than not they wanted to adjust it. Generally, the players agreed without too much fuss. Nor was it was just about money. It was about travel conditions and not being able to get decent training gear. Some people will perceive this as a bunch of well-paid athletes pouting and complaining, but all we wanted was the chance to perform at our peak for our country. The agreement we had with BA was designed to help us do that, but officialdom kept coming up with the changes. Like at the 1998 World Championships in Athens, I got the feeling John didn't understand how much this dispute, no matter how minor it seemed to some, could harm team morale. It was certainly something we just did not need going into the Olympic Games.

Out of nowhere, a solution to the Hong Kong stand-off was presented to us with the Diamond Ball trophy after we beat Yugoslavia in the final. The tournament official handed over the trophy and an envelope, which contained some of the prize money, in cash. So I figured we could bridge the shortfall by distributing the prize money to the players right there and then and everyone would be happy. It was probably about $1000 per player, which was not a lot of money, but the guys had taken a stand on principle. I contacted John Maddock and told him of our intentions, but he wouldn't agree to it, putting up an argument based on tax implications. Eventually, John agreed to let me distribute a small amount of the money to the players, which helped appease the immediate concerns, but it did little to ease the players' us-against-them mentality.

With some cash in our pockets and our confidence high, we flew back to Melbourne for the game against the US and its swaggering, millionaire NBA superstars. Despite the disillusionment with BA, we were on a high after winning in Hong Kong and looking forward to the game. We stayed at Crown Casino, we were playing in front of fifteen thousand people at the arena and millions on TV at home and overseas. This was big and the message from Boomers coach Barry Barnes was that everyone would get to play, so relax and enjoy the experience.

But right from the start, as the teams crossed over at the end of our training session to allow the Americans to start theirs, there was a negative vibe from the visitors. The US coach Rudy Tomjanovich was as friendly as ever, but the players were cool to the point of being cold when it came to greeting the Aussies. We all acknowledged them and said 'g'day', but they just brushed us. It later emerged that some of them had a bee up their bums because they didn't think they were being fully respected. Some people, especially in the media, disputed the notion that the Americans were a continuation of the Dream Team that originated with the 1992 US Olympic team. Others, including me, had suggested the 2000 Americans were beatable. Clearly, they didn't take kindly to all that and they tried to intimidate us and many others.

The lack of goodwill did not take long to surface in the game the next night at Rod Laver Arena. It actually took all of two possessions. US forward Vince Carter almost tackled me and took exception to being run into a high-post screen. On the ensuing play, the ball came to me at the top of the key outside the three-point line. I took a shot, Carter ran at me to close-out the shot, I kicked my legs out to try to draw a foul. As a non-athletic, slow veteran, I had to do whatever I could to get an advantage. So I exaggerated the contact and went to the floor. As I fell, we got tangled up, with my arm hooked around Carter's head and neck, so we ended up on the floor together. There was no call by the referee, which I wasn't impressed with, but Carter was even less impressed that he was on the floor with me. He jumped to his feet and stood over me in a menacing fashion, indicating where I should go and what I should do with myself. Both were physical impossibilities, I might add.

Anyway, the sight of Carter standing over me did not register as a sporting gesture with Shane Heal, who showed his qualities of mateship by being prepared to stick up for me whether I was in the right or not. While Boomers team-mate Sam Mackinnon took a diplomatic approach to removing Carter from the scene, Shane was more proactive and, funnily enough, offered Carter similar advice to what Carter offered me. Within a second, there was pushing and shoving to go with the trash talking and verbal threats and it was close to going over the edge. The tone was set on the court and off. The Americans would play us upstarts hard for the full forty minutes and the crowd, which had paid big money ostensibly to see NBA players, turned from star-gazers to Boomers barrackers. That they chanted 'Carter's a wanker' every time he got the ball showed how far the fans turned against them when they should have and could have had the audience in the palm of their collective hand.

During the Olympics, the international response was not favourable towards the Americans for their brash and confrontational behaviour. In terms of how good they were, how well they won and upholding the spirit of international competition, the Americans clearly didn't demonstrate the things people expected. People started to turn. The US had far superior talent to any other team at the Olympics but did themselves no favours by lacking humility. That might be the way of the NBA, but it cuts no ice on the international stage where the etiquette and protocol are much different and more sporting. As individuals, guys like Alonzo Mourning, Tim Hardaway and Ray Allen were terrific blokes. As a team, their behaviour, with chest pounding and preening, was arrogant and dreadful.

The postscript to the Boomers–US game in Melbourne, which we lost 89–64, was a confrontation I regretted almost immediately. Before flying to Sydney the next day, the Boomers and Opals were feted at a farewell breakfast, where I bumped into Damian Keogh, a former Boomers team-mate and a friend. Keogh was also a BA board member and, given what had happened in Hong Kong, I gave him a bake. I had a real hard crack, telling Keogh in no uncertain terms to get his boys on the board in order. It was unfair to unload on Damian and I regretted it straightaway. Once my anger had subsided, I called him on his mobile phone to apologise. By then, we were in Sydney and on the home stretch to the start of the Olympics.

Since the 2000 Olympics, the question I have been asked most is: what was it like to carry the flag in the opening ceremony? It's diffi-cult to explain in terms of emotions and memories, but what happened before we marched into and around Stadium Australia had a greater impact on me than actually carrying the flag.

In preparation for marching, all the athletes and officials assem-bled inside the SuperDome, which was adjacent to the main Olympic stadium. Every team was allocated blocks of seating inside the SuperDome, which was already set up for the gymnastics com-petition, so it was a bit like we were there to watch a make-believe showdown between Nadia Comaneci and Mary Lou Retton. I sat with the Boomers amid the greater Australian team and watched the opening ceremony on the big screen that hung from the roof. The only drawback was that there was no sound. To make up for that lack of noise, the teams created their own, taking turns to perform traditional songs or chants. The efforts of the Africans, New Zealanders and Australians were met with applause, but every-one booed when the Americans started chanting 'U-S-A, U-S-A'. To say their image was hurting a little bit might have been an understatement.

The singing and chanting was a nice way to break the monotony of the long wait. We were probably there for two or three hours waiting for the call, which took longer to arrive than normal given that Australia marched last as host country. Eventually, the first teams, led traditionally by Greece as the founder of the Olympics, assembled on the concourse and headed to the stadium. Finally it was Australia's turn and the announcement over the public address system calling the home team to mass on the concourse was greeted by a lusty mixture of relief and outright excitement.

There was no dictated order for where individuals would march within the team, but the rule of thumb was that the women were at the front followed by the blokes, all in general height order. No big deal. So as we gathered, the Boomers, being the tallest blokes in the team, were at the back of the massive pack. The only thing was I had to be at the front to carry the flag. Which made sense. So I said to the Boomers, 'Boys, have a good march. I'm at the front of the bus for this one, so I'll see you when we get there.' Then I turned to head to the front of the ranks.

As I started walking to the front through the entire team of more than five hundred athletes and officials, it was like the parting of a human sea as my team-mates made way for me to get to the front, grab the flag and lead us into our home Olympics. What a thrill. As I made my way along, team members cheered, applauded and slapped high-fives with me. To be acknowledged that way by Australia's greatest athletes was probably the best reward I have ever received in sport. Walking into the stadium to the roar of 120,000 people was incredible – but that, for me, was the highlight of carrying the flag: the feeling of unity and recognition that we were about to do something so special. I don't believe the athletes were necessarily cheering for me as captain of the Olympic team, but it was a symbol of what we were doing and what we were trying to achieve over the next fortnight. If you asked gold medal shooter and Melbourne Tigers fan Russell Mark, he joked that they were cheering because they had sat around for three hours and were finally getting the chance to march. Either way, it was a great moment.

As I got to the front of the team, the flag was waiting to be handed over. Another adrenalin rush. The only problem was that I didn't know what I was supposed to do, except carry the flag and not let it touch the ground, which I think I learned in primary school. There were never any instructions about what was supposed to happen. Fortunately, just before I entered the stadium, John Coates came across and told me to basically do what I wanted and just enjoy the moment. The only protocol was to dip the flag in front of the dignitaries who were seated in the stands adjacent to the finish line on the athletics track. Surely even I could remember that.

Lots of volunteers assembled to see us walk the few hundred metres from the SuperDome to the main stadium and the looks on their faces and the excitement in their cheering and clapping added to the buzz that built as we got closer to the stadium. As we reached the ramp that took us below the stadium and onto the track, many of the performers from the opening ceremony gave us a roaring reception, underlining the sense of national pride that the Olympics generated.

Being at the front of the team, I got a clear glimpse of the crowd and the atmosphere hit me in the face like a wet salmon. It was awesome, powerful and the most natural high any of us might ever have. We paused before entering the track to allow the other teams their moment and to maximise the effect of the Australian Olympic team's arrival. During that pause, I looked around and took in as much as I could, trying to comprehend what it was all about. Then we were moving again. A lot of people would move a lot faster around this track in days that followed, but not many got as big a reception as we got that night.

The people in the stands directly opposite where we entered the arena got the first glimpse of us, sparking a domino effect of a massive roar and camera flashes sweeping around the stadium. The roar got louder and louder and it was like that giant wave of noise carried the entire Olympic team around the track that soon belonged to Cathy Freeman. My only concern was the first one hundred metres, where I was supposed to dip the flag. Given that I was a little distracted by events around me, I thought I did well to remember to dip it just after the finish line with a minor, token effort. I was too busy having a good time.

The perception that athletes actually march at an opening ceremony is wrong. It was more like a pumped up stroll. For me, it was more like power walking as I waved to the crowd and tried to pick out anyone I knew. I was having such a good time, I almost forgot about my team-mates behind me and had to temper my excitement and let them catch up.

Unfortunately, I couldn't pick out Melinda and my two eldest daughters Courtney and Phoebe, who were with my mum and dad in the stands. But one of my greatest keepsakes from the Olympics is the home video Melinda took of the kids' reaction to the Australians marching. It was late and they were tired, but when we marched in, they fired up like a couple of sparkplugs and yelled out to daddy and waved and cheered. It was an emotional time for us all and to have that family perspective of the opening ceremony is priceless. When people talk about once-in-a-lifetime experiences, that was one for the whole Gaze family.

There was a lot of debate about who would light the Olympic cauldron. Cathy Freeman was mentioned as a candidate, but as we marched, I looked over my shoulder and saw her at the front of the team. Being as perceptive as I am, I figured she wouldn't be the last person to receive the Olympic flame after its journey from Mount Olympus.

After I delivered the flag to the infield with all the other nations' flags, I merged back into the group and joined the Boomers to watch the rest of the opening ceremony and the lighting of the flame. We saw Australian Olympic legends Betty Cuthbert, Raelene Boyle, Dawn Fraser, Debbie Flintoff-King, Shane Gould and Shirley Strickland and, then, bugger me dead if Cathy Freeman didn't step out of the darkness to be last in line to receive the flame. Unbelievable. I don't know how she did it. For a moment I thought she must have had a stunt double. It was a stunning moment.

Every Olympics since Los Angeles in 1984 has provided a spectacular and/or dramatic lighting of the cauldron, which is a symbol of the enduring Olympic spirit. We had Muhammad Ali in Atlanta in 1996 and the archer in Barcelona in 1992 and now we had Cathy

Freeman standing under a waterfall at Sydney in 2000. Except, as the cauldron rose to its resting place at the top of the stadium, it stopped with a clunk so loud we could hear it on the ground. We begged it to get going again and when it did, it was probably the most relief a whole nation had felt since peace was declared in 1945.

The entire opening ceremony was reflective of Australia. The feedback I got was that it really did make everyone feel good and it set the tone for the next fortnight. There were hiccups and controversies before the Games, but when the show got on the road, everyone banded together. To hear all the positive things had an impact on the athletes. But before we could feel too good about ourselves, we had to get back to the athletes' village. As we didn't have to play the next day, some of us walked. It was a decent walk, but a good walk that allowed us to unwind, reflect on what we'd just experienced and start to focus on what lay ahead. It was a long day, an emotional week and we were all tired. But the honour of carrying the flag was the most positive distraction I could have wished for in the build-up to an Olympics that carried a fair degree of expectation, pressure and anxiety for every Australian athlete and team, including the Boomers. Back at the village, I had something to eat, jumped into bed and went to sleep. It had been seven years coming, but it was finally time to get ready for my last Olympics.

chapter twenty-two

LET THE GAMES BEGIN ... PLEASE

THE numbers on the scoreboard changed so quickly it was like one of those time-lapse movie sequences. The only problem was that the numbers had changed in real time and the Boomers were in deep trouble against a team of Russians who looked like they would prefer holidays in Siberia to losing to Australia. So much so, they had turned a 24-point deficit into a two-point lead. In essence, the Boomers were on the verge of Olympic elimination as Russia took the lead, 71–69, with one minute, fifty-seven seconds left.

We lost the first two games of the Olympic tournament, which was not what we expected. We thought we would beat Canada to open the tournament, but lost 101–90, then we dropped our next game to world champion Yugoslavia, 80–66. A 1–1 start would have been ideal under the circumstances, but 0–2 left us on the edge and needing to win our next four games to make the medal rounds. We could still lose to Russia and make the quarter-finals, but then we would finish fourth in our pool and cross over for the knockout stage against the United States. So the reality was we could not lose to Russia if we wanted to win a medal. There were no ifs, buts or maybes. Losing to Russia was simply not an option.

I didn't think we played poorly against Canada, who performed very well behind NBA guard Steve Nash. We identified it as the game that could set up our tournament, but we couldn't get into any great rhythm. There were always nerves before the first game of the Olympic tournament and this was clearly a nervous start by the Boomers. In truth, the Boomers didn't expect to lose that game and it stung when we did. Losing to the Yugoslavs was no great surprise since they were world champions, although the further the tournament went, the more we suspected there was something amiss in the Yugoslav camp. Either way, we were faced with the prospect of needing to beat Russia, whom we'd never beaten at a major tournament, either as the Soviet Union or post-Glasnost Russia.

In both games against Canada and Yugoslavia, we lost control of the contests when they went on significant second-half scoring runs and we could neither stop them nor reply to them. There was no way we could do that against the Russians and hope to survive. We knew from all-too-recent experience not to let Russia get on top. Nor did we have a lot of time to analyse and repair problems. With games every second day during the tournament, the day between games was basically spent recovering with massage and pool sessions and shooting and walk-throughs. There was no time for a major overhaul, which was kind of ironic as we prepared to face the Russians.

We played Russia five times in the immediate build-up to Sydney and were 0–5. We lost twice at the official Olympic test event in Sydney in June and the alarm bells started ringing after a three-game series in Melbourne, Adelaide and Perth. We just couldn't crack the Russians and they had our measure. We were close in

Melbourne and Adelaide, but Russia gave us a touch-up in Perth and the worry beads were out.

There were extenuating circumstances during the pre-Olympic series. The Boomers Olympic team wasn't finalised, so some guys played more than others for the coaches to get one last look at them and the on-court chemistry was still awry. It was relatively early in our preparation, especially as it was the first time, after the change of NBL seasons from winter to summer, that we could go through an extended off-season preparation for the Olympics. Certainly, the coaches were still involved in the selection process, so we were not playing with a win-at-all-costs attitude – and that showed. Even so, we thought we'd be better than we'd shown against Russia and after the loss in Perth I had a dreadful feeling things were not great with our team. I wasn't the only one.

Having finalised the twelve-man roster, the coaching staff also culled some of the offensive sets we'd been using. Head coach Barry Barnes and his assistants Brett Brown and Alan Black felt we were doing a lot of things at a mediocre level rather than doing a few things really well. So they wiped out a significant portion of our offensive structure and decided to go with the shuffle options that had been the staple of the Tigers before I was born.

Changing the offence was considered controversial because some critics believed the shuffle did not properly utilise big men Luc Longley, Mark Bradtke, Chris Anstey and Paul Rogers. But Barnes, to his credit, realised we needed to do something different. We were talented, but we weren't as good as the other teams. Russia ran elements of the shuffle and I guess that provided some motivation for us to build an offensive foundation that was a little different and could exploit some of our strengths, namely perimeter shooting and mobile big men. Barry had his ideas and philosophies on running the shuffle, but he wasn't down pat on the intricacies, so he spoke to Bradtke and Heal and me about it. He also got my dad involved in tweaking and tuning the Boomers' version of the shuffle.

Though the decision was made and the change invoked, that did not necessarily mean there would be a smooth transition and we would live happily ever after. Not in this little Olympic fairytale that spirited us from Australia to the picturesque Italian Alpine village of Bormio for a four-team tournament involving the Boomers, Italy, Turkey and Angola. In front of a small audience in a tiny gym, we beat Turkey and Angola without being spectacular. There was a feeling among the group that things weren't right. Even more frustrating, perhaps, was that while a settling process always has to be gone through, this time it was taking longer than usual. The main undercurrent was that some people were miffed that they weren't playing as much as they wished or in different roles to their NBL teams.

Then we played Italy in front of a full house and the lid came off the gym and the Boomers. We lost by thirty-two and were terrible. There was just no other way to describe it. Italy was the European champion and playing at home, but we would have struggled to beat the Ringwood District champion that night. We were miles away from where we wanted to be and the frustration was no longer cloaked. At the buzzer Chris Anstey booted the ball into the stands, prompting Barry Barnes to make a bee-line for him. Barnesy gave him as good a verbal pasting as Italy had just done to us on the scoreboard. Vesuvius might have been at the other end of Italy, but something was about to blow a lot closer to Bormio.

By the time Barnsey reached the locker room, he had cooled a little, but he still laid down the law about needing to improve as a basketball team and acting with more class and dignity as representatives of Australia. After Barnes said his piece, Andrew Vlahov asked the coaches to leave so we could have a players-only meeting. As captain, I wasn't comfortable having that meeting right then and there, but Vlahov was a senior player and felt it was a good time for an open and frank discussion. I had never been on a team that didn't have one of these players-only forums, but I never felt that having them straight after a game was a good idea. Invariably, they are held after a loss, when emotions run way too high and you can't really be rational about what you're trying to communicate. It's just the wrong time to do it.

Regardless of what I thought, the meeting went ahead. Everyone had their two bob's worth and the gist of the airing was that the players felt they did not have a good understanding of their roles. Some who said they didn't understand their role were only getting two minutes a game. If you're only getting two minutes consistently, it would seem your role was defined as not playing much. Where some of the confusion may have arisen was that, while players were given good court time during the selection process before we went to Europe, it was to give them a chance to make the team. They might have assumed that their eventual roles and court time would be similar, but the refining process had made it clear that was not so. Egos were bruised, but people really just needed to accept their place within the team. I needed to be diplomatic with the players in what was clearly a case of being able to please some of the people some of the time but not being able to please all of the people all of the time.

As captain, I was saddled with the job of conveying to the coaching staff the players' concerns about getting roles established. I went back to the hotel to do so and I was faced with a no-win situation. No matter how delicately or diplomatically I put the players' views across, it would be difficult to be seen as not being critical of the coaching staff. The coaches explained that we were working through a process, but the loss to Italy and the players-only meeting might have prompted the coaching staff to accelerate that process. I don't think at that point the coaches had a clear-cut view on players' roles, if only because some guys weren't performing as well as they should have been. Simply, we weren't finely tuned and it made it hard for everybody.

While I had the post-game post-meeting powwow with the coaches, the rest of the team decided to have a bonding session and it turned into a late one. They went to a pool hall, knocked back a few beers with the locals and had a pretty good time, which helped lighten the atmosphere among the group. But next morning, there was a definite sense of foreboding among the coaches. As the players' excursion out on the town was after a nasty loss, the coaches weren't happy. I don't think anyone got plastered, but a few blokes showed signs of weariness and the tension at the front of the bus was palpable.

That morning might have been the most crucial of the European tour and our Olympic preparation and I give Barry Barnes great credit for how he handled it. After the loss and the frustrations encircling that result, the whole thing was in danger of going irretrievably pear-shaped. Barnsey knew that a few blokes were a little tired and suspected some were hungover, and you just knew he wasn't pleased about it. With a bloke like Barnesy, there was every chance he would blow up and get in some blokes' faces. His reaction to this situation was crucial and he chose to let it ride. He bit his tongue and opted not to make an issue of it. He wasn't happy, but he recognised we were grown men who were responsible for our actions and he sat on it. It was exactly the right thing to do and it was a turning point of our campaign.

We went from Bormio to the south-western French surf city of Biarritz, near the Spanish border, for two games (one official, one unofficial) against France. We had a couple of injuries, but there was a different mindset and we knew it was important to bounce back after the Italy debacle. It was always going to be tough to win in France and both games were physical and hard-fought. We split the games with a narrow win and a close loss, which restored our respectability, and we returned to Italy, this time to the Adriatic resort town of Roseto for a tournament, feeling better about ourselves and what we were doing.

We played Italy first-up in Roseto and, although we lost, we were much better than in Bormio. We went from losing by thirty-two to losing by five, then we beat Croatia to end the tour on a high with some palpable evidence of improvement. Roseto was where we solved another piece of the offensive puzzle by switching the roles of Luc Longley and Mark Bradtke. It was a move that didn't make sense to some, but we moved Luc to the feeder position on the perimeter and put Bradtke in the post. To most people, it would have been logical to play Luc, as our biggest big man, in the post. But Luc probably didn't have a full grasp of the intricacies of playing the post in the shuffle, whereas Bradtke had spent nearly ten years playing that spot for the Tigers. Neither player felt totally comfortable, so we spoke to the coaching staff and suggested they switch spots in the offence. One of Luc's strengths was his passing ability and if he played as the feeder, he would be the key passer and when the play continued, he would end up inside anyway.

It was the last tinker of a tour that started tentatively and ended with some confidence and promise that we were finally on the right track as a team.

So here we were in Sydney deep in a dog fight with Russia, knowing a loss would basically snuff out the Boomers' Olympic flame. Before the game, you could tell there was a resolve among the guys and that was demonstrated early as we got off to a good start. Our confidence grew with every made shot, our defence was very good and contained their strengths, and everything was going as scheduled. We were up 47–30 at the half and pushed that margin out to twenty-four points in the second half as we seemingly headed towards an enjoyable victory. It didn't turn out to be quite that easy.

We didn't shut down, but once we had such a big lead, it was like we subconsciously said, 'Let's try to bring it home and milk the clock with time management.' It was a sound strategy in theory, but while we tried to nurse home the win, the Russians threw caution to the wind and were hitting three-pointers at an alarming rate. We helped out with a few turnovers and suddenly we were on our heels, the Russians were full of confidence and momentum had turned 180 degrees. Russia tore off a 41–15 run that ended when they took the lead 71–69 with a few ticks under two minutes to go. The overwhelming feeling in the Dome was that we had cast away our Olympic campaign. The reality was that we were made of sterner stuff than to just tip our hats to inevitability.

Our recovery started when Luc Longley made one of the all-time great passes to Bradtke. Posted up facing away from the basket, Longley slipped a behind-the-back pass to the cutting Bradtke to tie it 71–71. That basket stemmed the Russian flow a little and we got a break when they didn't score on their next possession. Little did we know Russia had scored its last basket.

We took a time-out and Barry Barnes called for us to run 'Fist', which was a high screen-and-roll play for Shane Heal, who would either get room for a shot or pass to the screener rolling to the basket. We ran the play and Shane could get neither of the two preferred options, so he passed the ball to me high on the left wing. I was a long way out and Luc came over to set an on-ball screen for me to dribble off. As he set the screen, my defender stepped back to go behind the screen. It was a bad choice by the Russian.

I didn't realise how far I was behind the three-point line and I guessed there was about twenty seconds left (there was actually 38.9 seconds to go). But as the defender stepped off to give me room, instinct kicked in and I let it fly. As soon as the shot left my hand, it was dead on track and I knew it was home. Bang! We were up by three and the place went nuts. This was the Soviet Union at the Glasshouse in 1987 all over again, only ten times more important.

I knew it was a big basket, putting us ahead 74–71, but I also knew there was still lot of time to go and we couldn't relax on defence. Russia missed again, we got the rebound and Russia quickly fouled to stop the clock. The problem for Russia was that they hadn't committed enough fouls to be in the penalty situation and make us shoot free-throws. They committed some rapid-fire fouls and eventually I went to the free-throw line with 5.1 seconds left, knowing I only needed to make one to ice the game. I don't think

I'd missed a free-throw in the tournament, so naturally I clunked the first of the pair. Fortunately, I nailed the second and our 75–71 victory was complete. Our first win over Russia in a major event kept our Olympics alive.

Although our tournament was rejuvenated with that win over Russia, we still had to beat Angola and Spain. Angola, our old nemesis from the 1986 World Championships, made us work for our eleven-point win after being down at half-time. Spain, we knew, would be tough, despite the fact that the Europeans had had an ordinary tournament. But on the way to the Dome for the game we had a little inspiration.

Whatever expectations we thought we carried at the Olympics were minuscule when compared with the load heaped on the slim shoulders of Cathy Freeman. Our game against Spain started not long after Freeman's career-defining moment in the women's 400 metres final. The bus that carried us to the game was equipped with a television and we all intently tuned into Freeman and her quest for gold. The race was run and won on our final approach to the Dome and, as we disembarked the bus, we heard the sustained cheering of the crowd in the main stadium just across the road. There was a massive sense of relief for Freeman after her victory and it lifted our spirits as we prepared to play Spain for a spot in a quarter-final that didn't involve the United States.

Alas, the boost provided by Freeman's win didn't last long. Soon after tip-off, we were down eleven in this must-win game as Spain shot the lights out. We managed to claw back to within four by the half and the second half went our way when Shane Heal and I hit a bunch of three-pointers in a 23–4 scoring run to lead by as much as eighteen before settling for a 91–80 win. We had our quarter-final spot. As it turned out, Canada upset Yugoslavia earlier in the day, so they finished first and second in our pool, with Russia doomed to the unwanted fourth place and a showdown with the US. The Boomers finished third and were drawn to play Italy in the quarters.

While Russia was nothing but trouble during our Olympic build-up, Italy represented a benchmark of our progress. After being smashed by Italy in Bormio, we lost by only five in Roseto. By the time we played the Azzurri at the Diamond Ball tournament in Hong Kong a couple of weeks before the Olympics, we beat them. It was significant progress by anybody's measure. It was such that we felt confident of beating Italy again in a game that would send the winner to the medal rounds and the loser to the consolation games.

Italy slipped during the Olympics when it was upset by China, but we knew we faced a talented and dangerous team in this European champion. Those two facts were driven home with Ferrari-type power when Italy went on a 14–0 run during the second half to lead by four points. The Boomers were asked and answered some tough questions during the Olympics and the Italians popped one worth much more than the proverbial $64,000. How much did we want to win this game and make the medal round? Answer: more than you could know.

There are two clear memories of the second half against Italy as we banged in some big three-pointers to stay in the game. One was that the guys really made an effort to get me shots (I had twenty-two points in the second half); the second was the support from a SuperDome crowd that was boosted by a large section of Australian athletes and swimmers, including gold medallist Kieren Perkins, who rates that day as one of his favourite Olympic experiences. You never forget those days when you get in a shooting groove like I was in against Italy and you never forget days when it seems like a whole nation is willing you to victory.

The Italians' four-point lead became one as the game edged into the final minute. Then it took a decided swing to the Boomers with 44.6 seconds left. That was when Mark Bradtke stepped to the free-throw line and made both shots to put the Boomers ahead by one. We surely needed only one, maybe two, more defensive stops and we would win. You could sense the Italians were edgy and they didn't score on their next possession. The ball came to me, I was fouled as I tried to dribble into space to kill time and I went to the line with 13.5 seconds left. If I made both, I knew at least we couldn't lose in regulation. Italy would have had to make a three-pointer and we'd still have the last possession unless they hit a shot at the buzzer. I made the first free-throw. I made the second and we led by three, 65–62. Italy took the ball up-court, threw up a three-point shot to tie and missed. Game over. The Boomers were in the Olympic semi-finals.

The excitement and realisation that we had reached a very important stage of achieving our medal goal was there for everyone to feel and see. This was as memorable a Boomers victory as I was involved in and we shared it with the crowd, basking in the cheers and congratulations while offering our thanks for their brilliant support. High-fiving members of the Australian Olympic team courtside was a sweet feeling. For once, it seemed, the Boomers were centre stage at the Sydney Olympics and it was a great time to do it. We were just one win away from an Olympic medal.

chapter twenty-three

MEDAL OR BUST

OVER the years, some people questioned Luc Longley's commitment to the Boomers. Make no mistake, when Luc was with the Boomers for the 2000 Sydney Olympic campaign, his commitment was total. So much so that when Luc recognised the team's need for extra training gear, he took the initiative and ordered and paid for, out of his own pocket, T-shirts and tracksuits. The couple of thousand dollars it cost Luc would not have made a big dint in the bank account of a bloke who made millions during his NBA career, but it was the thought that counted more than the money. That was typical of Luc and why the blokes on the Boomers thought so much of him.

The gear Luc ordered was distinctive and unique to the team. Having seen the standards set by the Chicago Bulls in their commitment to winning, Luc wanted the guys to look professional, feel professional and be professional, which meant we needed to present ourselves in a professional manner. It was the old motto about looking like a good basketballer if you wanted to be a good basket-baller. We also wanted something on the gear that identified the 2000 men's Olympic basketball team and our team only. We also wanted something that provided motivation. We went with a screen print: M.O.B. If anybody outside the group asked what it meant, the stock answers were that a gathering of kangaroos, which boomers are, is a mob, or it stood for Men's Olympic Basketball. For the twelve players and the small band of coaches and support staff it meant something else entirely. It meant Medal Or Bust.

We didn't want to let the world know about our in-house motto, but after beating Italy in that stunning quarter-final, we were very deep into the medal or bust stage of the Olympic tournament. In fact, if we didn't get a medal after making the semi-finals, where we faced France, there would be plenty of people who would consider the Boomers' Olympics a bust.

The Olympic quarter-finals are decidedly make or break. If you lose, your tournament is done and you're playing for the minor plac-ings. If you win, you go into the semi-finals with two chances at a medal. Win the semi and you are guaranteed silver at worst. Lose the semi and you can still pick up a bronze in the play-off for third and fourth. We had two chances at winning our first Olympic medal in Sydney, but the effort came at a cost.

The emotional and physical demands of the Olympics were enor-mous in Sydney, where there was extra pressure on the home team. After losing the first two games, we were always playing to stay alive in the event. The physical efforts required, given the intensity of the competition, made it extremely demanding and we got to a point where, as a group, we knew we'd achieved a lot. Conversely, the public expected us to make the semis without understanding the dif-ficulties we faced to get to that point. Among the team, there was a sense of relief in reaching the final four, but that didn't mean we were satisfied. Far from it.

France was the surprise of the 2000 Olympics. We knew the

French were good after losing to them on the pre-Olympic tour of Europe, but they were less than impressive during the Olympics and were lucky to make the top eight. They were about ten minutes away from being eliminated when China, with a young Yao Ming, now one of the biggest and most easily identified players in the NBA, in the line-up had them down and out only for France to rally and get out of trouble. Then in the quarter-finals France upset Canada, who had topped our pool and was seemingly cruising. We would have loved another crack at Canada after our opening-game loss, but we also thought we were a pretty good show against France.

But France had clearly done its homework on the Boomers. The French had gone through their slump, weathered the storm, gained momentum and never gave us a chance, winning the semi-final 76–52. France was tall and athletic, took away our strengths and gave us match-up problems. I couldn't change my mind without someone being in my face defensively and we never really got into a flow. The semi-final was the day after we beat Italy, so we had little time to prepare for France and we were physically drained. That's not to say France didn't have the same things to deal with, but we didn't have the juice and we ran out of legs. We were down just four midway through the first half when France uncorked a 13–0 run and it was just about game over. The French shot better than us, they out-rebounded us, they outplayed us. Nor did we help ourselves by shooting only fifty-two points. We weren't going to win too many games or medals with that kind of malnourished score.

Adding to the pain of defeat was a knee injury to Luc Longley, who was forced out of the bronze medal game against Lithuania. Losing a bloke the size of a small building left a bit of a hole in the Boomers line-up, but we remained buoyant and determined to beat Lithuania. We had beaten Lithuania, our old and friendly rival, two weeks earlier in an exhibition at Wollongong, but they played much better as the tournament reached its climax. The X factor with the

Lithuanians was how they would respond to their semi-final loss to the United States.

In contrast to the Boomers' effort against France in our semi, Lithuania took the powerhouse, NBA-laden US all the way to the buzzer and the verge of the greatest basketball upset of all time. The game was tied with little more than a minute to go, then Ramunas Siskauskas had three free-throws for Lithuania. He missed the first two and made the last for an 81–80 lead. Vince Carter made a shot from the corner to put the US back in front, 82–81, before Antonio McDyess converted an offensive rebound for 84–81. Lithuanian guard Sarunas Jasikevicius made a drive with 10.8 seconds left for 83–84, then Jason Kidd made only one of two free-throws with 9.4 seconds left to make the score 85–83. Lithuania gained possession only for Jasikevicius's long-range shot at the buzzer to finish short, along with Lithuania's hopes of an upset. The close call also vindicated my pre-Olympic suggestion that this US team was beatable.

If we thought Lithuania would be dispirited or flat after that emotion-sapping loss to the US, we were wrong. The Lithos came out and were all over us from the tip-off. If any team was lacking spark, it was the Boomers and, truth be told, we were rarely in the game, losing 89–71. There was no consolation in the fact that I top-scored for the Boomers with twenty-two points in my last game for Australia. The bottom line was that we didn't achieve our goal of winning a medal and the disappointment of that cut deeper because of the way in which we lost. Against France and Lithuania we didn't perform to our potential and suffered significant losses.

Four years earlier in Atlanta, we had lost to Lithuania in the bronze medal game, but in vastly different circumstances. That game was close and we were devastated to lose. In Sydney, Lithuania had us covered well before the end, but the disappointment was still palpable, especially from those on the outside looking in. As for the insiders, I was very proud of the Boomers' result in Sydney. Finishing fourth at the Olympics is something that shouldn't be underestimated, but I think our ordinary performances in the medal round caused that to be overlooked.

We should have received some credit for finishing fourth, but there was a lot of post-Games criticism, particularly of coach Barry Barnes, and claims that the offence was outdated and Barnesy didn't play certain players enough. This was not unusual as there is always someone with a gripe or who wants to second-guess the coach. How anyone could second-guess Barry Barnes was beyond me. Barnesy was head coach at two Olympics and we finished fourth at both of them, equalling our best Games performance. I know plenty of coaches around the world would love to have that on their CVs. Sometimes fiery, sometimes cranky, Barnesy was from the old school and grew up in the tough inner Melbourne suburb of Richmond, where nothing came easy. But Barnesy made something of himself as a basketball player and coach and he was one bloke I always respected, admired and liked. Away from the court, Barnesy was funny and friendly, but training and games were a time for serious, intense business and competition, and Barnesy never shied away from that fact. Some blokes might have considered Barnesy to be a bit old-fashioned and stuck in his methods, but you could never doubt the integrity and intent of Barry Barnes when he was coaching the Boomers.

Unfortunately, once the machine of negativity started rolling, it was hard to stop. But consider what we had achieved in a tournament so tough that Yugoslavia, the world champion either side of the Olympics, and perennial power Russia did not make it past the quarter-finals. We beat Russia and Spain in big, big games; we beat Italy, which was reigning European champion, in the quarter-finals; we did some remarkable things just to get to the semi-finals. That we didn't get a medal seemed to tarnish our performance for some people, but that's not a fair assessment of our overall performance. We finished fourth and that was still the Boomers' equal-best finish at an Olympics.

That kind of rational thinking was still a few days away. In the immediate aftermath, disappointment was clearly evident. Initially, we were mostly numbed by the result and the performance against Lithuania. That it was my last game for Australia did not have a great deal of impact on me at the time, mainly because, even though I had indicated the Olympics would be my international farewell, I hadn't thought deeply about it. The key focus for the Boomers was winning a medal, not me playing my last game for Australia. At the time, there was no sadness that my international career was over. It wasn't like there'd been any fanfare about my retirement, except for a couple of newspaper stories in the middle of the tournament, and it hadn't really sunk in at that point.

I had always set my basketball goals from Olympics to Olympics, but being thirty-five in Sydney, I knew I couldn't go another four years to Athens. So rather than work on a year-by-year basis with the national team, I felt it was time to move on and give someone the chance to come into the team. In hindsight, if I had known Australia would field such an inexperienced team and fail to qualify for the 2002 World Championships, I might have stayed a bit longer. That's not to say I would have made the difference, or even made the team, but I would have been keen to help Phil Smyth, who took over as coach from Barry Barnes and inherited a team stripped of experience and talent by retirements and injuries. Phil did ask me about playing, but I declined. I think his enquiry was more out of courtesy. He appreciated that I'd done my time and he didn't want to put pressure on me or make be feel obliged to help out.

Nevertheless, as the Boomers slumped in the locker room after losing to Lithuania, nobody really knew what the next five minutes held in store, let alone the next five days, five weeks or five months. We sat in stunned silence and, with nowhere to go for the first time in what seemed a long time, the team just hung around the locker room oblivious to the gold medal game between the US and France that raged just outside our door.

After a while, a few beers were cracked open and there was a realisation among the guys this was the last time we would be together. Some of us had been together in the national team since just before the 1988 Seoul Olympics and some of us for only a few months. But we all shared a special bond of togetherness and sacrifice. We sat in a circle, taking turns to say something, and that was when the emotion started to flow. For more than an hour, everyone took a turn to speak and some found it harder than others. Andrew Vlahov went to four Olympics and beat the odds and bad ankles to get to Sydney. He was very choked up, having announced his international retirement, and coach Barry Barnes had to take a break during his speech to avoid breaking down altogether.

I was more of a listener in the circle of truth and was brief when it came my turn to speak. It was interesting to learn what the whole experience meant to the other players and there was a real sense of closure, especially for the guys who had been together on the national team for so long. Death is a profound thing and is not an appropriate analogy for this situation, but it was the end of a significant relationship for guys like Andrew Vlahov, Mark Bradtke, Luc Longley and me. It meant we were not team-mates any more. We were still friends, but not team-mates, and that common bond was removed forever.

Everyone, I believe, expressed their true feelings, but it was all good. Some guys might not have been entirely happy with how little they had played or what their role had been on the team, but all twelve members of the 2000 Boomers were thrilled to have been part of the Olympic experience. Everyone had an appreciation of what we'd endured. It was an experience they truly could cherish as a significant part of their lives.

The whole Olympic experience was so much more than the lead-up and the actual Games for the team. It was being involved in village life, getting immersed in the Olympic atmosphere, enjoying the buzz and the thrill when an Australian won a medal. It was about opening your eyes and absorbing what was going on around us. In Sydney, it was like you couldn't avoid being exposed to all that, living shoulder to shoulder for three weeks with the greatest athletes in the world. It was one of the greatest motivating factors to be had and the Australians couldn't help but be inspired.

Most days, after a feed at the village food hall, we would wander back to our accommodation and during the stroll we often noticed this long-haired bloke in Australian team gear, kicking back, puffing on a cigarette. Even among a village of ten thousand people, it was not common to see somebody sucking on a coffin nail, but we suspected he was a team manager or official and not reliant on his lungs for performance. So imagine our reaction when we turned on the TV one night to find a close-up of our smoking mate filling the screen, standing at the top of the long-jump runway working the home crowd into a frenzy. Next minute we were all clapping in time with Jai Taurima as he won the long jump silver medal in one of the more astounding performances of the Games.

When you talk about athletes achieving a personal best, it might be by one-tenth of a second or by five millimetres. Jai Taurima, who jumped 8.32 metres in 1998, sailed 8.40 metres in Sydney in 2000 to win that silver medal and I put much of that down to performing in front of the home crowd. I use the story as part of my presentations and speaking engagements as an example of how the Olympics help you achieve great things. You can realise your potential, in part, because of the atmosphere. My belief is that if I took Taurima and placed him at the same time on the same day at the same venue, but in front of only five thousand people, there's no way he would jump that far. But with the intangibles of jumping in front of 120,000 people, things happen. It's a great example of people achieving remarkable goals. He was proof that great things happen in atmospheres of greatness and there is no greater environment in sport than the Olympic Games.

I went home without a medal after five Olympic Games. It would have been nice to get a medal at some stage, but that does not detract from my feelings or experiences. I guess the greatest moment of disappointment after losing the bronze medal game in Sydney came during the rehearsal for the Australian Olympic Committee function to say thanks and farewell to the Australian Olympic team. As Australian team captain and flag bearer, I was asked to say a few words and present the flag to the captains of the Paralympic team. All the Australian medal winners were at the rehearsal and I felt like a bit of a shag on a rock as the only athlete there without a medal. I felt right out of place.

At times like that you tend to recall the line about it's not the winning but the taking part that matters. That's true for so many Olympians, who regard it as a high point of their careers to get to one Games. I went to five and they are all highlights of my life, let alone my sporting career. But soon after the Sydney Olympics, I almost had to remind myself I had been to five Games. It only seemed like yesterday that I was the wide-eyed teenager trotting off to Los Angeles for the 1984 Olympics. While I was doing TV commentary for the Boomers versus New Zealand series during 2003, it dawned on me that the players on the court were doing more than trying to win a game. They were, twelve months out from Athens, trying to win a spot on the Olympic team. I realised it might have been the only chance at the Olympics for some of them. Then I thought about going to five and I felt an enormous appreciation of what the Olympics meant, but I still found it hard to realise I had been to so many.

I also had a sense of envy watching those guys vie for spots on the team. While I knew deep down I couldn't have continued through to Athens as a player, that didn't mean I didn't want to be there. I did actually go to Athens to do basketball commentary for the Seven Network, but it's hard to shake the Olympics as a competitor when you've been to one, let alone five. I knew the players were heading into a load of hard work that could be a grind and very demanding, but there's a big reward at the end of it and that reward is not necessarily a medal. Sure, I'm disappointed I never got to experience winning a medal, but I have zero regrets. Sometimes we get caught up in the tangible results of first, second and third, while considering fourth to be a failure. When you go out and give your best and achieve the best result ever, as the Boomers did at four of my five Olympics, then you've got to feel fulfilled. It's over and done with and I'm happy.

There was also a deep sense of satisfaction and pride every time I played for Australia, whether it be at the Olympic Games or a low-key tour of Europe. It wasn't so much pulling on the uniform that meant so much, but it was hearing the national anthem and looking at the flag. I always had a sense that it meant more than just winning and losing and scoring points. There was a bigger picture that this was representing what we're about and it almost transcended the sport in some respects. Representing your country means you're reinforcing our culture, our nation, what we stand for, our ethics. In some way, you feel like you're obliged to represent everyone in the right way. I would like to think I managed to do that.

So, the bottom line was that there was no Olympic medal. But it was a long, long way from being a bust.

chapter twenty-four

FOR LOVE, NOT MONEY

OFFERS to play in Europe came regularly during my career. Some were lucrative and most were tempting. But the strangest offer was also the offer that should have been the easiest to take. I got a call out of the blue in the early 1990s from the general manager of Greek club Aris Salonika. Aris needed to win an important game and the GM was putting together the best team he could from anywhere he could. I was on his list with an offer of about $20,000 for one game. One game. He wanted me to fly from Melbourne to Athens, play the game, take my $20,000 and go home again. Talk about easy money.

I didn't take the Aris offer because the NBL season had started with the Tigers and my commitment was to them. There was relatively easy money to consider throughout my career and I usually did the same thing with that easy money: considered it, then turned it down to keep playing with the Tigers.

Like in 1998 when I went to the world championships in Greece, where a few conversations had my attention. Not just because of the seemingly continuous plume of smoke that hung in the air before sneaking up my nostrils, either. These conversations centred around an offer that was the equivalent, taking into account tax and exchange rates, of a $1 million deal to return to Greece after the world titles to play for Maroussi, coached by Kostas Petropolis, my former coach at Apollon Patras. I turned it down. For a million dollars, most people would be prepared to volunteer as passive smokers. But it wasn't the smoke from Kostas's cigarettes that was my excuse. I was going home and playing for the Melbourne Tigers for nothing.

While the glimmer of an offer from the San Antonio Spurs finally eventuated some months after it was tentatively broached in Athens, my intention had been to serve the Tigers in the NBL and I played the first seventeen games of the 1999 season before heading to Texas. But during that time with the Tigers, I didn't see a pay packet. In fact, I didn't get paid by the Tigers for the next three seasons as the club went through a difficult period. I had an obligation to the Tigers and the NBL and it was only the chance to play again in the NBA that truncated that situation. Had it been a money factor, and although I did well out of the shortened NBA season with the Spurs, I would have taken the million dollars from Maroussi. But money, as has been the case throughout my career, was not the biggest issue. Nor was my sanity, as some might be suggesting. It was my sense of obligation, belonging, convenience and in some ways, I suppose, honour that kept me with the Tigers.

Some people had trouble accepting and understanding why I turned down big-money overseas offers even for one season in preference to wearing the red of the Melbourne Tigers. When I look back, I have mixed feelings about some of the financial opportunities I passed up. I may reflect what I could have done with that money, but I also wonder what might have happened had I stopped playing for the Tigers.

I was never really motivated about the money on offer from Europe. By now, you probably reckon I should be twirling the propeller on one of those beanie caps, but the fact of the matter, and maybe the most important factor, was that I enjoyed playing with the Tigers in the NBL. Another factor was what might be termed my own feelings of insecurity about losing my position and standing in the NBL. I was protective, in a sense, of my turf and did not want someone to come in and take my place. It wasn't being selfish as much as it was a fear of needing to prove myself again from scratch if I left and came back. That might sound weird for a bloke with my reputation, but I took nothing for granted.

I always wanted to go on Boomers tours because I was not willing to give up my spot or give the impression I didn't want to play for Australia. I worried that if I asked to be rested from a tour, the coaching staff might take that as a sign I was losing interest or having self-doubt about my ability at international level. I never considered I was an automatic selection for the Boomers. That's not modesty talking. That's my insecurity. Even as I was heading towards my fifth Olympics, I thought I needed to make sure I was still an established part of the team. I only recognise now that I could have skipped a tour here or there and things probably would have been fine.

Also, if I couldn't be available for the Tigers, I wasn't available for Europe. The NBA, big as it is, was on the same notice. Sometimes there was probably an element of disbelief among my peers that I would place the Tigers and the NBL ahead of these overseas offers and opportunities, but it was basically non-negotiable.

From a financial standpoint, I would have made a lot more money if I'd played in Europe for five to ten years instead of in Australia. For almost fifteen years from 1986, there were always chances to play in Europe on deals that ranged from reasonable to lucrative. In fact, I was asked to go and play in Italy for Roseto after the 2000 Sydney Olympics. Needless to say, I knocked back Roseto, just like I turned down almost every European offer. The ones I accepted with Apollon Patras in Greece and Udine in Italy were more about circumstance and timing than anything else. When I went to Udine, we didn't yet have children, so Melinda and I could just go as a couple. When we went to Greece we had our first child Courtney, who was still a baby and easy to cope with. But after that, family became a major consideration in any European offer. Even with $1 million on the table from Maroussi in 1998, it wasn't enough to uproot our growing family. It also wasn't enough to get me away from the Tigers.

I never made big, big money with the Tigers. Not that money was ever a consideration. If it had been, I would have taken the money the St Kilda Saints offered me in the early days of my NBL career to jump ship and join the enemy. It was an almost ad hoc approach that was made by Saints club stalwarts Andris Blicavs and Eric Hingston in the stands at Albert Park on that occasion. I don't know whether they really thought they had a chance to get me to the Saints or what, and I did take it as a huge compliment, but I wasn't moving. It was almost impossible to consider committing to another organisation.

In the early days of the NBL, we played for free until the late 1980s and then I might have picked up $20,000 or $30,000 a season. Even in the mid-1990s when the NBL was probably at its peak and there was money around, I still only earned about $50,000 from the Tigers. There were probably only two seasons out of twenty-two that I earned more than $100,000 with the Tigers. As an MVP and leading scorer I was underpaid by the market rate, but I didn't mind. I don't declare these figures boastfully. It's just the vast majority of people would not believe me if I told them how much I was or wasn't being paid.

Fortunately, I have been well supported by some fantastic sponsors over the years and their endorsement deals have boosted my income. Who knows, without supporters and sponsors like National Australia Bank, adidas and K-Mart, who looked after me so well for so many years, I might well have ended up playing more in Europe and not playing so many years in the NBL. But I never felt deprived or handicapped. That said, had it not been for the stint with the Spurs in 1999, I might have had to consider one last fling in Europe given that I did not see any money from the Tigers for three straight seasons. That's when you start to think US$400,000 tax free for a season in Europe would be a worthwhile option.

Such thinking was only ever brief, though. After all, the compelling aspect of any decision to play overseas was whether I could play with the Tigers. I never felt comfortable about leaving the club, save for the impossible-to-turn-down opportunity with the Spurs. But I wouldn't change the way I did things. After all, how do you change your love for the club you have played for since you were six? In my case, it was a bond that was impossible to break. It was a bond that made playing for free my only option if I didn't want the Tigers to disappear.

When the NBL decided to move its season from winter to summer, only two clubs, the Tigers and the Sydney Kings, opposed the switch. It was foresight by the Tigers and Kings that some people might regret was not supported more strongly. For when the NBL moved seasons and squeezed three seasons into two years as a way to make the transition from winter to summer, I believe it contributed greatly to some of the financial problems clubs have endured since 1998. It was simply way too much of a financial strain on the clubs. This certainly was the case with the North Melbourne Giants and South East Melbourne Magic, who merged to make the Victoria Titans, as it was with the Tigers, who cut costs in various areas and tried different formulas to make sure the club remained viable.

Although I was not privy to a lot of the details, I believe the Giants and the Magic at one time or another approached the Tigers about a merger, but the club was never interested, and rightly so. It just wasn't in the Melbourne Tigers' best interests to give up any part of their identity. The irony of that stance though, was that the Tigers nearly went out of business altogether a few years after the Giants-Magic merger. It was a prospect that left me face-to-face with the greatest basketball loss I could ever imagine. It was a prospect that left me in tears as I contemplated the shocking notion that the Tigers would cease to exist.

During the 2002 NBL season, I started to hear whispers that the club was in financial strife, but the exact depth of the problem had never been made clear. That was until one night, when I attended a meeting with my dad, Peter Sheahan and Tigers chief executive Grant Cadee at our offices and training complex in North Melbourne. The whole awful truth was laid out for me to see. The club was in a dire situation. The Tigers were about $2 million in the hole and facing an uncertain future at best. My dad and his fellow board members had tried to shield me from the situation for as long as they could, but now it was all out in the open.

As board members and the CEO, my dad, Peter and Grant had put together several strategies and options for the club to get out of the financial mire. One of those options was to sell the club. The meeting became an emotional minefield as the Tigers' diabolical financial situation was explained in greater clarity. My immediate reaction was one of shock. As I began to consider the consequences, the gravity, pressure and emotion mounted to an overwhelming level and I broke down. I thought the Tigers were done. From what I could tell, it was over.

From the filtered information I had received before this meeting, I knew the Tigers had some serious financial problems but I was always given feedback that indicated that it was manageable. I could not understand how the situation could have reached this level, which to me was extreme. The sheer magnitude of a $2 million debt – actually hearing the number – was chilling. Once my initial emotional reaction subsided, it turned to numbness at the uncertainty of what might happen to the club. I'm an emotional person and clearly I didn't react well to that piece of news. There was a few minutes of silence and there was an attempt to try and reassure me that it would be okay and things were in place to correct the situation.

I also had a sense of embarrassment, helplessness and responsibility in this situation, even though I had no direct control over the direction or operation of the club. Yet that sense of embarrassment, helplessness and responsibility came about through a perception that I was an owner of, and major stakeholder in, the club. It was only a perception and I was concerned I would be held responsible for something I had no control over.

I was a member of the Melbourne Basketball Association Inc, which was a Monday night competition operated by my dad and which held the Tigers' NBL licence. The MBA is a non-profit operation and offers its members no pecuniary gain. With only a minor role, in terms of Tigers ownership, I never assumed or wanted any ownership of the Tigers. Given the club's history, I always considered the club in the amateur sense of being a non-profit operation. The Tigers had always been a family-orientated club, with everyone pitching in to help, and it wasn't until the late 1980s that they started to evolve towards professionalism by employing people to look after marketing and sponsorship in a bid to keep pace with the flourishing NBL. I would often be around the office to lend a hand and take an interest, which probably only served to strengthen my emotional ties.

When the club first went professional, I was asked to join the board, which I did, more as a link to the players and the team than for my undeveloped business acumen. Although I did not attend every board meeting, it was a good learning process for me and I was able to be the link the board wanted me to be. But after a few seasons, I stopped going to the board meetings because, as a player and an employee, I didn't feel it was appropriate to be there. So you can understand my concern with the perception that I was a hands-on owner and decision-maker when the fact of the matter was that I wasn't.

Even so, that did not mean I was able to walk away from that emotional meeting and get a good night's sleep. Quite the contrary. I felt somehow responsible for making sure we secured the club's future. While others more adept at business dealt with the financial institutions and creditors to give us time to organise a way out of our debt, there was one person who decided to go on the front foot as only he could, and I went along with him.

Nigel Purchase has been my best mate, brother-in-law and business partner for the past twenty-five years. It is probably not too much of a stretch to say he is also the bloke who played a significant role in saving the Tigers from becoming extinct. Certainly, Nigel's enthusiasm, drive, loyalty and love for the club were a major driving force in him and me hitting the streets and trying to sell the club to somebody who would make sure it stayed around forever. Nigel's line was that we could not allow some stranger to come in and buy the club. We needed somebody who understood and appreciated the history and background of the club and would be respectful of that. We needed someone, or some people, who would be prepared to get involved for the right reasons and for the long term, with a vision and belief for the future.

Nigel and I didn't have a lot of business expertise, but we had a lot of passion for the Tigers and we aimed high. Among the business people we had meetings with were trucking magnate Lindsay Fox, who might have wondered about the business sense of a couple of basketball duffers, but at least gave us a fair hearing; and major shopping centre developer Tony Gandel, who was a Tigers supporter. Lanard Copeland and I attended Tony's son's bar mitzvah, so it helped that we were familiar with each other when we went knocking on his door. We wanted about $2.5 million to give the club a healthy future, but at that early stage of the project, the most important thing people could give us was their time. Nigel and I were honest and forthright and told potential investors how we thought it could work. We didn't know any other way than to lay our cards on the table and I think people appreciated it and respected we were up front and left the BS at the door.

While we knocked on a lot of doors, our most welcoming receiver was Seamus McPeake, who was a long-time sponsor and recent Tigers director who ultimately drove the campaign to raise $2.5 million. It became fairly obvious through our initial enquiries that it was going to be too hard to get one person or business to stump the whole $2.5 million, so we aimed at getting a hundred investors at $25,000 each. We got some investors on that scale and we lost others who pledged but never followed through. That was where Seamus came up big and made sure that we got the rescue bid over the line, getting a few others involved and taking on his own large slice of financial commitment. Businessmen David Minear, who became chairman, and Grant Stephenson and the MBA, made some of the crucial financial investments for the club to keep going. Actually, quite a few people put their hands in their pockets for a $25,000 share and I thank every single one of them.

Once Seamus was involved and committed, he took control of the club and became the quasi-chief executive. One thing I'll say about Seamus is that he never backed off from his commitment and he never backed off from making the tough decisions. One tough job was telling some of the players that the Tigers didn't have the money to pay their contract, so he asked them whether they would take a cut. Fortunately most of them accepted his plan. As a successful businessman, Seamus knows the bottom line and that is that you can't spend more than you earn, which is what was happening with our home games at Vodafone Arena. The venue was costing us a fortune. Attendances averaging around six thousand was not enough to pay the bills. It was killing the club and we needed an alternative. Nigel and I were considering venue options when we realised we had seen a lot of netball games on TV but had never been to their venue. So we drove to the State Netball and Hockey Centre in Parkville and as soon as we walked in, the penny dropped. The Tigers could play there. Seamus came over, he agreed with our assessment and the deal we got to play at The Cage, despite its smaller capacity, was vastly better than that at Vodafone Arena.

Two seasons after all the turmoil and tears, and losing close to $800,000 over one season, the Tigers made a $100,000 profit. That's a pretty impressive turnaround. But it would not have been possible, and the Tigers might not have been around as an NBL club, if Seamus and Nigel had not played their crucial roles. There is no question that Nigel, with his initial spark followed by some soldier-ing footwork, was very significant in saving the club.

Nigel and I have been friends since we played against each other as juniors when he was with Eltham and I was with the Tigers. We were picked in the Victorian under-sixteen team, but Nigel never played because of a knee injury. Then he joined the Tigers, meaning we spent the vast majority of our playing days together. Actually with me, Nigel and Ray Gordon, we formed a pretty solid threesome on and off the court and have stayed close throughout our lives. In fact, I stayed so close to Nigel that, as everyone knows by now, I married his sister, Melinda, who got a fairly rude introduction when Ray and I stayed over at the Purchase house one weekend. Nigel had a weight boot to help strengthen his knee after surgery so, boys being boys, we took it in turns to see who could lift the most weight with the boot. Finally, I stacked so much weight onto the boot that I was straining to straighten my leg. Actually, I strained so much that I let rip an involuntary fart that momentarily stunned us all, including Nigel's mum and dad. But as soon as everyone started laughing, I knew I had backed a winner. Even if Melinda still insists that it was the most sense she's ever heard me speak.

On the basketball court, Nigel and I developed an excellent relationship, especially in the NBL, where, in our offensive system,

Nigel was largely responsible for getting the ball to me in position to score. From my point of view, Nigel was one of the best passers in the league. He saw the floor well, he read the play, he had good instincts and he made me look good a lot of times, hitting me with passes other people couldn't envisage, let alone execute.

While Nigel could be precise, he also had a knack for the freakish. Many people would be aware of his length-of-the-court three-pointer against the Brisbane Bullets, which received enormous media coverage. But Nigel also made perhaps the most freakish basket in NBL history when he scored a three-pointer *for* the Canberra Cannons at the Glasshouse in 1988. The Cannons scored on a free-throw, then applied a pressing defence, which made it hard for the Tigers to get the ball up the court. The ball ran loose towards a sideline and Nigel gave chase to try to save it. I was standing in the defensive key and realised what Nigel was trying to do as he reached out and scooped the ball back into play over his head. For a split-second I thought the ball was coming to me. Then I realised the ball was going only one place: the basket. Nothin' but net. Strangely, in the same game, our import Alvis Rodgers inadvertently tipped-in a basket from a Cannons missed free-throw, meaning we gave them five points in what I think was a three-point loss.

Those baskets kind of represent Nigel's personality of being a little removed from the norm and not always deferring to convention. Nigel is a happy-go-lucky bloke who, no matter how serious the situation, always manages to find something humorous. We go to some serious business meetings and I often leave wondering not about the success of the meeting, but how the people took Nigel's attempt at humour. We'll be in discussions with people and he will just come out with something that catches us off guard. It's usually an ice-breaking moment, but sometimes I wonder if Nigel's humour is appreciated by everyone. He certainly keeps a sense of perspective with him at all times, that's for sure.

That's just Nigel and it's one of his endearing features, even if it does frustrate the shoes off me sometimes. Probably the best skill Nigel has is that he's a people person. Whenever he meets people, even if it's a brief encounter, they will usually walk away with the firm impression that Nigel is a good bloke. There is no question about that. Nigel Purchase is a great bloke.

While I worked with Nigel to get some people interested in investing in the Tigers, probably the most important thing I did during that bleak time was defer some of my salary. Actually, I think I deferred about two and a half years of salary. I always considered I would play for the Tigers for nothing, or close to it. Now, with the club in such a dire situation, that became a reality. During the 1999 season the club was late on a couple of months' salary. Because, in all likelihood, I was going to the NBA with the San Antonio Spurs and would receive an NBA salary, I was not concerned and was happy to wait to receive my payments. But the financial plight of the club didn't improve and for the next two seasons after I returned from the NBA, I wasn't paid by the Tigers. I had been relatively well rewarded during my time with the Spurs and I was happy to have an open agreement with the club that I would be paid once their finances improved. If that didn't happen, it didn't happen. I signed a contract for each season, but the money never came.

That was okay. As I've said, playing for the Tigers was never for the money and my situation was insignificant when you consider my dad never received a brass razoo for coaching the team for twenty-two NBL seasons and thirty-five overall. He never took a cent. In contrast, I did okay financially playing overseas and through my endorsement deals, so it wasn't as if I was destitute. When it was obvious hat the Tigers couldn't pay me, I accepted the choice not to demand payment, hoping it would ease the financial burden a little. The Tigers, to their credit, recognised the financial sacrifice and have always promised to make good on the lost wages when they are able to do so in the future.

The most important thing is that the club appears now to be on an even keel with a healthy future. The Tigers and the NBL have had to endure some harsh financial lessons over the journey, but hopefully both are better for these. I have not agreed with all the moves made by the NBL, such as the move from winter to summer and the buy-outs of the Geelong, Hobart and Gold Coast franchises in 1996. The league should have been about expansion, not contraction.

Nor has the NBL had any sustained success with free-to-air television. Everyone is a genius in hindsight but if the NBL could go back in time they would probably rethink their decision to switch from Channel Seven to Channel Ten at the end of the 1991 season. From the late 1980s to 1991 the league had good coverage with the Seven Network, which gave it a niche in the highly competitive business of sport. Its games were played on Sundays as a lead in to Seven's AFL coverage and its popularity and ratings were significant and sustainable. This prompted Seven to trial some blockbuster games on Friday nights, which were also well received. When Channel Seven's rights were up for negotiation Channel Ten became a player in bidding for the rights and made a bold offer which included a significant increase in rights fees and the promise to telecast more NBL games, including live games in prime time on Saturday nights. Despite Channel Seven matching the financial offer of Ten, the NBL were lured to Ten on the back of a promise to be on prime time. Unfortunately the ratings did not meet expectations and after a short period of time the TV chiefs scrapped prime-time games during the regular season. I don't know whether the league has ever recovered from the misjudgement of trying to showcase the NBL as a prime-time product despite the incredible growth in attendances that the league was about to witness.

Attendances peaked in the mid to late 1990s and it was a buzz when fifteen thousand people filled Rod Laver Arena for games. I don't know that the NBL was responsible for all of that. At the time, basketball was culturally popular without necessarily being a popular spectator sport. The Michael Jordan phenomenon was at its zenith, hip-hop fashion and music was working its way into Australia's youth culture and all this helped the NBL, but I think it also hurt. When a survey of Australian schoolkids revealed Jordan was the most popular athlete in the nation, that was viewed as an inappropriate thing by sections of the community, who felt we should have an Australian sporting icon for our kids to follow. When the American fashion trends faded, the NBL had not developed its own identity or strategy to keep pace and keep the fans.

There is no question that the NBL is a quality basketball competition and is thriving in the smaller markets such as Townsville, Wollongong and Cairns, while work always needs to be done in Melbourne and Sydney to try to keep the teams in the community consciousness. Not to mention getting people to the games. Ticket prices, I believe, have had an impact on crowds at NBL venues, as has the lack of free-to-air television coverage. The NBL product has not been as accessible to the masses as it could and should have been.

What ultimately matters is that the Melbourne Tigers survived the roughest patch of their existence, edging away from the brink of extinction to maintaining its place as a flagship of the NBL and being ranked as perennial championship contenders. The Tigers have a culture that endures, even though the culture will undoubtedly be adjusted from time to time to best accommodate the club's needs. The Tigers have tried to preserve some history by retiring the playing numbers of Warrick Giddey, Dave Simmons and Ray Gordon, but the club's history goes further than that with guys like Ken Watson, John Maddock and Ray Tomlinson whose pre-NBL deeds need to be acknowledged as crucial to the Tigers' culture and foundation of doing things right and in the best interests of the sport.

I started playing for the Tigers when I was six and the most important thing in life was running up and down the court, whether

I had the ball or not. Thirty-odd years later, whether I was paid or not, the most important thing in my basketball life was just to complete my professional playing career with the Melbourne Tigers.

chapter twenty-five

THE LAST LAP

I never enjoyed losing. Never. I was not a bad loser, but that didn't mean I had to like it. I liked it even less when the Melbourne Tigers blew a big lead against the Sydney Kings early in the 2005 NBL season. We were up by twenty-seven at one stage and led by twenty starting the final period. Then we stopped scoring and lost by one as Jason Smith hit a three-pointer with about ten seconds left. It was a killer blow that took the Tigers into the cesspool of reality and bitter disappointment. It took me even deeper.

The next morning as I walked through Sydney Airport for an early flight back to Melbourne, I was surrounded by commuters and travellers hurrying to and from the departure and arrival lounges. The airport might as well have been deserted for all the notice I took of those around me. I was deeply disappointed by the loss the previous night and, just five games into the new NBL season, one thought dogged me constantly as I waited for the call to board.

'I should not have played this season,' I thought. 'I have made a mistake.'

Retirement was more than an option at the end of the 2004 season. In my mind, it was a reality and I told the club as much. Had I not been persuaded to change my mind about playing into a twenty-second NBL season, I would not have had to endure that embarrassing loss and I would not have had to endure a twenty-four-hour period after that loss that again had me on the verge of retirement, no questions asked.

The immediate aftermath of that dreadful loss to the Kings in Sydney was disappointing, to say the least, with suggestions that my dad should be removed as Tigers coach. Call me biased, but to even think about forcing him out was ludicrous. That said, I understood the frustrations with the loss. There were ten of us who had played and were angry and upset about the loss. We also shared the responsibility.

For most of that game, certainly the first three quarters, all the things we thought might happen with our team were there. Our form was great, we flowed, we played the kind of basketball we and others expected from such a talented and experienced roster. We went into the game 2–2 and carrying a few question marks, but the first three periods against the Kings eliminated them completely. The fourth and final period magnified them beyond all belief as we went from an unlosable situation to being under pressure, to tightening up to the point where it seemed we could not play the game.

It was one of those situations we could see unfolding right in front of us, only we were totally powerless to do anything about. My initial reaction to the loss was shock, then I felt a truly gut-wrenching sensation like I was going to vomit. It was a loss that did not go down well with anyone. We stayed that night at the Darling Harbour Holiday Inn, which was right across the street from the Sydney Entertainment Centre, and we returned there with heads down and shoulders slumped.

It was at the hotel that talk questioning my dad's position as coach started to float around. Some people felt he should take the ultimate responsibility. I spoke to Lanard Copeland and Mark Bradtke about this speculation, and both of them were unequivocal in their support of my dad staying as coach. And, it went without saying, so was I.

At that stage of my career, the situation was something I didn't need and certainly didn't want. I just wanted to play and do my best. As far as the business of basketball and coaches and responsibilities was concerned, I didn't want to know about it. Not just because my dad was involved. There was much more to it than that. When I got home from Sydney the day after the game, I telephoned the Tigers chairman David Minear, who had not been in Sydney for the game. The bottom line to the conversation was that if my dad went, I would retire immediately.

It was not a threat to ensure my dad's position just because he was my dad. My stance was about two things: backing the coach regardless of who it was; and finishing my career, under the circumstances presented by the Tigers, when I had wanted to retire the previous season. Simply, I did not want to go through this emotional roller-coaster after every game and, unless it was dealt with, that was what would happen. There was no point wanting to fire people after every loss and hugging and kissing after every win. We needed some balance and we needed everyone involved in the club to realise that it was going to be a challenging season and that, despite some impressive reputations among our playing roster, we didn't have an overwhelming advantage over our competitors. Forget about how good we were supposed to be and deal in reality. Otherwise we would all have been in straightjackets before the season ended.

To his credit, David Minear backed my dad without hesitation or reservation. But it still took me a little time to feel comfortable. Throughout that twenty-four hour period I constantly thought about my situation. Had I known this was how it would be, I would not have come back for one more season. With my body already showing signs of wear and tear, this extra emotional baggage so early in the season was too much. After all, I had determined this would be my last NBL season, even if nobody else knew that.

Over the previous few seasons, I had tried to figure out when to retire. Finally, at the end of the 2004 NBL season, when the Tigers were eliminated in the second round of the play-offs by the Bullets in Brisbane and I finished the game on the bench after a nasty poke in the eye late in the game, the time had arrived. I had a clear sense it was time to move on. It was not an emotional reaction to the play-off loss. It was a calculated realisation of where I was as a player that led me to believe I should retire from the top level in Australia. Clearly, I felt my days of controlling games and having an impact, as I once did, were no longer there. That's not to say that I couldn't have been influential, but doing things on the basketball court had become more difficult and, in some aspects, diminished more than slightly.

The other aspect of my retirement consideration was, ironically, to do with the Tigers' coaching situation. Even though I never tied my continued playing with my dad's continued coaching, I was conscious of the fact that if he stepped down at the end of the 2004 season, it would cause me to think harder about my future. But if he went, it did not automatically mean I would follow. I had not determined to never play for the Tigers under anyone else. That would be totally disrespectful to a great bloke like Al Westover as the coach-in-waiting. Even I had wondered what it would be like to play for the Tigers under another coach. It was just that I felt it would be easier for the coach who followed my dad if I wasn't there, either. I didn't want a new coach to have the pressure of cutting back my minutes or changing my role or maybe telling me he didn't want me at all. It would be easier to just retire.

About a week after our play-off exit to the Bullets, we had our usual post-season individual meetings between players and the coaching staff and executive. Going into my meeting with my dad, assistant coach Al Westover, majority owner Seamus McPeake, chairman David Minear and general manager Mark Robinson, I had decided I was done. My career was finished. It was time to move on. Somehow, I came out of the meeting without having retired.

After general discussions about the team and what we needed to do to improve for 2005, I laid my position on the table and said I felt I should retire. I had concerns about my long-term health due to so much wear and tear on my body, which was basically wearing out. I also wondered how my body was coping with the anti-inflammatory drugs I took to ensure I made it from game to game during so many arduous seasons. I also explained I didn't want to be a distraction to the team if things went pear-shaped for me during the season, placing extra unfair pressure on everyone around me. I didn't want to finish my career on the bench and I didn't want to finish it scrubbing around as a pitiful figure on the court. Frankly, I just felt the Tigers might have had a better chance of winning the championship without me and it was in the team's best interest for me to move on.

While my dad was non-committal, everyone else in the meeting encouraged me to play on. In fact, there was a strong desire from some to make sure our deal with massive Chinese electronics company Haier, who wanted to use me for some TV commercials in China, remained secure, which was one significant reason for me to keep playing. I listened to their points of view, which were at odds with my own thoughts about my future, and I left the meeting without making a commitment except to play on our tour of China and then make a decision. That those in the meeting opposed my retirement was good because I did have a desire deep down to keep playing. Their wish for me to keep playing was just the boost I needed to free myself from any doubts that I could go on for one more season.

When people started speculating that the 2005 season could be my last, there was a notion that it would have been the cream on the cake if the Tigers could win the championship. It would have been nice, but the fact of the matter was we tried to win the championship every year. That had certainly been our mindset every season since 1997, when we won the second of our titles, but factors and better teams conspired against us. The reality was that it was never easy winning an NBL championship, regardless of what some people might have thought.

The NBL changed after our 1997 Championship win, with the move of season from winter to summer, and we had little time to revel in our triumph over the South East Melbourne Magic. The 1998 season started in January and ended in June, because the NBL didn't want a massive gap between seasons in the transition, then we started again in October. It was a huge strain physically and emotionally on the players and coaches. In hindsight, we didn't prepare well for the season, we lost Lanard Copeland for some games to knee surgery and we scraped together a 16–14 record before being swept by the Brisbane Bullets in the first round of the play-offs.

Making the load even worse for the elite Australian players was that, between the end of one season in June and the start of another in October, the Boomers played at the Goodwill Games in New York and World Championships in Athens. Funnily enough, the Tigers started 10–0 and looked good before finishing 17–9 and second on the ladder. I only played the first seventeen games before heading to the NBA with the San Antonio Spurs, but the Tigers made the semi-finals. We were beaten in the semis by the Victoria Titans, but the game scores were 80–77 and 94–87, so it was much closer than it appeared as a 2–0 series result.

That performance gave us hope that 2000 would be a good season for us. But Marcus Timmons threw us off balance by wanting to get out of his contract for something better in Europe. Marcus played in Poland, but finished the season in the NBL with the Perth Wildcats. We tried several players to fill Marcus's spot and finally settled on Bennett Davison from Arizona University. He was the most athletic player I ever played with. Bennett could jump over two-storey houses. He made amazing dunks that brought a reaction from the fans and if we could have kept him, he would have been a very good player in the NBL. After his one season with the Tigers, Bennett went to Europe, where he played in Slovenia and Italy. Even with Bennett providing the highlights, we finished a mediocre 14–14 and lost to the Titans, 2–1, in the first round of the play-offs with no margin greater than nine. The Titans made the grand final but lost to the Perth Wildcats. The grand final MVP was none other than former Tiger Marcus Timmons.

It was false optimism to believe we could turn a 14–14 record into a title in 2001 because the Tigers failed to make the play-offs. By going 13–15 and finishing seventh, it was the first time we missed the finals since 1988. We had more import problems after losing Bennett Davison and, after tryouts and short-term signings, ended up with Phil Handy and Clarence Tyson. It was one of those seasons that was bad on and off the court. We couldn't win when we needed to and, behind the scenes, the club was falling into a major struggle financially that would soon take its own personal and emotional toll.

The Tigers revived for 2002 but petered out after a strong start, to finish 16–14. I was a spectator for a fair bit of the second half of the season after going down with an ankle injury during a road game in Townsville. The game had only just started when I felt like I had been kicked in the ankle. There was nobody near me, but I was done for the game and, as it turned out, pretty much the rest of the season. I had surgery and came off the bench for a few minutes here and there with some painkilling injections, but I still had problems, and more surgery sidelined me again. It was frustrating for me, but the team did a great job with Marcus Timmons back in the line-up and playing a great finals series.

We beat the Titans in a memorable first-round play-off series, then lost in the best-of-three semi-finals to the West Sydney

Razorbacks after winning game one by twenty-one. I was a passenger in the play-offs, coming off the bench with a numb ankle full of painkillers, which really made me think about what I was doing. I was getting drugged up to the point where I wasn't sure that it was the right thing for me and the team. I tried to power through, but I always worried that I would damage myself physically and the team's chances of winning.

We had hopes of making more noise in 2003, but we limped through a 15–15 regular season and went out in the first round of the play-offs to the Sydney Kings, who eventually won their first NBL championship. We took the Kings to three games, but we just didn't have enough guys playing well. We were inconsistent, which made the season one long struggle. People questioned our age and veteran status, asking if we were too old and past our peaks. The age factor was just something for the critics to grab hold of. It was more form than age that was our undoing.

The age factor was again out there, even before the 2004 season, when we signed Darryl McDonald and Chinese swingman Wu Zheng, which bumped our average age up a notch or two. We were referred to as Dad's Army and there were gags that the Tigers had a team capable of winning the title ... in 1988. We believed we could win the title in 2004. Wu had a calf injury that he brought from China and never played a game, so we signed Canadian forward Dave Thomas, who had played with the Canberra Cannons.

DT lowered our age and upped our athleticism, which helped us go 20–13 in a pretty good performance. There were two things about that: it was only the third time in twenty-one NBL seasons that the Tigers had won twenty or more games, which shows how hard it is to achieve; and winning those twenty games only got us into fifth place on the ladder, which meant we had to play one-game, knock-out basketball in the first two rounds of the play-offs. We beat the Adelaide 36ers at home in the first round, but lost in the second round on the road to the Brisbane Bullets. We played well against the Bullets, leaving us to wonder how it could have panned out in a best-of-three series. That was the hand dealt to us and we played it as best we could. It just wasn't good enough. That game in Brisbane ended with me on the bench nursing an eye I couldn't see out of. As far as I could see in my mind's eye, the end of my basketball was coming into clear focus.

It wasn't like my basketball retirement would be a surprise. I had played a lot longer than the average NBL animal and my age and grey hair were a fair indication of my basketball mortality. It was simply a matter of when I would retire rather than if. The big if probably surrounded what I would do after basketball. As in what I would do for a career and a living, since basketball was pretty much all I had ever known, even though I went to university with the goal of graduating as a physical education teacher.

I suppose I have been lucky in that I was able to create some profile during my career and that helped me experience some things that could help in my basketball retirement. I have worked in the media, especially on television with Fox Sports on the NBL coverage and with the Seven Network at the Athens Olympics. The 2004 Olympics provided a test unlike any I had during the five I played at. After all, when I was playing, I never had to worry about pronouncing the names and providing background on a women's match between Korea and China. Not that I will ever be employed as a royal watcher by any media outlet. Not when, at a *Sports Illustrated* party in Athens, I was approached by a chatty and attractive woman who seemed to know who I was. Her face was familiar, but I couldn't put a name to her. After a while, it dawned on me in embarrassing fashion. It was Princess Mary of Denmark. Which just shows I do socialise in lofty circles. I just don't know who I'm socialising with.

While I knew I shouldn't have been counting on a TV career to feed the Gaze family, I had put in a fair amount of time with Australian Basketball Resources, the business I operate with Nigel Purchase. We try to cover all aspects of basketball, including camps, which have been our staple for a long time. But we took a big step during 2004 when we launched the Gaze brand basketball shoe in conjunction with Dunlop. It was an exciting venture and one we aim to develop and grow with other clothing lines featuring the Gaze brand.

I guess the one thing I and others wondered was what I could do in a hands-on fashion when it came to basketball. Many people have long assumed I would take over as coach of the Tigers when my dad stepped down. Let me state categorically that coaching the Tigers has never been my ambition. For one thing, I've been too busy playing. For another, I'm not naive or arrogant enough to believe you don't have to serve a coaching apprenticeship before becoming a head coach in the NBL. I always thought I would coach juniors and see what happened from there, but there is no guarantee I would enjoy it or be any good at it. Coaching is a skill in itself and, while I understand the tactics and basics, a good coach needs to get players to believe in his or her system and philosophy. Could I do that in the NBL? Who knows? You need time away to devise those philosophies and ideas and I'd like to visit the US and Europe to learn from coaches about their philosophies and techniques. Which is all well and good to consider for the future. My most immediate concern was getting through one last NBL season.

Probably every season for the last four or five of my career, things became more difficult on the court. It was so frustrating at times, when my mind recognised situations and opportunities like it always had but my body would not respond as quickly and allow me to execute in sync with my brain. That led to dealing with the self-imposed pressure of not wanting to embarrass myself or let down the team and my team-mates in terms of performance and results and inhibiting other players' development. I made adjustments to deal with a slowing body and I also learned to play fewer minutes and tailor my game accordingly. For twenty seasons or more I played more than forty minutes a night without fail. So playing anywhere between thirty and thirty-five was something new for me. I still maintained my desire to win and be competitive and effective. I just had fewer minutes to channel my energy into those areas. Playing fewer minutes was not an issue. I was quite happy to play between thirty and thirty-five minutes, sometimes more, and I was enjoying it. It lessened the physical demands, it gave me rest periods and it allowed me to still be effective at crucial times in games.

The first half of my final season was something of a roller-coaster in terms of results and emotions, highlighted by that big dipper against the Kings. A turning point for the better came after we lost to the Hunter Pirates in early December to leave us 6–9 and in a rut. It seemed there were different points of view and theories on what we should be doing and attitudes were clearly split on the court. That loss to the Pirates highlighted a number of deficiencies and my dad played a video to point out some home truths about body language and poor performance. It might have been a catalyst because we won nine of our next eleven games to be the hottest team in the NBL as the play-offs loomed.

If the play-offs loomed, so did the end of my career. While the media speculated the end was nigh, I was the only one who knew the truth. I had kept my own counsel throughout and was determined 2005 would be my final season. Not that I dwelt on it. Probably during the last couple of months of the season I contemplated the approaching end and reminisced without going over the top. After all, we were still striving for our goal of winning a championship. Not that ultimately failing to win the title was a downer in terms of my farewell. One reason behind my longevity was that I derived satisfaction and enjoyment from just playing rather than always needing to win to feel good. If my career and associated enjoyment were based exclusively on winning and championships, I would have retired a long time ago.

It's a cliché, but many aspects of life are about the journey rather than the destination. My career was no different. It's about all the experiences, good and bad. Take the trauma after that Sydney Kings loss. At the time it was not a pleasant situation, but compare that with the celebration of my six hundredth NBL game in January 2005. In terms of emotions, they were poles apart, but they were two major experiences I will never forget. One I will savour, the other I will no doubt learn from. If you went through life without a few tough times, it might make for a dull journey.

The most amazing thing for me over the journey is that the NBL has evolved into a competition that has allowed a privileged group of blokes the chance to earn a living playing the game they love. When I was a kid at primary school, I might have been the only one there who knew what basketball was. Not any more. I never ever envisaged, much as I would dream about playing for Australia, that basketball would become my livelihood and I would be allowed to pursue it around the world. When you grow up in a humble cottage attached to the basketball stadium at Albert Park you dare not believe something as great and magical as that could happen. That it did means I have so much to be thankful for.

To have been involved in contributing in some small way to the rise of basketball in Australia comes largely down to me being in the right place at the right time. I was very fortunate to have been along for the ride, blessed by my parents' genes and attitudes and the environment in which I grew up. Although it was never forced upon me, it was impossible to avoid basketball and for that I will be eternally grateful. I will also remain eternally humble that I have been honoured in several ways while people like my dad and Ken Watson, and other significant contributors, have toiled without the financial reward and recognition. It's out of whack. I merely played the game while these men were true custodians of the sport. It is they who have fulfilled their self-appointed charter of leaving the game in far better shape than that in which they found it. They have made a much more significant contribution to the sport than I have or ever will, but it is because of their work and efforts that I have never taken the game, its people or its facilities for granted. I just always felt that others, especially the servants who toiled anonymously for the game, were deserving of greater recognition than I was.

Which also made it hard for me to comprehend the title of 'Australia's greatest basketball player'. It is a flattering title, but one I've never used to describe myself. It's embarrassing to even think in those terms. I know I was a good player, but one reason I was able to be a good player was because I knew, recognised and abided by my limitations. Some people think they know their limit and sell themselves short, while others continually try to extend their limit and consider it a failure when they don't reach that extra level. The trick is to discover your limit and operate at that limit as often as possible. I think I was a reasonably smart player, which helped overcome some of my physical limitations, but much of my good fortune as a player came down to being in the right place at the right time, and being given the opportunity. People point to my statistics as support for their assessment of referring to me as Australia's greatest player, but I know it is an impossible thing to claim with any certainty because stats are not the whole story in judging a player and his greatness or otherwise. I know I would like to think I offered teams more than just scoring.

Don't get me wrong. I'm very proud of all those statistical marks I have achieved and those NBL awards I have won. They are great and are proof for future generations that I could play the game. But I never set out to do those things. It's impossible as an eighteen year old starting out in the NBL in 1984 to have a goal of becoming the all-time leader in games played and points scored. It's unrealistic to do that and even contemplate it. I never went into a game wanting to score twenty or thirty or forty points and I never went into a season wanting to win the scoring title. I went into every game wanting to win that game and I went into every season wanting to win the championship.

Even though I won fourteen NBL scoring titles, there were times where I felt it wouldn't be a bad thing if I didn't top the scoring because I was concerned about the perception, in view of the attention given to scoring stats, that it was my prime motivation. It wasn't. It's all well and good to say after the event that it wouldn't have been the end of the world not to be leading scorer, but I was conscious of people thinking I was selfish and one-dimensional when I didn't believe that to be true. It was great to be recognised and feted, but that was never why I played basketball. Ever since I was a kid I played basketball because I loved the game. I always will love it and I always will play, even in a social comp, because I can't yet comprehend not playing the game that has been my life.

Given my emphasis on team goals and achievements rather than individual glories, some people will point to the fact the Melbourne Tigers only won two NBL championships during my career. Certainly, there is a strong belief that the Tigers should have won more. It's a good debating point, but the reality is that we had our chances and didn't win, so the inevitable conclusion is that we weren't good enough. You get tested on the court and either you're good enough or you're not. If Lanard Copeland's shot went down against the Magic in 1996, there's another championship. If I don't go to the San Antonio Spurs, maybe we get another title. If I don't rip up my ankle, maybe we win another championship. I don't know. It's just too simplistic, ignorant and arrogant to assume that would be the case. There are many variables that can make a pretty subtle difference and you can come up with a million hypothetical scenarios when you're playing what-if. It's the reality you need to live with. Either way, to have won two championships was a great achievement for the Tigers.

People believe that having Lanard Copeland, Mark Bradtke and me in the Tigers' line-up should have been enough to win multiple championships. It is flattering that people saw us as players who made our team a constant contender. But one thing I want to stress is that I believe you could never look at Copes, Hogey and me and say we were failures. There was never a game we didn't think we could win. When you talk about the fortunes in life, I feel extremely fortunate to have played for so long with quality players and people like Lanard Copeland and Mark Bradtke. I certainly don't feel any less fulfilled as a basketball player because I only won two NBL titles. When you take in twenty-two NBL seasons as a whole, where the Tigers went from bums to two-time champions and regular contenders, I'm proud of that.

As my last NBL season progressed, there was every reason to believe the Tigers could win a third championship. We recovered from a so-so start to the point where none of the other seven teams in the play-offs would have been keen to play us. I was pleased to contribute meaningfully to the team and maintain some consistency at a reasonably high level throughout. It was important that I did that, if only to prove to myself that I did make the right decision to play one more season. Perhaps most important was that I still enjoyed the game, I still had the desire to play and I still had the competitive juices flowing through my body every time tip-off approached. I was happy to know I would leave before I stayed too long.

It has been suggested that I should have announced my retirement before the season's end to give the fans a chance to say farewell and thank you. I appreciate the sentiment, but I just didn't feel it was the right thing to do. Even though I knew in my head and my heart that it was the last lap for me, I always intended to wait until after the season to make an announcement. Simply, I didn't want to become a distraction, either to myself or the team, with a procession of pre-game ceremonies. Also, I get uncomfortable in such situations, feeling I do not deserve such attention simply for doing nothing more than playing basketball for a long time. Having said that, the standing ovation the Melbourne fans gave Perth Wildcats veteran Ricky Grace as he left the court for the last time was nothing short of sensational. It was a magical, moving and proud moment. It hit home for several of us that the fans do have an attachment and an appreciation of what we do and that we do have an impact.

Yet I did not really want that in my final game. For one, I would have been an emotional wreck. For another, it would have been to invite recognition that is equally deserved by others who have been just as committed, put in just as much work and played at just as high a level as me. I understand people wanted the chance to say thank you. But I don't need anyone's thanks. I should be the one thanking all the people who supported me, watched me, helped me, played with me, sponsored me, touched me in any way during my career. I have an acute feeling I've got more out of the game than I probably deserve. I felt enough of an impostor as it was, without courting more applause.

Which was why, as the final buzzer in my final game ended my NBL career, I simply left the court with my team-mates with a little wave to the crowd, just as I did hundreds of times over twenty-two seasons. There was no need to make a big show, no need to linger. After all, the disappointment of defeat and bowing out of the play-offs to the Townsville Crocodiles was the greatest emotion I felt right at that time. We played poorly early, got back into the knock-out game with a big fourth-quarter run but finally lost by twelve points. For the record, my last points in the NBL came from the free-throw line (fitting for those who reckoned I was a protected species with the referees) with two minutes and thirty-eight seconds left in the game.

Even over the last two minutes with the result beyond our reach, the disappointment of the impending loss nudged aside any pause for reflection on my career or self-pity. After twenty-two seasons, it was still hard to quell the competitive fire, even in supposedly poignant moments like that. Probably from the midway point of the season I did have momentary reminiscences at venues I was visiting for the final time, knowing I was playing for the last time against people I liked and opponents I respected. Yet losing, as always, still hurt more than anything in the immediate moments after the buzzer.

It wasn't until I reached the locker room that the realisation started to settle in that I was done. Not that anybody else knew that, regardless of what many people suspected. I was a little teary-eyed in the locker room, without being a babbling mess, especially when I looked over at Mark Bradtke and Lanard Copeland and realised we had just played our last game together. I was tempted right then and there to stand up and announce my retirement to my team-mates and coaches, including my dad, but thought better of it. I had committed to a process and that was to delay an announcement until I had a post-season meeting with the club. The subject of retirement was inevitably raised at the post-game media conference and I gave my usual reply about not knowing for sure but the odds were that it was time to call it quits. My dad, never shy in voicing an opinion about anything except his own coaching future, publicly called for me to keep playing. Much as I love and respect my old man, that would not happen.

Back at the team hotel, we had dinner as a team and then we gathered on the roof-top pool deck for one last time to say farewell to the 2005 season for the Tigers. At the roof-top gathering, Mark Bradtke expressed his desire for me to keep playing, which was nice. But as I lay in bed that night, I knew I had made the right decision. I was sore, feeling beat-up and emotionally drained. Young though you like to think you are, it's times like that you know for sure your teen years are somewhere back in the Ice Age.

Not that I wouldn't do it all over again. Even the tough times. Without those tough times to endure, it certainly would have been a dull journey. I definitely would have liked to have won more championships, but I don't know how much more enjoyable that would have made my career. More than anything it was a privilege to go through such a journey and there is no way I could be ungrateful for anything that happened along the way. It was an absolute privilege and an honour to be able to share with my team-mates the highs and lows of one last NBL season.

There was only one brief moment that night in Townsville that I contemplated scrapping my retirement plans. That was when someone asked whether I would have liked my son Mason to have remembered seeing me play. It was almost enough to tempt me to keep playing, especially as he loved going to the games in his little Tigers singlet without really knowing too much about what was happening out on the court. Then, as always, reality set in. I had had my time. I had been on more flights than an experienced airline pilot, eaten so many pre-game pasta meals I might have been Italian, taken more shots than a fashion photographer.

Nobody could have envisaged all that when my mum took me to my first training session as a six year old. Bear in mind that I ran home crying that day only for my mum to take me back a week later. After almost thirty-five incredible years of basketball as my passion and privilege, it was finally time to go home.

Acknowledgements

From the start, when initial telephone calls were exchanged with potential publishers, to the finish, with the launch of this book, this project took more than three years. This means that many people have been involved, directly and indirectly, knowingly and unwittingly, along the way. Hopefully nobody is omitted from the list of thank-yous. If so, I apologise unreservedly and thank you again.

Knowing where to start with this list of acknowledgements is as difficult as it was to come up with the title for the book. Starting with those most influential in my life, I thank my dad and mum, Lindsay and Margaret Gaze. Their assistance in remembering names, places and anecdotes and for opening the family scrapbooks that provided personal photographs was invaluable. I also owe major thanks to my sister, Janet Gaze-Daniels, who not only cast a keen and critical eye over the manuscript, but also set the tone of the book with a beautifully written foreword. My wife Melinda was also crucial to the finished product, by not only providing sustenance and patience during the long hours involved, but by filling in some of the gaps that have been created in my memory. I also thank her just for being there, which is the most important thing of all.

I thank my former Boomers coach Barry Barnes for his assistance with game tapes. My long-time friend Brett Brown helped fill in a couple of blanks and Craig Miller from USA Basketball hunted down some vital information. The often arduous task of research was helped by the online archives of newspapers and organisations around the world such as the *Seattle Times*, the *Seattle Post Intelligencer*, the *San Antonio Express-News*, the *Washington Post*, the *Herald Sun*, *The Age*, the *Sporting News*, the *Newark Star-Ledger*, the *Astbury Park Press*, the *Setonian*, the *Australian Basketballer*, the *1988-89 Big East Basketball Yearbook*, the Italian Lega A, the NBA, the NBL, Basketball Australia, Seton Hall University, and ESPN.com. To all the writers and stats people who contributed to that collection of information and material, I thank you. Special thanks, too, to Ed Leonard, who collated, bound and sent me the collection of newspaper files on Seton Hall's memorable 1989 season, while Patrick Smith's work on the previously-published *On The Road With Andrew Gaze* was a valuable resource.

Over the years, I have appeared in hundreds of photos, though not by design. Some of these are reproduced in this book, so I would like to thank the photographers, whose work appears here courtesy of the *Herald Sun* and News Ltd.

There were several people who worked tirelessly behind the scenes to make this book a reality. My representatives at Octagon management, Justin Cohen and Matthew Fearon, saw the project through with the utmost professionalism, while the crew at Hardie Grant were brilliant in their devotion and diligence. Sandy Grant and Julie Pinkham provided massive support and enthusiasm from day one, while editor Sally Moss did a terrific job of tightening the manuscript. Most gratitude and thanks is reserved for commissioning editor Mary Small, whose patience was severely tested, but still managed a smile and made sure the book got to the finish line on time and in excellent order.

The most important thank you goes to my co-author Grantley Bernard because quite simply, this book would not have happened without him. Throughout my playing career I have often been asked to pen stories for newspapers and in most instances I have insisted on writing them myself. When I was first approached to write this book I thought along similar lines and wanted to do it alone. This notion did not last long as the reality of deadlines, writer's block and literary skill became apparent. I turned to my friend Grantley to fill the void and he has delivered. His enthusiasm, passion and commitment to the project were inspirational and his patience was appreciated. Thanks also to Grantley's wife Cheryl and daughters

Abbey and Sophie. Many weekends with the family have been lost because of this book and I am forever indebted to them for supporting Grantley's involvement.

The people who have helped me the most and the longest, apart from my family, have been those from the basketball community. So to every fan, coach, referee, team-mate and opponent, I say thank you. I couldn't have done it without you.

Andrew Gaze

My wife Cheryl believes I would have helped write this book for free. She is right. But I still would have needed her love, patience, understanding and support to get the job done. The same goes for my daughters Abbey and Sophie, who have often found it impossible to get use of the home computer.

Two other women were very important to my efforts. Margaret Gaze helped with her enthusiasm and produced the right scrapbook at the right moment, while Melinda Gaze welcomed me into her home even as I continually robbed her and the four Gaze children of time with her husband and their father.

The greatest thanks belongs to Andrew Gaze, who asked me to be involved in writing his life story and made the process a thoroughly enjoyable one. It was a privilege and an honour to be involved.

Grantley Bernard

Statistics

NATIONAL BASKETBALL LEAGUE
612 games for the Melbourne Tigers (1984–2005)
18,908 points
Seven Most Valuable Player awards (runner-up four times)
Fourteen scoring titles
Two championships
Rookie of the Year
Fifteen All-NBL first team selections
Two All-Star Game MVP awards
Named the greatest player of the first twenty-five seasons

INTERNATIONAL
297 games for Australia
Captain from 1993–2000
Five Olympic Games
Four World Championships

OVERSEAS
Played for Seton Hall University (1989 NCAA Championship
runner-up), Udine (Italy), Apollon Patras (Greece), Washington
Bullets (US NBA) and San Antonio Spurs (1999 NBA
Champions).